Tuning a
Racing Yacht

MIKE FLETCHER WITH BOB ROSS

Tuning a Racing Yacht

NEW EDITION

ANGUS AND ROBERTSON · PUBLISHERS

ANGUS AND ROBERTSON · PUBLISHERS
London · Sydney · Melbourne · Singapore · Manila

First published by Angus and Robertson (Publishers) Pty Ltd
in 1972
New edition published by Angus and Robertson (UK) Ltd,
16 Ship Street · Brighton · Sussex

Copyright © M. F. Fletcher and R. W. Ross, 1972, 1978

ISBN 0 207 95770 3

Printed in Great Britain by
Hazell Watson & Viney Ltd,
Aylesbury, Bucks

Set in Monotype 11 on 12pt Plantin series 110 by
HBM Typesetting Limited
Standish Street, Chorley, Lancashire

Contents

To racing yachtsmen everywhere–
and to the wives, families,
and friends who put up with them

Foreword

AUSTRALIAN yachtsmen, conscious of the long and expensive air miles that separate them from the mainstreams of European and American thought, have been voracious readers of overseas books on sailing theories and techniques. However, on travelling overseas they have often found, as I have, that the theories and techniques of the sport in our own land lose nothing by comparison with those of the internationally recognised pundits. Indeed, Australian ideas have been taken up by the overseas competitors, particularly in fittings and other yacht equipment.

Just as Australian yachtsmen have won international respect, so has the industry that keeps them supplied with boats, sails, and equipment. From this industry comes Mike Fletcher, formerly a designer of yacht fittings, now a sailmaker and one of Australia's top yachtsmen with national championships in Gwens, Moths, and Herons to his credit.

Mike is one of the men in Australian yachting who know how to make things work, and he is just as happy crewing in yachts like Dragons and Thunderbirds—as the "engineer" who tunes the rig and calls the tactical shots—as he is helming.

His ideas on tuning yachts have been transferred to print by Bob Ross, a journalist who has been reporting the Australian yachting scene since 1960 and who is also an enthusiastic sailor.

The subject is a difficult one, a challenging one for anybody to tackle in the face of so many conflicting ideas. This book, by methodically discussing all the elements of a racing yacht's rig and then the techniques of bringing these elements together to send a boat along at its fastest, will help all racing yachtsmen, beginners or experts.

I first met Mike Fletcher while sailing against him in a Finn Dinghy during the 1960 Olympic trials. I gained a very healthy respect for his ability in all aspects of yachting. And as this fine book shows, he has spent the past 17 years most fruitfully.

It was my pleasure to meet Bob Ross shortly after I moved from Adelaide to live in Sydney in 1962. I hope that, with Mike Fletcher, the friendship will be enduring. I'm sure their book will achieve the great success it deserves.

JIM HARDY

Preface

THIS second edition of Tuning a Racing Yacht has been revised and enlarged, with a complete new chapter on ocean racing and sections about classes that just did not exist when the book was first published in 1972. Since then, Mike Fletcher has added three serious ocean racing campaigns to his heavy bag of personal sailing experience. He captained the Australian Admiral's Cup team in 1975 and was principal helmsman aboard the outstanding offshore yacht *Bumblebee 3*.

His own success on the water has been matched by the success of his sails and the growth of his Elvström sail loft in Sydney, which remains a focal point for much of the innovation in Australian sailing.

Since our first edition, Mike has become Australia's first national yachting coach, and he was appointed coach to the 1976 Australian Olympic team. His coaching duties have included lectures and practical on-the-water tuning sessions in all parts of the country. These have refined his ability to impart clearly to wide audiences of sailors his very practical perception of what occurs on the water.

This edition includes new techniques; among them using wool tufts and leech ribbons in sails for tuning purposes.

While the new ideas flow continually on the highly competitive currents of yacht racing, basic precepts do not change. However, we look at them again in this edition in the light of new experience.

Fletcher has either sailed or helped tune all of the classes featured in detail in this book. Nothing is secondhand.

1977   BOB ROSS

Introduction

PEOPLE go sailing for different reasons. Some just seek peace and quiet, an escape from life's everyday sound and fury. Some sail for the challenge, physical and mental, of battling with the elements. Others cannot be enticed onto the water unless there is someone else out there to race against. This book is aimed at those with this competitive spirit.

As soon as there is competition, you must try to sail faster and this is where the frustrating process called "tuning" begins. Tuning is probably shrouded by more mystery and misconception than any other word in the yachtsman's vocabulary. Yachtsmen generally tend to over-complicate and surround their tuning problems with highly technical and confusing discussion that has no bearing on the immediate issue.

Tuning means looking for more speed. Having more speed than your opponent means you have found more correct answers to a hundred and one tuning problems on your boat than he has found on his.

These problems can be grouped into some basic compartments that must be understood for success at all levels of racing: Mast, correct sail shape, tuning a mast, tuning the sails to a mast. These basics can make five minutes' difference around a course and if the fullness of your sail or the bend of your mast is wrong, you should not be worrying about a little wrinkle in your sails. Forget the little things until you have solved all the basic problems—tuning really is solving problems and if you can recognise the problem, you are well on the way towards solving it. It is no use copying an idea or change of adjustment on someone else's boat unless you understand why it has been made. It might be wrong for your type of sail and rig.

Once you have put right these things that determine basic speed, including crew-work, you have to transfer your attention from technical detail to intuition. From there, you must tune your boat from the way she feels, learning how to achieve more power, how to reduce power; how to make the boat lively when she is dead and pacify her when she is too lively.

This might mean, say, altering mast rake and centreboard position to correct the balance of the boat.

Really to get the feel of your boat and assess, in terms of performance, the changes you make to her, you must sail as often as you can. Practise on weekends after the race and during the week. Just sailing in races a week apart is not frequent enough for real progress. The memory becomes dulled by the complications of everyday life and you are liable to go on, week after week, with the same faults unnoticed.

You can learn twice as much about the tune of your boat in two hours of practise sailing as you can for the same time on the race course, with its tactical distractions.

In these tuning sessions, get off the boat now and then, study your gear from another boat or from the shore, take photographs, analyse faults, decide on remedies and be firm in trying them.

It is easy to be discouraged, but you must never let your enthusiasm slide. As soon as you do you're on the skids with it, towards the tail of the fleet.

Lack of money shouldn't be the drain on enthusiasm that it is with so many yachtsmen. Sure an unlimited supply of money allows you to try every new trend, but the sailor of limited means with a good hull is more likely to develop his tuning skills through altering his sails and rig until he gets what he wants than old moneybags who just buys and discards until something clicks.

It all takes time, but the trying can be fun.

MIKE FLETCHER

How Sails are Made

WHY does one yacht sail faster than another? There are many answers—shape of the hull, skill of the crew, ability of the helmsman, and so on, but the real reason is usually found in the shape of the sails. These are the yacht's engines, the means of gaining power from the intangible wind to drive the hull through the water. So tuning to improve the speed of a yacht must be heavily directed at varying or controlling the shape of the sails by means of the spars, rigging, and sheets.

The story of most sails begins in the same way. Before any sail is made, the sailmaker must bring together all the information he can about the type of boat it will drive, the spars it will set from, and the prevailing conditions of wind and water in which it is going to be most used. The customer can help greatly at this stage: the more correct information he can feed the sailmaker, the greater the chance of gaining a race-winning suit of sails.

Over the past decade, sail plans have made few really revolutionary advances but have steadily developed along roughly similar lines. Sails have become taller on the luff and shorter on the foot. This narrower sail has made life easier for both sailmaker and yachtsman. It is easier to shape in the loft and easier to control once it is on the boat, with its relatively parallel width of chord most of the way up the sail. Headsails have tended to come in off bowsprits and onto stemheads to balance the shorter boom. The jib take-off point on the mast has tended to go higher, making the slot effect of the jib operate over a bigger proportion of the mainsail than it did in the old low-aspect rigs where the headsail went only two-thirds of the way up the mast. The longer luff also allows the foot of the jib to be shorter for a given area. While the benefits are there in boat-pointing ability and ease of handling through tacks, sheeting has become more critical, and the sail is much more susceptible to variation in fullness due to forestay sag.

Before going further we should consider why a boat sails against the wind. The simplest explanation is that the sail, set at an angle to the centre-line of the hull, is curved so that the wind goes in at the luff and bends around the sail on both sides and exhausts at the leech. The forces resulting from this wind flow are divided, some being directed forward, some sideways, and some backwards. If the forward pressures are greater than the backward ones and there is a keel or centreboard in the water to stop the boat going sideways, then the boat must go forward.

This is as technical as we need be in a book whose aim is mainly to explain the hundreds of practical measures that make one boat three or four minutes faster than its rivals.

DRAWING A SAIL PLAN

While sail shapes have fallen into a fairly narrow pattern, the area and manner in which sails are arranged on a boat still have to be designed to suit individual circumstances. First you must find the hull's centre of lateral resistance. This is a difficult proposition for the amateur if he tries to follow the complicated calculations employed by the professional designers—more so in a dinghy where the silhouette area of the underwater sections changes quickly with the step up from displacement speed to planing speed and with alteration of crew position, but there is a simple, non-mathematical way of checking any hull.

You must choose glassy water with absolutely no wind. Launch the boat with mast stepped but without centreboard or rudder, and have the crew seated in their usual fore-and-aft sailing-to-windward positions, but inboard, so the boat heels to its normal sailing angle. One of the crew holds a line by which another person pulls the boat sideways through the water. The crew member changes the position

1

of the line fore and aft until the boat tows directly sideways, with neither bow nor stern tending to swing toward the direction of the pull. The attachment point of the line will then be the hull's centre of lateral resistance and the point, theoretically, for the centre of resistance of your centreboard or keel. I don't believe the rudder blade should be considered when calculating the centre of lateral resistance. It is just there to steer the boat.

Now, back to the drawing board and mark the centre of resistance and the centreboard position on a profile drawing of the hull, which, for accuracy, should be about 1 in. to 1 ft. in scale.

Decide the height of the mast and length of the mainsail boom. A good rough rule is to make the mast height one and a half times the length of the hull, and the foot of the sail about 40 per cent of the luff length (Fig. 1). Very tall rigs are superior in light winds but much harder to hold up as the wind strength increases. The top half of the sail also becomes harder to control, particularly in a dinghy where it is difficult to get enough sheet pressure

Figure 1. Basic dinghy sail plan, applying rough proportion rules.

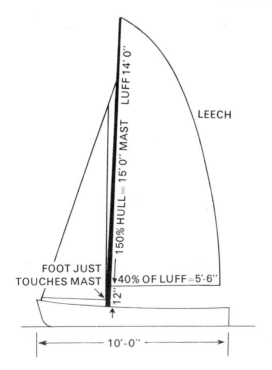

on the relatively light and flexible mast to make the upper part of the leech stand up. Spend a couple of days checking over existing rigs on similar-size craft before tackling these problems; it is easier to see the advantages and disadvantages on a full-sized boat. Pick a position for the mast, again just arbitrarily, and sketch it in.

Draw in the sails so they look right for this size and type of boat. Will it be a family sailer? Then you want a moderate-sized rig, without overlapping headsails, for ease of handling. Perhaps you have in mind a high-performance racer with plenty of power in crew-weight or keel to resist heeling? Then you'll need a tall rig without overlapping jib. If it is a racing boat with not much power from a smaller crew, or less ballast, you'll probably go for an overlapping genoa with small mainsail. The choice will probably also be governed by class restrictions (Fig. 2).

Once you have decided on the size of your sails, the next step is to find their centres of effort. First cut the sail outlines in cardboard to the same scale as your hull drawing; then swing the mainsail template freely from a pin fixed through one corner to the end of a table, hang a plumb-line from the pin, and mark this line on the template (Fig. 3). Repeat the procedure, pinning the template from the other two corners in turn. The intersection of the lines from each corner, besides being the centre of equilibrium of the irregular shape, is also the centre of effort (CE) of the mainsail. The jib shape is near enough to being a triangle, and the centre of effort of the jib can be found on the template merely by measuring halfway along each of its sides and drawing lines to the opposite apexes of the triangle. The point of intersection of these lines is the centre of effort.

The combined centre of effort of main and jib can be found by the following method. Place the templates on the hull drawing and join the CEs of each sail (call these two centres, *A* and *B*). Now divide the length of the resulting line in the same proportion as the main is to the jib (Fig. 4). Supposing the main was 75 sq. ft. and the jib 25 sq. ft. you would draw a line *AC*, 75 units long, at right angles to *AB*, and another, *BD*, 25 units long, also at right angles to *AB* but on the opposite side to *AB*.

Connect *CD*. The intersection of this line with *AB* is the combined centre of effort.

Project a line downwards from this point to compare the combined CE with the centre of lateral resistance (CLR). The combined CE should be forward of the CLR—but at this point theory stops and guessing starts. Even top designers have different ideas on how much forward of the CLR the CE should be—I have heard arguments for from 0 to 10 per cent of the waterline length. This, obviously, must vary for different types of hull shape (there could be quite a difference between a fixed-keel displacement yacht and a planing dinghy), and you should be guided by previous experience with the class, or type of boat. Juggle your mainsail-jib template on the hull drawing until the combined CE is just forward of the CLR, and finally draw in the mast position. This should be near enough, in most boats, to allow for the final adjustment of balance between sails and hull by varying the rake of the mast once it is in the boat or, at worst, moving the mast slightly forward or aft; most new big yachts have mast-steps so built that the mast can be shifted 18 in. or so to correct balance after trial sailing. In a dinghy, shifting the centreboard fore and aft in the centre-case is usually the easiest method of finally adjusting balance—the correct position is the one where the boat sails fastest.

These simple methods of calculating the balance of sails to hull, besides being a guide to the sailmaker, are also useful in tuning—they can get you back within fine tuning tolerances if your boat has gradually crept way out of tune. If you found the combined CE of the sails was, say, 3 ft. behind the centreboard, you'd know something was drastically wrong. This can happen! Your boat may have been burying her head, so you've shifted the mast back and found the boat going better—but this is only because you have the lesser of two evils; the boat is trimmed properly fore and aft in the water but she's still out of balance. What you need is a new centreboard position, drastically further aft. You can find this easily by the methods outlined above.

Big overlapping headsails on yachts complicate this method of finding the combined CE, as some of the area near the clew is often aft of the CLR, and this tends to contribute to weather helm rather than reduce it. Putting bigger and bigger headsails on yachts in an effort to cure weather helm in fact makes it worse. Remember the basic rule—moving sail

*Figure 2. Contrasting rigs. **A**, International Contender, a single-hander with plenty of power from trapezing crewman to keep it upright, which allows it to carry a big sail area (112 sq. ft.). **B**, Flying Dutchman; this 20 ft. Olympic dinghy has a large overlapping genoa jib with moderate mainsail to keep the rig's overall centre of effort low, enabling a two-man crew to hold this large boat upright in a fresh breeze. **C**, International Soling class, with keel to help the crew, has plenty of power to resist heeling and can take a tall rig without an overlapping jib. **D**, ocean racer's big overlapping genoa jib is mainly prompted by the rule that allows a big sail-area gain in overlap without a handicap penalty.*

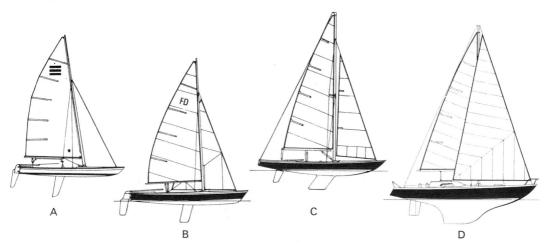

A

B

C

D

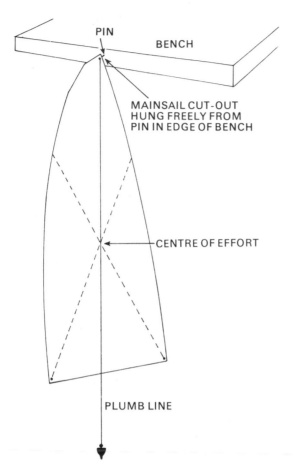

PIN
BENCH
MAINSAIL CUT-OUT
HUNG FREELY FROM
PIN IN EDGE OF BENCH

CENTRE OF EFFORT

PLUMB LINE

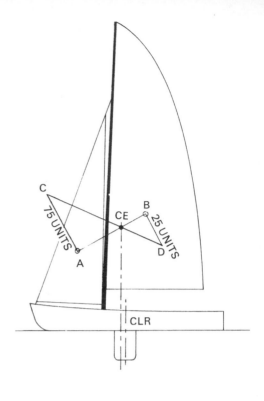

C
75 UNITS
CE
B
25 UNITS
A
D
CLR

Figure 3 (left). Method of finding a sail's centre of effort.

Figure 4 (above). Method of finding the combined centre of effort.

area aft increases weather helm and moving it forward reduces it. Conversely, moving a centreboard forward increases weather helm, aft reduces it.

Armed with a rough sail plan reached by these rule-of-thumb methods, the amateur should then go to a sailmaker, or a designer if the yacht is a big one, for expert assessment before he has the sails made.

There are other things the sailmaker has to know. Almost all yacht sails are restricted in some way or other—one-design classes have tight restrictions limiting the height of the mast and the width of the sail (half-height or three-quarter-height measurements). Jibs are normally restricted by measurements along luff, leech, and foot. Restricted classes such as 5.5s, Moths, and International 14s, where hull shapes are variable within limits, have their sails limited only in area. Besides knowing the restrictions themselves, the owner should know how the class measurers interpret them. Some

regulations are not clear as to how the half-height should be determined, where the width of the headboard should be measured, or whether or not the bolt ropes are to be included in measurements. The owner must know how to measure his own sails correctly, not only to save himself from being wrongly disqualified after winning a series but so that he can keep an accurate check on the shape of his sails before the series starts. You would be surprised how many yachtsmen don't know how to measure their own sails and how many sails we have had back as incorrect from official measurers who have themselves measured them incorrectly.

The sailmaker will also want to know exactly how much the mast and boom his creation is to set from will bend under sailing loads. If a stock aluminium section is being used, and the sailmaker is up with the latest trends in the class (as he should be), he will probably already know how much the mast is going to bend. But

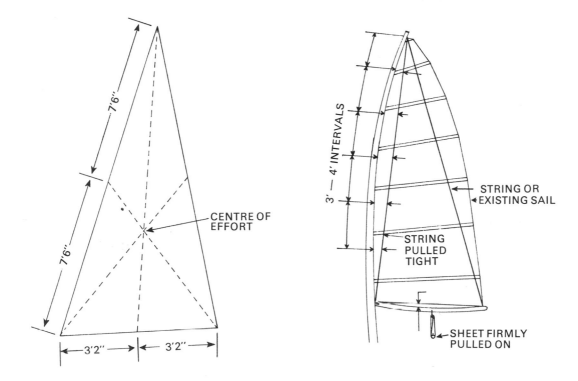

Figure 5. Method of measuring mast and boom bend to assist sailmaker. The distance from string to mast is measured at 3 ft. to 4 ft. intervals. Boom bend is measured at the point of maximum bend.

if the mast is made of wood, or of some obscure aluminium section, the mast bend should be measured to give the sailmaker really accurate information.

Mast bend can best be measured while the mast and boom are rigged in the boat, or perhaps in some testing device if the boat is still unfinished. You only need to attach the forestay, and have a piece of wire or rope running from the top of the mast to the end of the boom to simulate the pressure of the leech on the mast. Pull on the mainsheet as hard as you comfortably can with one arm (this will be a little harder than you would normally sheet while sailing) to simulate the extra pressure from the wind in the sails and the swinging power of the crew. The amount of pressure on the mainsheet varies from class to class and for different mainsheet systems. You can usually feel, as you apply pressure to the end of the boom, a point where the mast will bend no further without excessive force. The pressure applied at the end of the boom on most two-handed centreboard boats is about 50 lb. With this pressure applied, run a string line from the after edge of the top of the mast, at the point where the headboard of the mainsail will be, to the gooseneck—as though you were stringing a bow. Mark off the mast at 3 ft. or 4 ft. intervals starting from the head (because this is a fixed point, whereas the gooseneck position can vary up and down), then measure and record the distances from the points on the back of the mast to the string line (Fig. 5).

These measurements will indicate to the sailmaker the amount and also type of bend he has to allow for when cutting the luff curve of the sail—while an untapered mast section may yield in a fairly regular bend, a mast finely tapered in the top sections will form more of a parabolic curve towards the top.

Boom bend can be measured at the same time. While the rig is tensioned by the sheet, stretch a string line from the end of the boom to the gooseneck. Normally the only measurement of the boom's deflection the sailmaker needs to know is that at the point of maximum bend. He'll also need to know the sheeting arrangement—whether it is end-boom, mid-boom, or some variation of both methods.

At some point while you are measuring the spars the question will undoubtedly be raised, either in your own mind or by some outsider: Should the sail be cut to suit the mast or the mast altered to suit the sail? While the answer is very much a combination of both these alternatives, you cannot get good results from a good sail on a bad mast, although strangely enough you can get reasonable results from a bad sail on a good mast. In highly developed classes masts tend to develop within quite fine limits among the top performers, and sailmakers specialising in these classes have developed a sail that suits the ultimate mast.

In big yachts mast bend is not as great as it is in dinghies, but is just as important. You cannot measure a big yacht's mast bend in the same way we have outlined for dinghies; however, one-design keelboats are tending to use standard aluminium spars for which the bend characteristics become well known to the sailmaker. Besides, they have more rigging on their masts than dinghies to control them. The sailmaker will want to know what type of rigging the mast will carry. Is the top to be stiffened with jumpers? Is the bottom of the mast controlled with diamond or jumper stays? If the mast is well controlled, the sailmaker will probably cut the mainsail slightly flatter, as he knows that the rig can be used to stiffen the mast so as to give the sail more fullness for light weather.

The sailmaker should also know the weight of the crew and the condition of wind and water his creation will normally encounter.

CLOTH WEIGHTS

The sailmaker now has all the information he needs and is ready to cut the sail. First he must decide on the weight of cloth to use. It is better to tend towards a heavier cloth, particularly in highly tuned racing classes. The sail will retain its shape longer, and the control you have over the sail through the luff and foot-tensioners will be more positive because of the stability in the cloth.

Some yachtsmen have been misled by the dramatic developments of lightweight cloths for 12-metre yachts. "If a 12-metre can carry a 3 oz. headsail, why can't my 12 ft. dinghy have a $\frac{3}{4}$ oz.?" seems a fair enough question, but the comparison is not valid. Twelve-metre yachts and ocean racers carry these very light headsails because they do much of their sailing off-shore where they are being tossed around by the sea. In very light weather off-shore the lightest possible headsails are essential because they don't slat backwards and forwards with the action of the boat. But for in-shore racing, if the breeze is light, the seas are normally flat and the weight of cloth is not particularly important. In fact, a heavier-cloth sail will sometimes take its shape better than a light-cloth sail as you heel the boat over in the lightest of airs. The dramatic reduction from 10 oz. to 7 oz. mainsail cloths in the 12s was to reduce weight aloft. Carrying 70 to 80 lb. of sail aloft can contribute significantly to the heeling moment of a 12, and reduction of even 10 per cent in cloth weight means a considerable saving. In a sailing dinghy, saving weight through sail-cloth is meaningless because the boat is sailed more upright, and advantages gained in control over sail shape far outweigh the advantages of having lighter cloth.

The weight of the cloth used depends on how much pressure is going to be put on the sail. This can vary considerably, even between small-boat classes. For a boat like a 16 ft. skiff, with four men in the boat and two of them on trapezes, you need a solid cloth to withstand the quite extreme pressures they can impose. But a Cherub or a Moth, relatively light boats with light crews, can get away with light cloth.

Keel yachts must have heavier-weight cloth because of the tremendous pressures exerted on the sails when a ton or two of boat is being pressed to its maximum hull speed. It is not going to jump up on top and plane like a dinghy to release this pressure. Special types of cloth are made for keel-yacht headsails and mainsails. Headsail cloth has to be very stable in the bias (the line at 45 degrees to the edge), so that it will stand the strain put on it in all directions radiating from the clew. This is known as a balanced cloth; the weft or "fill" yarn (across the cloth) is the same strength as the warp yarn (along the cloth). The mainsail cloth is constructed with a fractionally heavier weft yarn, making it stronger across the cloth but a little less stable on the bias. This extra strength is necessary to stand up to the concentrated pressure running up through the leech to the mast-head when sheeting pressure is applied to the boom. This pressure concentrated in the leech becomes very high in larger yachts when winches are used to sheet home the mainsail in strong winds (Fig. 6).

The tall, narrow, high-aspect ratio mainsail of the modern ocean racer demands a cloth with extremely high strength in the weft direction. Mainsail cloths are laid at right angles to the leech—practically, at right angles to the line between the front edge of the head-board and the clew. The cloths in a high-aspect ratio sail meet the mast at an angle much closer to a right angle than a low-aspect sail. When the low-aspect sail is sheeted in, the sheeting pressure falls almost across the bias line of the thread weave pattern at 45 degrees and the cloth tends to stretch evenly at luff and leech.

With a tall, narrow sail, much higher sheeting pressures are needed to keep twist out of the sail and this pressure works more directly down the line of the weft threads towards the leech. If the cloth is not woven with very high strength in the weft direction, the drive in the sail shifts back to the front of the batten line,

causing hard vertical creases, and a lot of Cunningham eye is needed to pull the drive back to its correct position, about 45 per cent from the mast. A mainsail with the correct stretch-ratio cloth for this type of sail can be sheeted in hard in strong winds with hardly any Cunningham eye needed as the cloth stretches in the right ratio at luff and leech.

Dinghies and small keelboat classes favour a general-purpose cloth whose stability is increased by surface finishing during manufacture. The cloth is rolled under very high pressure, and treated with finely controlled heat and resin fillers to give smoothness to the surface. This high stability is very desirable in dinghies to ensure constant shapes in the sails over a big range of wind strengths. It's also worth having on bigger yachts, although it makes the sails difficult to handle and the hard-finish cloth cracks and breaks down quickly through being rammed into sail-bags after repeated headsail changes. That's why the ocean racers tend to go for softer-finish fabrics.

This type of manufacture is taken to its hardest-finish form in Bainbridge's yarn-tempered cloth—so heavily resinated and finished with very high temperature and pressures that it is mechanically welded together.

Figure 6. **A,** *showing direction of normal cloth layout for mainsail and genoa;* **B,** *parts of a sail;* **C,** *bias distortion, caused by stretch along the foot and luff.*

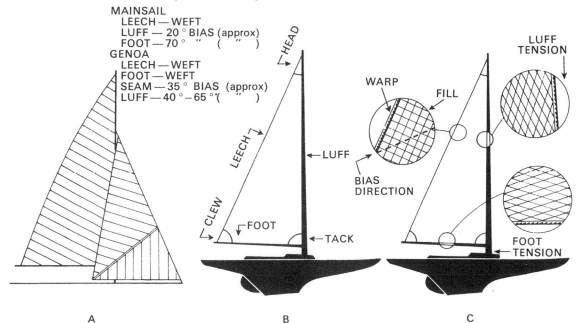

MAINSAIL
  LEECH — WEFT
  LUFF — 20° BIAS (approx)
  FOOT — 70°   "   ("   )
GENOA
  LEECH — WEFT
  FOOT — WEFT
  SEAM — 35° BIAS (approx)
  LUFF — 40° – 65° ("   )

A   B   C

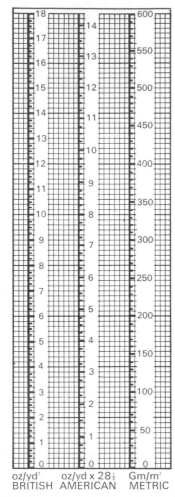

oz/yd²   oz/yd x 28½   Gm/m²
BRITISH   AMERICAN   METRIC

Figure 7. Chart of equivalent cloth weights.

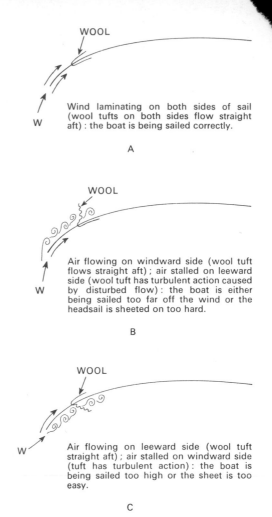

Wind laminating on both sides of sail (wool tufts on both sides flow straight aft): the boat is being sailed correctly.

A

Air flowing on windward side (wool tuft flows straight aft); air stalled on leeward side (wool tuft has turbulent action caused by disturbed flow): the boat is either being sailed too far off the wind or the headsail is sheeted on too hard.

B

Air flowing on leeward side (wool tuft straight aft); air stalled on windward side (tuft has turbulent action): the boat is being sailed too high or the sheet is too easy.

C

Figure 8. The effect of air flow on wool tufts in a sail.

It is very stable in the bias direction so is particularly useful for small headsails on dinghies, one-design keel yacht classes like Solings and Etchells and even on some of the smaller ocean-racers for short-term high performance. The cloth will not stand up to the flogging during sail changes and stuffing into sailbags of long-distance ocean racing aboard bigger yachts. It is so stable that the shape can be built precisely into the headsail with the knowledge that it will not move and require minimum variation to luff tension; no more than $\frac{1}{4}$ in. through the wind range from 0 to 20 knots. So yarn-tempered headsails can be built with a very low angle of entry with the drive well back, for high pointing.

Yarn-tempered sails must be carefully handled to retain the hard finish. The best way to store them is to roll them onto a tube of PVC or cardboard, about 4 in. diameter, a little longer than the foot of the sail. Put ties through the tube near each end, to secure tack and clew; pull the foot reasonably tight along the tube and then roll up the sail over it.

Sailcloth is made almost exclusively from the synthetic fibres Dacron (or Terylene), for mainsails, jibs, some staysails where minimum stretch is required and Nylon, for spinnakers, lighter staysails and drifters—reaching or running sails where some elasticity is needed.

Weights, incidentally, vary from country to country for the same cloth. The American cloths are calculated on a 27-in. sq. yd. and English and Australian cloths on a 36-in. sq. yd.

Wool tufts working well on a genoa. However, another tuft in the upper area, near the cross-trees, should be added to help in trimming to control twist in the top. This is particularly important on tall headsails such as those carried by 5.5s and Solings.

Disturbed air from mast interference and the use of too-full semi-stalled mainsails for ultimate downwind performance make it nearly impossible to have mainsail tufts working effectively. Here, the two after tufts are streaming while the forward one, just on the edge of the turbulent air from the mast, is going straight up. However, tufts are very useful downwind for trimming the sail to the most favourable angle.

The weights we refer to are US, per 27-in. sq. yd. (Fig. 7).

On boats up to 12 ft., I normally use 3·8 oz. mainsail cloth with a 5 oz. jib, even on boats as small as a Heron. Headsails are currently made of heavier cloth than mainsails because they are subject to more abuse and pressure. The shape must be built in to stay from the start; you cannot rely on the sail stretching into shape as in the old days of cotton sails.

The weight of cloth does not increase dramatically for dinghies from 12 ft. to 20 ft. A 16 ft. skiff mainsail might be 5¾ oz. with 6 oz. headsail. But a sail for a Finn or an OK dinghy would still be only 3·8 or 4 oz. because with its one-man crew and very flexible mast there is never going to be any great pressure on the sail.

For keel yachts up to Dragon size you need 6·5 oz. cloth in the mainsail. Headsails are of roughly the same weight (for instance 6·5 to 7 oz. cloth in the headsails for Solings and Dragons), because cloths of this weight are plenty strong enough for both jobs. Light-weather sails of lighter cloth weight are less favoured than they used to be. The danger is that you might be caught by a sudden increase in wind strength with your light-weather jib on and ruin it as well as your chance of winning. So a specialised light-weather sail these days is more likely to be one of the same weight but with more drive cut into it. Then it can be carried in stronger winds if necessary with reasonable results.

A problem of the heavy-cloth headsail is that it is difficult to "read" in light weather, because the cloth doesn't lift and show when you are too close to the wind as quickly as a light-cloth sail does. This can be overcome by having wool tufts through headsails near the luff (Fig. 8).

It is generally better in all small-boat classes to go for the heaviest weight possible, provided the sail will fill smoothly when you heel the boat over in light weather—an 8 oz. cloth under this test would be no use in a Heron; the creases it carried as it came out of the bag would still be there when the breeze reached 10 knots.

Parachute spinnakers should be of the lightest possible cloth. With the great fullness built into them they have a lot of cloth to be held up by the wind alone—a critical business in a light air. That is why most boats carrying 'chutes, such as 5.5s, Flying Dutchmen, 505s and Fireballs, normally use 1 oz. cloth ($\frac{3}{4}$ oz. US)—the lightest standard cloth available. A $\frac{1}{2}$ oz. cloth has been developed, but not many classes other than ocean racers are using it owing to its very restricted wind range; as soon as the breeze gets up to 5 or 6 knots the spinnaker has to be changed because the cloth just stretches and blows completely out of shape. A 10-knot gust could ruin a very expensive spinnaker. Many classes impose a minimum spinnaker weight— $1\frac{1}{2}$ oz. per square yard for the Dragon and $\frac{3}{4}$ oz. per square yard for the Soling—to avoid this sort of expensive incident.

Some of the smaller boats carrying flatter-cut double-luff spinnakers—which are not true parachutes, and therefore not as full—are suited best by a $1\frac{1}{2}$ or 2 oz. cloth. This isn't liable to collapse in light weather, can be carried shy and in strong winds, and is less liable to tear and stretch out of shape. With the wire-luff flat-cut spinnakers used on skiffs and some other Australian and New Zealand classes, the best choice is $2\frac{3}{4}$ or 3 oz. Terylene, as the sail is just like a genoa jib and there is no fullness to be supported by wind alone. In a light breeze you just have to lay the boat over and the "flattie" will flap into shape.

A cloth developed especially to keep its shape under the heavy pressure of reaching is Dynac. This Bainbridge cloth is a nylon weave coated, as are most modern spinnaker cloths, but with a hard finish to give it stability.

Available in $\frac{3}{4}$ oz. and 1·5 oz. (US) weights, it has less stretch than standard cloths of comparable weight but a much lower tear strength.

It is used mostly for reaching spinnakers in highly-competitive classes like the Soling and 470. These boats still carry softer-cloth $\frac{3}{4}$ oz. spinnakers for square running. In light air, the hard Dynac fabric tends to shake itself free of air and the spinnaker tends to collapse easily.

Dynac is not favoured by classes using spinnaker launching chutes because it is prone to tear on being hauled in and out of the chute.

CUTTING THE SAIL

Having selected the cloth, the sailmaker lays out the design on the floor of his loft. He marks out with chalk the basic triangle of luff, foot and leech to their maximum size. Then he draws in the luff curve and foot curve to help give the sail fullness, taking into account the amount of bend the mast and boom are expected to take under sailing pressures.

He calculates the extent of the roach (that part of the sail projecting beyond the straight line drawn down the leech) by measuring the half-height across from the luff or, in a sail governed by a total area restriction, working out the area of the basic triangle, adding the area of the luff and foot curves, and subtracting them from the total allowed to find how much is left for the roach. The leech is then divided

Right. Sail cloths being laid over a diagram marked on the floor of the loft and cut roughly to size.

Centre top. Seam tapers are carefully measured and drawn on the cloth along a bent batten to give an even curve.

Centre bottom. Seam tapers show clearly as gaps between cloths of this sail being laid out.

Far right. Excess cloth from the tapers is trimmed off with a hot knife and the cloths are "struck up"—pencil marks are drawn across the join so that the machinist can maintain accuracy as the cloths are sewn together.

into sections according to the number of battens you are allowed, and the leech shape designed. This may be governed by three-quarter-, half-, and quarter-height restrictions. If so, the leech is laid in a fair curve so that it falls through these three points. It may be necessary to make one of these two measurements less than maximum to give a smooth curve—less luff curve in the bottom section tends to kick out the quarter-height, leaving a bump in the roach which could not be supported if only short leech battens are allowed.

Next, the sailmaker begins laying down the cloths which in a mainsail should run at right-angles to a line between the clew and the head of the sail. He draws this line and lays in the bottom cloth at right-angles to it so that the off-cut of the tack corner is turned over and used at the clew. The remaining cloths are just rolled out flat and cut, allowing enough outside the diagram for any final variations in leech and luff shape and enough overlap at each seam for shaping.

Then the shape is induced into the sail, by two modifications: (*i*) luff and foot curve, which induce fullness when the sail is set on spars that are straighter than the curves; and (*ii*) seam taper which, by shaping the edges of the cloth panels, introduces three-dimensional fullness, particularly in the lower third of the sail where mast bend doesn't play such a big part in controlling the fullness. We'll discuss seam taper more fully in the following chapter on mainsails.

After the sail is shaped, it is "struck up"— that is, the adjoining cloths are stretched to an even tension and small pencil marks ticked from one to the other, so that as the sail is being machined one edge is not stretched farther than the other, causing small puckers along the seams. The machinist then sews the panels together and the sail is laid back on the floor for final marking out.

Allowance must be made here for slight stretch all round. The sail is laid over the original diagram, maximum lengths of the three sides marked, and the luff and foot shortened. If it is a heavy-weather main that has to be set between black bands, you might shorten a sail with an 18 ft. luff by 3 in. so that it can be stretched out hard in strong winds and still fall within the restricting black bands on the mast. If it is to be a general-purpose sail, you might shorten the luff by 1 in. so that it will have enough tension for the lower wind range, and add a Cunningham eye so that the luff can be stretched further to control the shape for varying wind.

The sailmaker now finally draws on the luff curve, checking measurement restrictions very

carefully. He then finally draws the leech shape, and fits reinforcing in the corners. The luff rope and tape to which it is attached are struck up for the correct tension; luff ropes are normally stretched on fairly tight so that when the tension is released at the gooseneck the sail will shrink with even puckering all the way along the bolt-rope to give a fuller sail for light weather.

The sail is now finished on the machine, batten pockets sewn on, and handwork finished. Sails are almost universally sewn with zig-zag stitching which holds the cloth edges flush, as well as together, protecting them from damage against fitting or other projections. This stitch is also easy to undo for alterations or repairs. The thread is normally a Terylene or Terylene-cotton mix. Cotton thread should never be used on Terylene cloth, especially in the medium weights, as it shrinks at a vastly different rate to cloth, causing the seams to tighten and the sail to distort. Cotton thread also becomes rotten through the damp-dry cycles all sails must endure.

Stitching on Terylene cloth stands out on the hard surface, where it is vulnerable to chafe. You must constantly watch for chafed-through stitching, particularly on headsails, where they rub against spreaders and shrouds.

Maintaining present-day sails is not a lot of trouble. Watch for broken stitches and repair them before they let go further or let an edge raise which could snag and lead to a major tear. Hose the salt out occasionally, fold carefully after use, flaking mainsails into the foot and rolling jibs along the wire luffs—and don't jam

them unfolded into bags. A good racing mainsail that is well looked after should last for two hard seasons. Headsails, because of the flogging they take, have a shorter life; perhaps a season and a half on a high-performance dinghy.

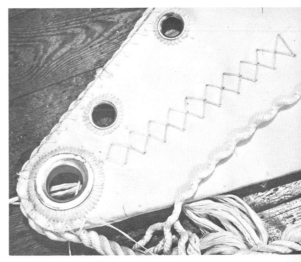

Right top. Machinist seaming cloths together, carefully following the strike-up marks and taper lines. Any variation from these marks will lead to small gatherings on the seams in the finished sail.

Right centre. Handwork on the corners of large sails must be strong. Here, strengthening rope is being hand-sewn around the clew to distribute the strain more evenly.

Right and far right. A mainsail being flaked into the foot. Such care avoids damage to cloth fibre and gives sail longer life. The flaked sail is folded again before being carefully placed into a sail bag.

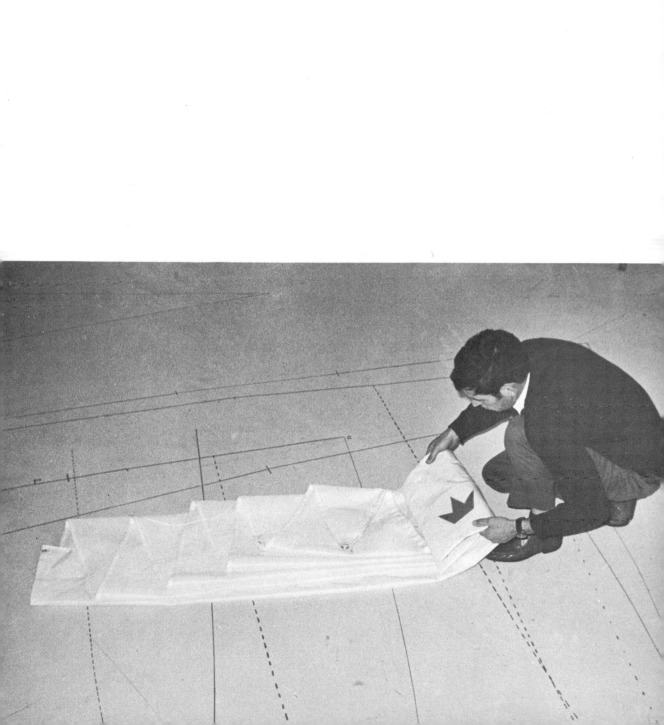

Mainsails

THE MAINSAIL is probably the most complicated sail on any yacht. Since the advent of the flexible rig we have come to expect it to do many different things—it must sail efficiently to windward in wind of between 0 and 25 knots without developing any vices and still be as full as the spinnaker for reaching and running. The sail will not do all these jobs on its own. It must be pulled, pushed, encouraged into a variety of shapes for every different set of circumstances. To help the sail handle this multiplicity of tasks, you must understand how the mainsail is constructed so that you may "read" the sail's needs and make the correct adjustments.

There are several ways of building fullness into a mainsail. The first and most simple, if not particularly efficient, method is to sew together a number of flat sheets of cloth and then cut a convex curve along the luff. In normal sailing breezes, when this type of mainsail is set on a straight mast, the difference between the curve on the luff and the straight mast is pushed back into the sail as fullness. This places all the fullness well forward, near the mast, leaving the leech very flat, loose, and powerless. As the mast bends, the sail gradually flattens, until eventually the mast reaches the same curve as the one drawn on the sail, at which point the sail is perfectly flat. Such a sail would also be very flat along the boom.

The second major method of cutting shape into a sail is to shape each cloth, developing the fullness in a three-dimensional form, just as if it were built out of sheet metal. This way the sailmaker can build a sail with any amount of fullness and with maximum depth anywhere he wants it just by altering the amount and shape of the tapering in each seam. This sail, set on a straight mast, will look perfect, but will only work in the exact wind strength for which it was designed, for as soon as the mast starts to bend, the sail will distort badly. It is impossible to flatten a three-dimensional shape without distortion (look at the mudguard of your car next time you hit something).

Between these two extremes are hundreds of combinations open to the sailmaker for cutting a versatile mainsail by blending luff curve and seam taper. The luff curve must suit the type and amount of mast bend expected, while seam shaping will control the position of maximum drive (Figs. 9, 10). Seam shaping shows in some sails by the varying amount of seam overlap, usually increasing in width towards the luff. But some crafty sailmakers trim the excess overlap from the seams after tapering the cloths so that the seams appear parallel, making it a little more difficult for the opposition to detect exactly how the sail is constructed. "Darts" running at right angles from the bottom in the middle of a cloth panel provide another method of building in fullness without taking a seam right across the sail. They are commonly used along the foot of the mainsail to allow a smooth transfer of shape to the boom, continuing the fullness as low as possible down the sail.

The proportions of seam taper and luff curve in a mainsail are normally well-guarded sailmakers' secrets. However, here are two basic rules they follow:

- Dinghy sail to set on a stiff mast: plenty of seam taper with a small luff curve.
- Dinghy sail for a bendy mast: not much seam taper but large luff curve.

In both types of mainsail you should find more seam taper down low, in the bottom third of the main; the lower part of the mast moves only slightly compared with the upper sections as the mast bends under sailing loads.

A soft-finished piece of cloth does not need as much seam tapering as a very hard cloth because the drive moves aft of its own accord as the wind pressure increases. The stiffer material resembles sheet steel and so needs more shaping to build the drive into the correct position.

What is the correct position? The mainsail's cross-sectional shape and fullness vary with the

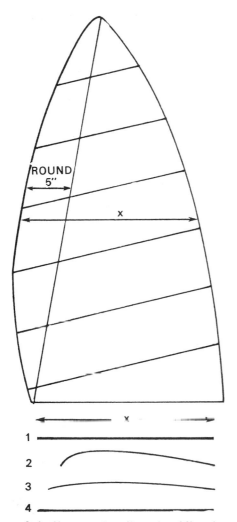

Figure 9. Luff curve. A sail made of flat sheets of cloth with a curve cut on one edge would lie flat on the floor (section 1). When set on a straight mast (section 2) the 5 in. of cloth in the luff round would be pushed back into the sail but the drive would remain too far forward, right against the mast, and the leech dead flat. The draft moves back as the mast starts to bend, say, $2\frac{1}{2}$ in. (section 3) and then becomes dead flat again when the mast has bent 5 in., equalling the amount of luff curve cut into the sail (section 4). Such a sail, with the drive right forward and leech flat, has been proved inferior to one with the drive farther aft (ideally, 45 per cent aft of the mast).

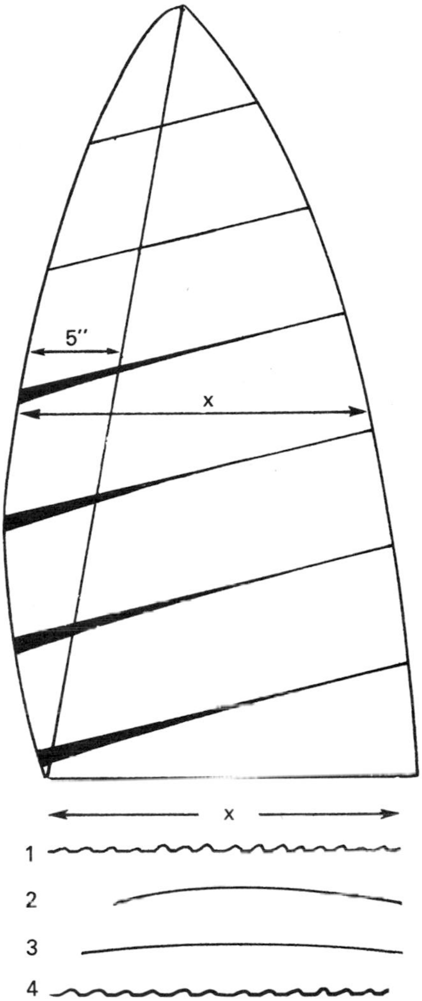

Figure 10. Seam taper. The shaded wedges of cloth are cut away and the seam edges sewn together. This results in a three-dimensional shape that will not lie flat on the floor (section 1). In section 2, with the sail set on a straight mast and the 5 in. of cloth in the luff curve pushed back into it, the maximum depth is farther aft than in the same section in Figure 9. Section 3 is flatter, with the mast bent $2\frac{1}{2}$ in., but the draft is nearly in the middle. With the mast bending to its maximum 5 in. (section 4), the sail is as flat as it will ever get, but with the built-in fullness still showing as wrinkles.

type of boat and rig. The una or "cat" rig as used on Moths, Finns, and OKs will probably be the only one with a perfect shape, having a smooth-flowing fullness back about 45 per cent of its width from the mast with the depth of fullness between 10 and 14 per cent of the chord width (width across the camber of the sail) (Fig. 11). Contrary to some opinion, I think this maximum depth position should be very nearly the same for strong winds and light,

Right top. The three-dimensional shape induced by seam taper is being distorted out of this mainsail because the mast is bending more than the designed luff curve.

Right bottom. Cunningham eye, pulled down by a line through the tack, which will be led by a system of tackles to the adjustment position in the cockpit of the boat.

Far right. Minimum luff tension being used deliberately to induce maximum drive in the mainsail, keeping crewman on the trapeze wire in light-moderate breeze. This is 1976 world 505 champion crew, Peter Colclough and Stephen Jones of England.

but getting slightly flatter as the wind strength increases.

Most yachtsmen say the drive needs to be further forward for strong winds. But I believe that in these winds the drive tends to drift aft of the 45 per cent position owing to mast bend and cloth stretch as the wind strength increases; increasing the luff pressure only restores the drive to its original position. You get the impression that it is further forward when you are rigging-up on the beach before wind pressure and mast-bending do their work.

A mainsail cut especially for heavy weather will be of a slightly heavier cloth with the drive built in further forward to help overcome stretch problems. The luff will also be cut

Figure 11. Depth and position of maximum drive shown as percentage of chord width.

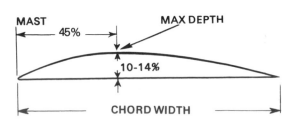

shorter to allow for more initial luff tension if the sail has to be set between black bands. A specialised light-weather mainsail will be cut from light, softer cloth with the drive built in mainly through seam taper. To keep the drive well aft, the luff will be maximum length, sometimes a little longer, so that when it is pulled to the black band the luff tension is at minimum, giving the sail an easy, smooth flow from the mast to the leech. This type of sail can be fitted with a Cunningham eye to allow extra luff tension to be applied as needed.

ADJUSTMENT DEVICES

Luff tension should be minimum in light weather—just enough to remove the wrinkles on the luff tape. As the wind strength increases, so the luff tension is increased to hold the drive in the right position. This tensioning stretches the cloth in the luff of the sail, removing some of the seam-taper built into the sail to keep the drive back towards the middle for light winds. A Cunningham eye sewn into the sail, 6 to 8 in. above the normal tack cringle, allows for more

luff pressure to be applied after the luff has been stretched out to its marks by tension on the gooseneck or tack downhaul. The Cunningham eye can be pulled down (by a light line just passed through the eye) as far as the tack, to stretch the sail out to its absolute limit. Don't be afraid to pull the Cunningham eye tight down to the boom, even if it takes what appears to be excessive pressure—a lot of this pressure is used to extend the luff rope which would normally have been stretched tightly onto the luff of the sail when it was built and then allowed to return to its original length.

Some skippers use sliding goosenecks instead of the Cunningham eye, leaving the boom free to slide up and down a track on the mast. Their theory is that the harder the sheet pressure, the more luff tension is required—as they pull on the sheet, the gooseneck slides down, automatically controlling the luff. This may be so, but in medium winds, when full power is required, tight luff tension may not necessarily be good. The gooseneck in these winds should therefore be locked against descending of its own accord when sheet pressure is applied.

The free-sliding gooseneck also fails badly

Right. Too much luff tension in a soft sail shows in a fold close to the mast.

Centre right. The same sail with insufficient luff tension. Creases run diagonally downwards from the mast.

Far right. Correct tension. Seams show drive in the sail is perfectly positioned, about 45 per cent of the sail's width from the mast.

when sailing free. The upward loading on the end of the boom from the leech of the sail will make the boom pivot on the boom vang, causing the gooseneck to slide down. This increases the luff tension and releases the leech tension, exactly opposite to the pressures you need for fast downwind sailing.

The Cunningham eye is used mostly on soft sails (short battens only) and is operated by a tackle led back into the cockpit where adjustments can be made while sailing.

The soft sail is more susceptible to faults from incorrect luff tensioning, as there are no full-length battens to smooth out the folds and wrinkles. Conversely, because of this smoothing effect, it is harder to detect incorrect luff tensioning in fully battened sails. Too much luff tension will show up in a soft sail as a crease or fold close to the mast, while in a fully battened sail it can only be seen by studying the shape—the drive will be well forward and the sailcloth as taut as a drumskin. It will be very

difficult to make the battens change shape from one tack to the other in light winds.

Insufficient luff tension in a soft sail will show up in diagonal creases running from the mast downwards and outwards towards the end of the boom. In a fully battened sail, these creases will be smaller and confined between the battens.

The tension on the foot of the sail can be varied in the same way. I like the foot to be cut a little shorter than the maximum to allow it to be stretched out to the black bands for strong winds. The foot tension has a direct effect on the fullness of the lower third of the mainsail and therefore it is essential that it be readily adjustable. As you stretch the foot, you increase the width of chord and reduce the depth at the same time, pulling tight tension folds into the cloth along the boom. These will blow out in strong winds, but the foot should be eased until the folds disappear in light or medium winds. Don't be upset in light winds

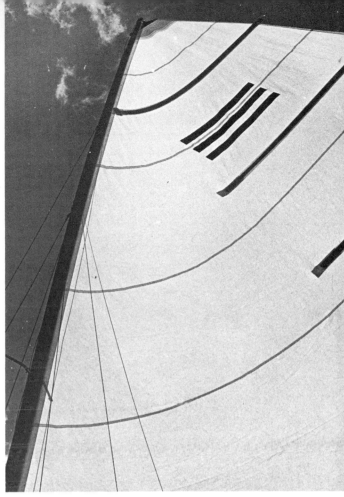

if the mainsail is up to a couple of inches short of the black band limiting maximum width of the sail at the end of the boom. You have no less area set, and it is much more important to have the correct shape. It is good practice to ease both the luff and foot tensions when running or reaching—the broader the reach, the more you should ease. When square-running, you should increase pressure slightly on the foot. This is to present the maximum sil-

Too much tension is being applied along the foot of the mainsail in the left picture. It shows as a tight fold along the boom. The tension should be eased until the fold disappears. In the picture on the right there is too little tension on the foot. It should be pulled out until the vertical creases disappear.

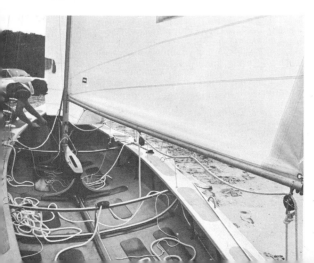

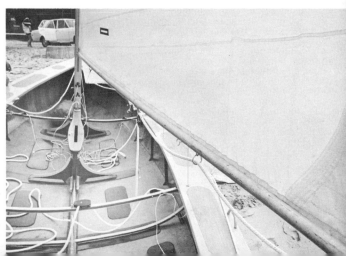

houette area of the sail to the wind when full-ness is slightly less important. Here again, a soft sail varies slightly from a fully battened sail. The more the foot and luff of the soft sail are eased, the fuller it will become. A fully battened sail on easing the luff will reach the point where the outward spring in the battens will completely flatten the sail.

DIFFERENT TYPES OF MAINSAIL

You must remember when deciding on main-sail shape that the position and amount of full-ness in a mainsail will vary for different types of hull and even for different sea and wind conditions for the same hull. You must also remember that the boat has to be fast both downwind and upwind. Sometimes compromise in sail shape is necessary to gain speed on one leg if this will give a better all round performance.

The hull that will plane to windward, such as a Flying Dutchman or Cherub, must have a mainsail powerful enough to make it do so in the lowest possible wind strength—the jump in speed is dramatic compared with that of a competitor who has not managed to reach the plane. However, in designing this fullness, the sailmaker must be careful not to make the bottom of the mainsail too full and so close the slot between the lower part of the main and the leech of the genoa. The FD keeps this lower part of the slot open by having a lot of mast bend down low. The mast comes forward and to windward near the bottom, giving a twofold benefit in coping with increased wind pressures —first, flattening the section of the mainsail that the genoa overlaps when going to wind-ward; and secondly, moving the whole of the mainsail bodily away from the leech of the genoa.

This excess bend sometimes shows up alarming creases in the three-dimensionally shaped lower section where it has been flattened past the stage where the luff tension can keep this creasing under control. I have tried flatten-ing this section of the main to remove the objectionable-looking creases, only to find that the immeasurably small improvement in per-

Insufficient luff tension on a fully battened sail shows as small creases confined between the battens. On this Australian lightweight Sharpie the battens are not in hard enough; more pressure on them would help remove some of the wrinkles.

Maximum fullness has been induced into this OK Dinghy mainsail by easing luff and foot tensions for a downwind run in a light breeze.

formance to windward is not enough to make up for the drop in performance on the reach due to the flatter bottom of the mainsail. With this type of mainsail the upper section still retains fullness, with undistorted shape, for maximum efficiency to windward.

In a boat such as the Cherub, however, where the genoa does not overlap so far, the problem is overcome just by having a very flat entry in the lower section of the main. This pushes the drive further aft—not good, theoretically, but more than justified by pulling the forward section of the main away from the genoa leech.

A boat without trapezes that doesn't have the power to plane to windward and has a relatively small jib, such as a Northbridge 14, presents a different problem. You must concentrate on making this fine, easily driven hull go high to windward by making the draft in the lower section of the mainsail shallow. This allows the small jib to be sheeted well inside the gunwale line for high pointing without back-winding the main or choking up the slot. With the Northbridge you don't have to worry as much about building in fullness for downwind speed, because it is an advantage under the class's area measurement restrictions to have a loose foot. This can be easily adjusted to any amount of fullness for better speed on the reach. The mainsail above the hounds is, however, kept relatively fuller, as the shape here is controlled by mast bend and not by the loose foot.

Smaller, light dinghies such as the Heron and Mirror cannot point high to windward owing to their rather full-bodied hull shape, so the mainsails are cut full to drive them through the water with a little more speed. The mainsails have a more even fullness from top to bottom. The bottom fullness is not as critical in this type of boat, because the jib-sheeting angle is necessarily wider, for speed rather than pointing ability.

Catamarans normally have easily driven hulls and travel at high speed to windward, which greatly increases the apparent wind strength (actual speed of the airflow across the sail of the moving boat). This means that their mainsail shape must be more shallow than for many of the mono-hulled types, with the leech kept as flat as possible so that the sail exhausts easily.

The power (through fullness) that makes a dinghy plane to windward is not necessary here. This open leech sometimes damages performance in very light winds, especially downwind. A leech line can be used to overcome this drawback. The best type is an external light wire line threaded through the ends of the full-length battens. Tightening the line presses the battens in towards the mast, making the sail fuller. The leech line should be used with caution when going to windward or tight reaching as the sail can be very easily stalled.

LEECH SHAPES

The leech shape is mostly governed by sail area or half-height and three-quarter-height cross measurements. The variation in restriction accounts for some of the off-beat shapes that are seen. The roach area for the Australian 16 ft. skiff, for instance, is calculated by taking two-thirds the area of a rectangle found by multiplying the maximum leech measurement by the maximum distance the round extends beyond the basic triangle. This makes it an advantage to have the leech coming out quickly at the peak to the maximum decided on, then running parallel to the straight line between the head and the clew, hooking in again at the boom (Fig. 12).

This type of leech shape throws a lot of pressure on the battens at the point where the curve is sudden. Take care that the battens are strong enough to stop the leech curling in this area. The 16s allow a free batten arrangement, so the battens are concentrated in the maximum curve areas at the head and clew.

In sails where the area of the roach is measured by breaking the round into various triangles, it is better to give the leech a more even shape so that the pressure is taken more evenly by each batten (Fig. 13). Still, the trend is to cut all sails with a fairly wide head to give a controlled sectional shape right to the top. Here again, the top three or four battens are critical. Sails restricted to short leech battens necessarily have a smaller round in the roach— normally about 40 per cent of the total length of the batten. Bigger roaches than this tend to make the leech fall away to leeward, forcing the battens back into the body of the sail and causing bad creasing at the inner end.

BATTENS

Battens are usually left to last in a yachtsman's list of equipment, and you see many poorly made, makeshift battens ruining carefully designed sails.

There are two types of batten systems—leech battens, used in "soft" mains, and full-width battens. Leech battens, which are short and do nothing but hold out the leech, normally come four battens to a set. The lower two need very little shaping as they are in the area of the main that needs to be kept as flat as possible. I prefer to have these made from ash, hickory, or glassfibre so that they can be stiff while small in section and relatively light. If they are too heavy, the sail's flapping during rigging or before a start, or even when tacking in strong winds, will throw a lot of strain on the batten

pockets and eventually burst them away from the sail.

If they are too big in section they will swell the pockets, throwing strain on the material in the sail immediately around the pocket. This has the same effect as altering the seam tapers in the leech, and causes loose cloth between the battens as it develops a tight spot 12 in. to 18 in. inside the edge of the sail (Fig. 14).

The upper two leech battens normally extend farther into the sail and therefore should be made more flexible at the inner end, allowing the tip of the batten to be bent by the sailcloth itself, blending it into the curve of the sail without causing a sharp ridge, while the outer end still holds the leech flat (Fig. 15). Sometimes, for example in Soling and Dragon classes, it is even necessary to reduce the width of the batten at the inner end to make it flexible enough for light weather.

Battens running full width through the sail are more complex in construction and performance. They are normally used with big-roach sails and have to help control the shape

Figure 12. Roach shape for a 16 ft. skiff.

Figure 13. Even roach shape.

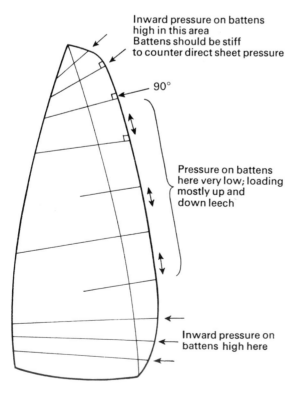

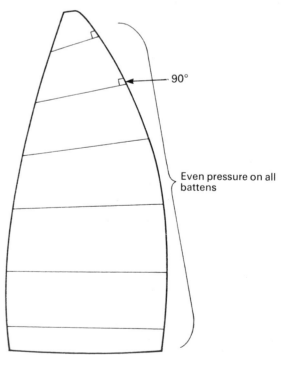

as well as hold out the roach. The pressure on them varies in different areas of the sail; hence their stiffness should also vary. The amount of pressure depends largely on the silhouette shape of the leech, as pressure from the end of the boom is transmitted around the edge of the sail to the masthead, imposing an inward pressure on each batten.

Figure 14. A, oval batten form slides easily into the pocket and causes no distortion; the pocket width is only slightly reduced. B, batten that is too bulky tends to force the pocket off the sail and, more seriously, shortens the leech and thus tightens it; this type of distortion can alter the whole shape of a sail. C, battens must not taper inside the pocket towards the leech; this causes looseness within a few inches of the leech and bad leech flutter.

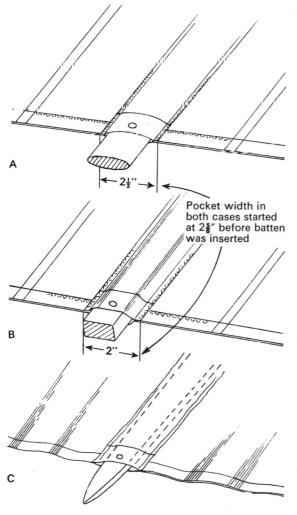

A

← 2½″ →

Pocket width in both cases started at 2⅜″ before batten was inserted

B

← 2″ →

C

Where the leech changes shape suddenly in a mainsail with a wide top, such as a Northbridge 14 or Moth, the battens will be under maximum pressure. To counter this, the sailmaker will plan several battens close together around the sharp curve. The battens themselves will have to be strong enough to hold the top out and up without allowing the leech area to curl. Continuing down the leech, the curve becomes more gentle and the battens can be spaced wider apart. If the leech has an even curve from top to bottom, as on the Tornado sail, there is even pressure on each batten, so they can be of fairly uniform stiffness.

If the leech is relatively straight, such as on a Finn, there is no inward pressure on the battens at all. All these battens do is hold the edge of the sail flat, so they need little shaping and can be very thin.

The best way to test the bending characteristics of a full-length batten is to hold it lightly by the thick outer end and push it against a wall. It should take a smooth curve to the exact shape you want in the sail. The degree of stiffness is a matter for experience and experimentation. I find as a general rule with battens four feet and more long that if you hold the battens horizontally by the thin inner end with one hand it should just support its own weight. The shorter ones near the head of the sail can only be judged by the appearance of the sail in this area. If they are too stiff, this section of the sail will be very flat; if they are too soft, the leech will curl in and the shape will be too deep. There can be some advantage in having separate heavy-weather and light-weather sets,

Figure 15. Leech battens should also be carefully tapered.

LEECH BATTEN TOO STIFF, CAUSING RIDGE AND PRESSURE ON POCKET

BATTEN WITH TAPERED INNER TIP FLOWS INTO SAIL

23

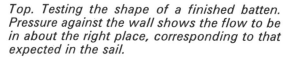

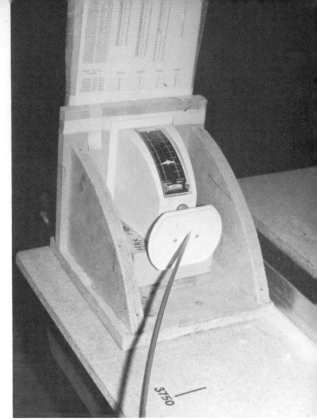

Top. Testing the shape of a finished batten. Pressure against the wall shows the flow to be in about the right place, corresponding to that expected in the sail.

Centre. A batten 4 ft. or more long should just support its own weight if held horizontally by the thinner end with one hand. The batten held in the right hand is about right; that in the left hand is too soft.

Bottom left and above. Method of checking batten shape. The batten is supported lightly by the left hand and pressed against a set of kitchen scales with the right. Bend for a given pressure can be faithfully reproduced in other battens.

especially if your sail is one of the wide-top designs.

Classes such as the Tornado have found batten curvature and tension so critical they have developed a method of checking them with a spring balance and noting the change in sail fullness and performance for varying loads. The batten is stood in a vertical direction and load applied with a spring balance to the tip. The test helps to reproduce accurately battens either as replacements or for experimental purposes.

MAKING BATTENS

In selecting material for your battens, you must look for something that is flexible enough to take up the flow of the sail, fairly easily worked so that you can control the shape during manufacture, yet strong enough not to break in a capsize or crash gybe.

Timbers suitable for battens are silver ash, tulip oak, and hickory for the short ones, and tulip oak or cane for the tapered top battens or full-length battens. Professionally made glassfibre battens have also reached the required standard. Glassfibre is particularly good for long battens, as it takes an even bend and has sufficient rigidity without being too bulky in the pocket, is almost unbreakable and does not warp as wood is inclined to do. The thickness of glassfibre battens can be altered by sanding them with a coarse paper around a flat block. If you want to save money, use wood for battens less than 6 ft. long, glassfibre for those over 6 ft.

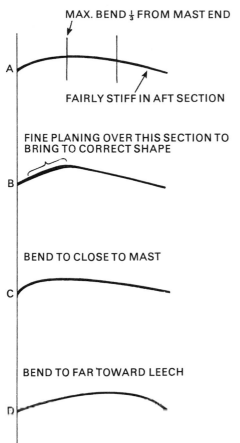

MAX. BEND ⅓ FROM MAST END

A

FAIRLY STIFF IN AFT SECTION

FINE PLANING OVER THIS SECTION TO
BRING TO CORRECT SHAPE

B

BEND TO CLOSE TO MAST

C

BEND TO FAR TOWARD LEECH

D

*Figure 16. **A**, battens should take this shape when pressed against the wall. **B**, if the batten looks like this, plane lightly where marked to correct shape. **C** and **D**, wrong flow shapes.*

Battens too stiff for this light air are forcing the sail outward from the mast, flattening the sail completely as well as causing tight creases from the batten end.

Figure 17. Correct finishing of batten ends is important if damage to sail pocket is to be avoided.

Figure 18. To reduce the stiffness of a leech batten without making it paper thin, the width can be tapered at the inner end as shown. This is quite often used at the inner end of leech battens to prevent splitting.

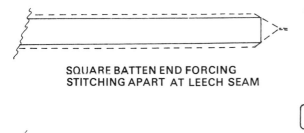

SQUARE BATTEN END FORCING
STITCHING APART AT LEECH SEAM

CORRECT TAPERING OF BATTEN END

INNER END LEFT FULL WIDTH TO PICK
UP ELASTIC IN POCKET.

REDUCE WIDTH TO INCREASE
FLEXIBILITY

Left. A Thunderbird carrying a maximum-fullness mainsail with easy-flowing leech—essential on this type of small yacht if weather helm is to be kept in check. The mainboom is sheeted close enough to avoid even the slightest back-winding from the jib.

Centre. This Star class carries a big main for its size, but the big fore-and-aft bend to the mast flattens the head and allows the leech to exhaust airflow. The crew pictured is working hard to keep the hull at a perfect sailing angle. Fullness in the bottom of the sail and the lower leech shape is being kept under control by the bending boom.

Far left. The crew of this Australian 16 ft. skiff have their fully battened mainsail set for maximum power in the light breeze. A good, even flow is being achieved from the boom to the top of the mast. The drive is well aft to allow close sheeting of the jib and to give a good angle of entry at the luff.

Bottom left. Full bottom of Moth sail, clew slightly eased, gives power for fast, planing reach.

If money is no object, make them all glassfibre.

Weight is a problem with full-length glassfibre battens. Tornado sailors have made a real effort to reduce weight by making battens from a glassfibre-foam laminate. A big piece of foam is tapered in thickness towards one edge, glassfibre laid up on both sides and then the battens sawn from the "sandwich" as strips.

Some of the earlier glassfibre battens, containing wooden inserts, were superior to the modern extruded ones, which have to be so thick to gain sufficient stiffness in long battens that the weight problem arises.

Mainsail has its leech hooking badly under the high pressure needed to make the leech of the high aspect sail stand up. This will cause weather helm and poor acceleration in response to gusts.

Maximum power in the bottom of the sail, leech opening at the top and flattened upper sail in Sydney Harbour 18-footer.

Headsails

THE HEADSAIL tends to be forgotten and misunderstood in yacht tuning. It lives in the mainsail's shadow in more ways than one. The mainsail, with mast and boom, gets most of our attention in both rigging and sailing, while the headsail is two-thirds obscured from view except on those yachts large enough to have one crew member constantly down to leeward, trimming the sail and studying its shape by the minute—which is the attention it really needs.

The dinghy sailor, who just cannot give the sail this specialised attention on the water, has tended to buy one new headsail after another, discarding the ones carried in lost races, hoarding like gold the ones carried in wins. This unscientific and uneconomic approach can be largely overcome by intelligent appraisal on the beach of the position of fullness, leech shape, and sheeting angle in relation to the mainsail, and then experimentation on the water. Studying the design and construction of the sail will help you understand it.

Except in off-shore racers, and in some specialised dinghy classes like the Flying Dutchman, the trend is to narrower jibs which do not overlap the mainsail. In development class boats, where the size of the sail plan is limited by a total area restriction, the tendency is to break up this area into 25 per cent for the jib and 75 per cent for the mainsail. This gives maximum windward performance with the smallest possible jib so that maximum area is left in the mainsail for downwind sailing.

The trend in ocean racers and bigger harbour-racing yachts. to big overlapping genoas has several advantages. The rules allow for the foot greatly to overlap the mainsail without handicap penalty. The International Offshore Rule, which gives more encouragement to larger mainsails, still allows a big penalty-free overlap. The maximum is 150 per cent of J (the measurement from the mast to the forestay bow fitting), now measured from the outside edge of the clew to the nearest

This development-class 5.5 metre shows the trend to tall, non-overlapping jibs which sheet forward at very close angles and do not interfere with mainsail efficiency. Inside tracks on the deck show that even closer sheeting is possible for lighter winds.

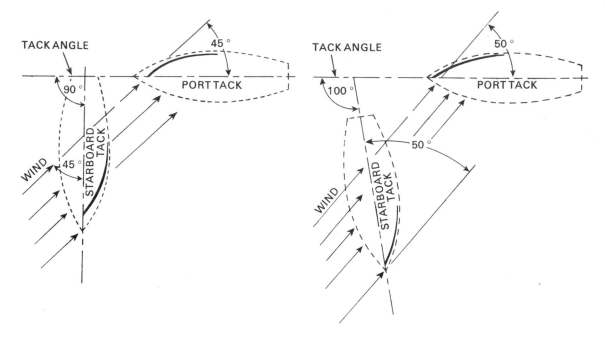

Figure 19. Tacking angle when angle of entry of headsail is 45 degrees.

Figure 20. Tacking angle when angle of entry of headsail is 50 degrees.

point on the luff wire.

With no mast in front of it to interfere with airflow, the genoa is a more efficient sail, area for area, than the mainsail. It has less heeling effect than the mainsail, because, owing to its triangular shape diminishing towards the head, it has a lower centre of effort. It can also be quickly changed for smaller and flatter jibs as the wind strength increases, or lighter-cloth fuller ones as the wind decreases.

The Flying Dutchman uses the big over-lapping genoa because it enables this 20 ft. long, powerful hull to be held upright and balanced by a two-man crew. But on most one design yachts and centreboard classes with maximum sail-area restrictions the non-overlapping jib has been conclusively proved more efficient.

Shaping a headsail is governed by several considerations—the pointing ability of the hull that it is made for, whether the hull is a planing or displacement type, and the length of the foot. But the angle of entry is the first thing to consider in both shaping and sheeting—the angle the leading 12 in. of the headsail makes to the centre-line of the hull, which governs how high the boat will point into the wind before the headsail lifts.

Disregarding, for the moment, the apparent wind variation caused by the boat's speed in relation to wind speed, we could say a headsail with an angle of entry of 45 degrees to the centre-line of the hull will enable the yacht to tack through an angle of 90 degrees (Fig. 19). But if the angle of entry is widened to 50 degrees, the tacking angle increases to 100 degrees (Fig. 20). So a small variation in the angle of entry makes a big difference to the angle a yacht has to tack through to progress to windward.

Taking into account the apparent wind, with the direction of the flow over the sails forced a long way forward by the boat's speed, the angle of entry will be lower than shown in the examples and will obviously vary for different wind speeds. In light winds the yacht might do 2 knots in a 5-knot wind, which will force the apparent wind a long way forward in relation to the true wind, and thus reduce the boat's pointing capacity (Fig. 21). So a light-weather headsail should have a lower angle of entry. This dictates, to some extent, the need in light weather for headsails with the drive back towards the middle, which gives a full sail with a low angle of entry.

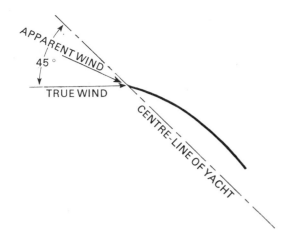

Figure 21. Direction of apparent wind and angle of entry of headsail in light winds.

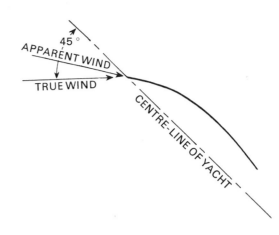

Figure 22. Direction of apparent wind and angle of entry of headsail in heavy winds.

In heavy winds, where the same hull may be able to do only 5 knots to windward in a 20-knot wind, the apparent wind is not so far forward, which allows the yacht to point higher or use a headsail with the drive further forward and a flatter leech, giving a wider angle of entry than before for the same pointing-angle (Fig. 22). This also gives the hull more power to handle rougher sea conditions without loss in speed or pointing ability.

If the angle of entry is taken as a constant factor in designing the sail, shape will then be governed by the length of the foot, the sheeting angle, and where the maximum draft is positioned.

Assuming the sail has the maximum draft 45 per cent back from the leading edge, and is widely sheeted, it must be flatter to hold the same angle of entry (Fig. 23). If this sail is full and sheeted wide, it will not point well. If the drive is too far forward, the angle of entry will become larger and pointing ability will be reduced. If the drive is too far aft, to keep the angle of entry low, the leech will be closed and stall the sail with consequent loss in boat speed. If a flat jib is sheeted at too close an angle it will stall very quickly and probably be too close-winded for the mainsail, causing the mainsail to back-wind.

For a headsail to work well, the curve of the sail must fit within the angle formed by a line representing the apparent wind at its point of entry and the exhaust line from the leech parallel to the centre-line of the hull. The less efficient the hull (in pointing ability) the greater the angle of the apparent wind to the centre-line, and hence the deeper the headsail that can be fitted within these limits (Fig. 21).

For longer-footed genoas to have the same angle of entry all the way up as well as having the capacity to be close-sheeted, the camber shape low down will need to be built in with seam taper and placed forward with a straight, flat area, for good exhaust, towards the clew. Moving higher up the genoa, where the leech starts to twist open more, the camber shape must be located further aft, towards the middle of the sail, to gain the same angle of entry as the bottom while retaining the maximum amount of draft.

*Figure 23. Both these jibs have the same angle of entry. **A**, being sheeted closer, can be much fuller than **B**, with its wider sheeting angle.*

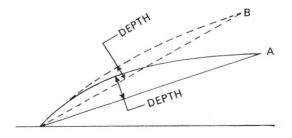

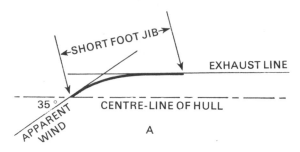

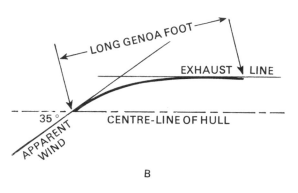

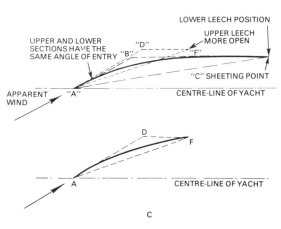

*Figure 24. The fullness of **A**, the short footed jib and **B**, the long footed genoa fits within the angle formed by a line representing the apparent wind (shown here at 35 degrees to the centre-line of the hull) and the exhaust line (parallel to the centre-line). **C**, tall, longer footed genoas need a variation in shape. The triangle ABC represents the boundaries of the shape necessary in the lower genoa triangle and ADF in the upper genoa triangle. Because the upper leech is twisted open more, the triangle ADF has its maximum depth much further aft. Therefore the sail shape drawn into it must be much flatter than the bottom shape drawn into triangle ABC.*

This is also true for taller, narrow jibs such as those carried by the Soling, Etchells and 5.5. However with these jibs, the foot is shorter and by using very hard-finished stable cloths such as New Yarn Tempered, the drive can be moved as far aft as 50 per cent of the cord width to gain maximum fullness for medium conditions.

CUTS

Over the years, sailmakers have had cloths running in every conceivable direction to try to stabilise headsail shapes or to develop something different that might click. The traditional and still most usual headsail design is the true mitre cut with the mitre seam from the clew bisecting the angle formed by the leech and foot sides of the headsail's basic triangle. This allows the straight edges of the cloth to fall directly in line with the foot and leech where the maximum strain is applied.

In larger headsails it keeps the stretch in these areas to a minimum, while the mitre through the slanting biased section of the cloths can be adjusted to control the fullness in the middle and out towards the clew. In large, overlapping genoas, however, it is disastrous to get too much fullness here, as the headsail will then not exhaust cleanly, causing excessive heeling and undue back-winding of the mainsail in stronger winds. The mitre cut is still very popular for medium- to fresh-breeze headsails on larger yachts, because the mitre seam is shaped in anticipation of the cloth stretching to some extent, as it always will. With such a headsail it is wise to have it up and working some time before a race start to allow it to stretch into its designed shape. When it is first hoisted, the mitre line will probably stand up in quite a tight ridge; this progressively disappears as the sail stretches into shape.

The pressures are not so great in smaller headsails, into which the sailmaker is able to build the exact shape required from cloth strong enough to hold this shape through the sail's wind range. The leech of most dinghy headsails is approximately at right-angles to the foot, so the cloths naturally run horizontally across the sail. This cross-cutting allows the

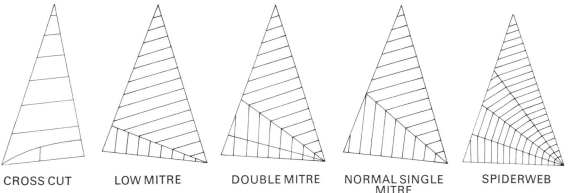

CROSS CUT   LOW MITRE   DOUBLE MITRE   NORMAL SINGLE MITRE   SPIDERWEB

Figure 25. Headsail cuts.

sailmaker to shape the headsail more accurately, building in three-dimensional fullness through seam taper and allowing him to position the maximum drive accurately.

Many ocean-racers are now also using cross-cut headsails, with harder-finish stable cloth and dinghy-style seam shaping employed to produce a flat-entry, deep-low-down genoa that gives excellent results. The hardness of the cloth is not such a problem to handle now with the introduction of twin-groove foils demanding that headsails have to be flaked out and placed in long turtles for efficient sail-changing.

There have been many variations in headsail cuts. Double-mitre headsails have been used for medium-sized genoas on Dragons and yachts with similar sail-plans, with the top mitre pinched to flatten the dangerous, low leech area, and the bottom mitre used to build fullness into the foot of the sail where it can be of most use.

The radial-cut headsail, in which the cloths radiate from the clew to the luff, was very popular for a time. Such a sail is very stable in shape, especially in strong winds, and this design is still used quite successfully for specialised heavy-weather headsails. But it is difficult and expensive to cut, and tends to develop ridges at each seam as the sail gets older. Any subsequent recutting to alter shape or cure leech faults is impossible, as there are no suitable seams running across the sail to adjust.

The deck-sweeper, a more recent headsail cut, is designed so that the foot touches the deck or goes as close as possible to it to stop the high-pressure air flow on the windward side from escaping under the foot and interfering with the low-pressure flow low down on the leeward side. While the theory sounds good, I think the practical gains are immeasurably small. However, to achieve the sweeping effect, clews have dropped closer to sheeting points, which is a real advantage in control. If the deck-sweeper adds sail area without penalty, as on a Flying Dutchman, it is worthwhile. But on classes where the headsail's total area is measured, I would rather have a couple of extra square feet in the top of the overlap area, where it is helping the leeward side of the mainsail, rather than have the same area lying uselessly on the deck.

FORESTAY TENSION

Once the sail is cut by the sailmaker, the major control on headsail shape is the tension on the forestay. Forestay tension controls the amount of sag to leeward in the headsail luff, which in turn affects the fullness of the sail. While a mainsail can be flattened as the wind strength increases by bending the mast supporting it, the headsail, unfortunately, is supported by a length of wire which is pulled aft and to leeward as the wind strength increases. This puts more luff-round into the headsail, making it fuller instead of flatter. As it is physically impossible to stop this completely, the sailmaker will cut just enough hollow into the luff of a medium-weather headsail so that it will not be too flat for light winds when the forestay is virtually straight, yet not be too full when

33

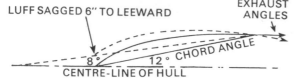

LUFF SAGGED 6" TO LEEWARD

EXHAUST ANGLES

12° CHORD ANGLE

8°

CENTRE-LINE OF HULL

Figure 26. Effect of a sagging luff on the angle of attack of a headsail.

the stay is sagging to its maximum in strong winds.

The problem of forestay sag makes it necessary, in most classes, to have three headsails—one specialised light-weather sail, a medium-weather all-rounder, and a specialised heavy-weather sail. The light-weather sail may be of lighter cloth than the other two, which makes it a little more responsive and slightly easier for the helmsman to "read" when sailing to windward in a light air. It will have a considerable amount of built-in fullness and positive luff-round to give flow, remembering that it will set on a basically straight forestay. This sail should be efficient up to 10 knots.

As wind pressure increases and the forestay starts to sag, making the sail too full, you should change to the medium-weather headsail which should be efficient through the 5 to 18-knot wind range. This sail would possibly have a similar amount of shaped-in fullness, but the luff would have hollow or negative luff-round, so that when the forestay sagged, say, two inches, the sail would set to its designed shape. If you are forced to carry this sail into a dying breeze, it often helps, if you can do it, to ease the tension of the rigging and allow the forestay to sag more than normal in light air to maintain fullness in the sail.

The heavy-weather headsail is normally cut from a slightly heavier cloth than the other two, with no built-in fullness, or very little, and enough hollow in the luff to suit the maximum forestay sag. This sail should be effective from 10 to 25 knots with the emphasis on over 20 knots. The two specialised headsails must perform reasonably well in wind speeds that overlap well into the most-used medium-weather headsail's wind range with maximum performance aimed at either the light or heavy end of the scale. This makes headsail selection less

critical and keeps you right in the running when the wind strength increases or decreases 5 knots or so during a race.

The sagging luff also affects the angle of attack of the headsail. Suppose you have your jib sheeted 12 degrees from the centre-line of the boat (Fig. 26). Move the luff 6 inches to leeward, as excessive forestay sag would cause it to do, and the angle made by the chord of the headsail arc to the centre-line would perhaps be reduced to 8 degrees. This is why the performance of some yachts with fine sheeting angles falls off quite quickly as wind strength increases. The forestay sag reduces the sail's angle of attack and the jib exhausts its airflow directly onto the leeward side of the mainsail. This is not such a problem on small boats with fairly wide sheeting angles, but it is very important on boats such as Dragons, FDs, and ocean racers where genoas sheet well back down the length of the boat and, necessarily, at a very close angle to the centre-line.

This extra fullness let into the headsail by forestay sag must also increase the angle of entry, reducing the sail's pointing ability. Conversely, if a medium-weather headsail that has been cut to allow for 2½ in. luff sag is set in lighter weather on a forestay that has been dragged up nearly straight, it will not only be flat and powerless but will have a very low angle of entry, allowing the boat to be sailed so high on the headsail that the mainsail cannot possibly follow it.

Realising the importance of forestay sag for headsail performance, how do we keep the forestay straight—or at least (as a dead-straight forestay is next to impossible except in the lightest winds) keep the variation in sag to a minimum?

First, don't be misled by the tension on the rigging when you are rigged on the beach or at a mooring; this has no bearing on forestay pressure (and hence sag) while you are sailing, although a lot of helmsmen think it has and spend hours with Highfield levers and stretching devices on their rigging at risk of bending their hulls completely in two. There is a simple proof to this proposition—the leeward shroud is always slack when a yacht is sailing to windward, no matter what tensions you apply to the rigging beforehand, indicating (in a typical

A sagging forestay, aggravated by the big sea the Flying Dutchman is ploughing into, has caused the genoa jib to become far too full for the heavy wind. The upper leech has fallen completely open.

The lee rigging is very slack on this Australian Heron, but the jib luff wire is quite tight. The slackness in the lee shroud keeps it from interfering with the sheeting angle of the jib.

three-shroud dinghy or small-keelboat rig) that the mast is being fully supported by the forestay and windward shroud. The pressures involved on the mast, forestay, and weather shroud are all due to side-loading from wind pressure and are broken up into compression on the mast and tension in the two wires supporting it. If the rig were set up very tight initially there may be only a small amount of slack in the leeward shroud; if set up loosely there would be a lot of slack in the leeward shroud—but the tension on the forestay under sail would be the same in both instances.

In a dinghy, the point of attachment of the shrouds to the hull is one of the main controls on forestay tension: the further aft they are, the more strain will be transmitted to the forestay. The direction of pull of trapeze wires can contribute to keeping the forestay tight. On some

classes, such as 16 ft. and 12 ft. skiffs where there are two men on trapezes, the windward shroud sometimes becomes quite slack, even in strong winds. This phenomenon can be shattering for both crew and mast, particularly if the mast is semi-supported by a spreader attached to the bar-tight windward shroud that suddenly goes slack! Trapeze-wire tension is, however, inconstant, distributed according to where the crew is situated fore-and-aft along the gunwale and likely to vary considerably for different wind and sea conditions. For each change in position you have a different amount of sag in the forestay.

Mainsheet tension, another well-known contributor to forestay tension, is equally unreliable. When it is most needed to help the forestay, in strong winds, the mainsheet normally has to be eased to relieve the pressure on the mainsail from gusts; this has a disastrous effect on the headsail, making it fuller when it desperately needs to be flat.

Many dinghy skippers have taken steps to control forestay sag and rig tension further by adding multi-purchase boxes to their jib halyards as well as the main shrouds. The halyard adjustment allows them to loosen the rig for light winds, encouraging maximum forestay sag. In these conditions, the vang can be used to control the twist in the mainsail, allowing the mainsheet to be hooked well to windward, controlling only the boom angle. This sheeting technique eliminates the transfer of mainsheet pressure through to the forestay. As the wind strength increases, the traveller is moved down and the sheet tension re-established.

The shroud tensioners are used to increase the tension of both shrouds to a point where the lee shroud is just tight. This gives more support to light spars in the upper wind range as it brings the leeward spreader into use for better mast control.

Aft runners go through the deck of the Swedish 5.5 metre Tomatoe. *Note the lengths of shock rubber led to the permanent backstay which holds the loose runner wires clear of the boom end and sail when they are released for tacking or gybing.*

On dinghies without these extra controls, the shroud position is still a very important factor. The only real restriction on how far aft they may come is the main boom's swinging range. If they are too far aft the boom will not come away far enough for square running. Many classes overcome this by setting the shrouds on slides along the top of the gunwale, allowing the leeward shroud to be pushed forward out of the way for square running.

The ultimate extension of this principle is the runner, extensively used on three-quarter-rigged yachts like the Dragon, and some of the 5.5s. This is undoubtedly the most efficient and controllable way of applying pressure to the forestay.

To the crew, runners are fiendish inventions, but they are worth all the cuts, bruises, and curses in terms of sailing efficiency. They can be used in two ways, both of which have their drawbacks: first, in a forward position, about 6 ft. abaft the mast, where they act like an after shroud. The athwartships rigging must be set up loosely to allow the mast to fall over to leeward, throwing pressure on the runner and forestay. Too much tension on the windward cap shroud will rob some weight from the runner and hence limit the force going through to the forestay. These forward runners normally work on slides and are almost impossible to release and haul on when gybing and coming hard on the wind around a leeward mark. But they are quite good when tacking to windward, as they don't have to be hauled on and let off with each tack.

The second system is to have the runners sited well aft, not on slides, with pressure applied more directly by winches, wheels, or Highfield levers. They must be pulled on and let go with each tack, and, if care is not taken when rounding up from a reaching to a close-hauled course, you end up with a mile of wire flapping around the leeward side, begging to be caught on a protrusion from another yacht, or perhaps the mark. This system is, however, the most positive method of controlling luff or forestay tension.

The further aft the runners go, the more direct will be the pull on the forestay, and the less compression will be exerted on the mast (see Fig. 27). Runners sited aft, by pulling the mast almost directly aft, leave sideways bend to be controlled completely by the athwartships rigging. By finely adjusting the cap shrouds and lowers, the mast can be made to lay off to leeward at the top, or come to windward below the hounds, or remain straight.

With the forward-runner rig, where the runners necessarily take the major side loading, the same degree of control is not available. So I prefer the aft-runner system. This type of runner normally goes through the deck near the centre-line of the boat alongside the backstay. The two runner wires are led down through two sets of rings, attached to the backstay by two short lengths of shock rubber, 4 ft. and 8 ft. above the deck, before going through the deck to the winch, wheel, or lever adjuster.

The shock rubber holds the loose runner wires clear of the boom end when they are

released for tacking and gybing. When the boom is eased, the slack wire is swept forward by the leech of the mainsail and not by the boom as it is with forward-set runners. This keeps the amount of loose wire to a minimum and high in the air, out of harm's way.

LUFF TENSION

After striving to hold forestay sag as constant as possible, you must now look at other ways of controlling headsail shape. Luff tension can be used in the same way as it is used to vary mainsail shape. Most modern dinghies use the luff wire in their jibs as a forestay, the luff tension on the sail being adjustable from the bottom by varying the tack position or with a Cunningham eye.

Keel yachts, from boats like the Soling upwards, carry rope or tape stretchy-luff headsails hanked to the standing forestay. With this system, the luff tension is normally adjusted from the top by varying halyard tension. The

Figure 27. Effect of varying the shroud position. The distance behind the mast of the main shrouds has a great bearing on forestay tension. In a simple three-stay rig with side loading, the mast is supported by the forestay and the windward shroud. Position 1, level with mast: the shroud is supporting the mast sideways only, exerting no tension on the forestay. Position 2, 2 ft. back from the mast: shroud and forestay are now supporting the mast together; forestay must now be in tension. Position 3, 4 ft. back; forestay tension is double that at position 2.

If the headsail luff is not stretched up hard enough, wind pressure will cause sag between the hank attachment points, making hard spots along the luff.

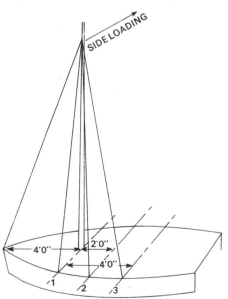

halyard should be organised so that the genoa can be easily lowered for light spinnaker reaching or square running where it would affect the efficiency of the spinnaker.

Larger off-shore and in-shore yachts now set their stretchy-luff headsails in twin-groove headstay foils (see Chapter on Ocean Racing).

Special care is needed when luff-tensioning yarn-tempered headsails. Most sailors used to standard-cloth headsails tend to over-tension the luffs. This pulls the drive too far forward, knuckling the sail badly from the luff and leads to an immediate break-up of the cloth structure. Minimal luff tension is needed: just enough to remove the wrinkles with adjustment in terms of a quarter-inch instead of two inches.

SHEETING ANGLES

The question most commonly asked about headsails is:- Where should they be sheeted? My stock answer, which is usually small comfort to the questioner, is: In the position that makes the boat go fastest and highest to windward. There is only one way to find this out—by lots of trial and error. However, there are a few basic

guidelines to finding roughly the correct position before on-the-water experiment.

Take no notice of the mitre in deciding the correct fore-and-aft position. At one time the right place was considered to be just aft of the extension of the mitre line. But this is no longer a very reliable guide since sailmakers have been widely varying the angle of the mitre seam (and even eliminating it altogether). The best rough approach is to lay the headsail on a flat surface and bisect the angle formed by the foot and the leech with both pulled tight, then set the sail with the boat on the beach or at mooring, and mark the spot where the extension of this line meets the deck. This is a fairly good starting point; a sheet led from here will impose even pressure on the foot and leech.

A tall, narrow headsail, such as on a Star, Soling, or 5.5, will necessarily have to be sheeted farther forward than this rule-of-thumb position. As the leech is probably four or five times as long as the foot, it needs a much higher proportion of the sheet pressure.

Most modern dinghy headsails have considerable fullness built in low, near the foot, and if the sheeting angle is taken too far aft, excessive pressure along the foot will cause this built-in

Far left. This Cherub is being perfectly handled in fresh wind. The full headsail is twisted open around the head to give a perfect parallel slot around the lee side of the mainsail. The puckers on the luff wire could be removed with a little extra luff tension.

Centre. Lazy E number 47 has insufficient cloth tension on her jib (and mainsail luff, too).

Left. The headsail is too full, sheeted too far forward, and on too hard, causing the leech to hook back, closing up the slot between headsail and mainsail.

fullness to distort and curl up. The sheet should be gradually moved forward until this built-in shape sets correctly. This, in turn, will give a more direct pull from the sheet on the leech, so you must be careful not to over-sheet, causing the leech to stand up bar tight and choking the slot between mainsail and headsail.

This forward sheeting of headsails has become a trend in recent years, aimed at making the bottom of the sail more efficient with built-in shape taking the place of the old-fashioned, flat, stretched-out shape of the past. While it has improved the performance of many dinghies, some skippers have discarded it as a failure. This is usually due to for'ard hands pulling on the headsail just as hard as they did with the old flat-footed headsail which needed a lot of pressure to make the leech stand up. The for'ard hand must trim this new type headsail very accurately—a $\frac{1}{4}$ in. of sheet makes a large alteration to the leech position in relation to the mainsail, so a new trimming technique has to be evolved to gain its full advantages.

The age-old technique of shifting the jib leads aft for heavy weather and for'ard for light weather still holds to a certain extent. As the sheet is shifted aft the foot of the sail receives a larger proportion of the pressure from the sheet; the foot stretches and allows draft in the lower section to be flattened by brute force. This is usually effective action if you get caught with a light-weather headsail in a freshening breeze, but always having to sheet a headsail this way to get performance indicates that the shape cut into the bottom of the sail is wrong—it may be too full or have the draft too far aft—and you would be better off having it recut.

The other big recent trend is to sheet headsails closer inboard in an attempt to narrow the slot between headsail and mainsail down low for a more parallel slot generally around the lee side of the mainsail. Here again you must be careful not to oversheet. If you pull it on too hard you will close the angle of the jib at the top as well as the bottom with a result that the sail will not exhaust from the leech. This effect will be worse than with the old wide sheeting angle, which gave an uneven slot, wide at the bottom and narrowing higher up.

Dinghy headsails tend to sheet between 10 and 17 degrees from the centre-line. This big variation is because a fine, easily driven hull can carry a smaller angle than a big, bluff-bowed boat that is hard to drive through the water.

And in flatter water with light winds, where hull speed is achieved easily, narrow angles of sheeting can be used to allow the boat to go high to windward without losing speed. As soon as the wind strength increases to a point where the main boom has to be travelled to leeward to de-power the rig, then the jib should be sheeted at a wider angle to keep the slot between jib and main constantly open. The only way to find the best angle for your boat is through trial and error—keep closing the headsail in until the boat starts to point too high and lose speed, then open it out slightly until it is going at its best again. The angles you find should be carefully marked on decks and sheeting tracks so that once you have proved a certain angle is best in light, flat water, you can easily home in on it.

LEECH FLUTTER

Leech curl and leech flutter are perennial headsail headaches—if one doesn't get you the other will. But how much do they really affect performance ? With a genoa, if the leech is dead flat it must eventually begin to flutter as the wind strength increases. If the flutter is only slight it will not affect sail performance although it may drive the crew insane after two or three hours. However, if the flutter becomes a heavy flog and begins to shake the whole sail, affecting its entire shape and making it very difficult to sail with, it must be fixed.

For smaller, harbour-racing headsails, the hot-knife leech is probably the best solution. The single layer of synthetic sail cloth is cut and sealed in one motion with a hot knife, leaving no seam at all along the edge. This allows the whole leech to stretch evenly and there is no extra weight from a seam to encourage heavy flutter. This type of sail demands extremely careful maintenance. You must check seams and the leech edge for chafe or signs of fraying after every race—a split seam or badly frayed edge could ruin this headsail.

The most efficient and long-lasting control is a leech line. This should be as light as pos-

sible and continually adjusted—just tight enough to keep the flutter under control. The small curl on the leech of the genoa from this leech line tension, I have found, does not detract from the sail's performance provided the overall shape is correct. But start worrying if a large curl develops six to nine inches in from the leech.

On smaller jibs, where battens are allowed, I prefer, if given a free hand by the class rules, to have a through batten to control the shape at the narrow head section with a couple of leech battens lower down to keep the edge of the sail free of curl. Weight and thickness of jib battens must be kept to a minimum; about $\frac{1}{16}$ in. $\times \frac{3}{4}$ in. glassfibre battens are ideal. If the battens are too thick, cloth will be stretched either side of the pocket, which in turn will cause looseness between the pockets and lead to flutter. If the battens are too heavy, their weight, flogging around through tacking in high winds, will stretch the leech and eventually burst the pockets away from the sail.

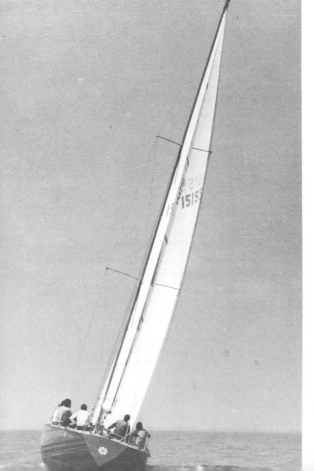

Far left. A small amount of leech curl, usually caused by the leech line to stop flutter, is acceptable in a headsail, but the 6 in. curl on this genoa leech is a performance robber.

Centre. Good, close-sheeted crosscut at the top of its range. The sheet leads are well aft to flatten the bottom and provide the right exit angle.

Left. Powerful, close sheeted headsail forming beautiful parallel slot with mainsail leech, in light breeze.

41

Spinnakers

THE SPINNAKER is one of the mysteries in the sailmaker's life. No matter what he does in design, cloth selection, and cut, the only real certainty about the final result is that some spinnakers go very fast from the moment they are first made until they eventually blow to bits, while others of identical size and, apparently, shape just never perform as well. Against that even-chance gamble to be faced on the loft floor we can reduce the variables with some proved knowledge of spinnaker styles and shapes.

There are basically two types of spinnaker—the flat spinnaker, which is peculiar to Australian and New Zealand classes, and the universally popular parachute.

FLAT SPINNAKER

The "flattie" is widely used in the Australian skiff classes (18s, 16s, 12s) and national classes like the Sharpie and Gwen 12s. It is normally cut to a total area restriction or to a class luff, foot, and leech length restriction in the same style as a genoa.

The flat spinnaker usually has a wire luff and is set from a much longer pole than those used by the international classes. The wire luff is tensioned like a genoa luff, with the pole held down tight by a kicker, allowing the shallow spinnaker to be used on very close reaches—almost hard on the wind. The long pole keeps the sail well clear of the normal headsail, with the leech falling out and around the mainsail like a large overlapping genoa. It is sheeted well towards the quarter. When the flat spinnaker is carried on a three-quarter reach or square run, the sheet lead is moved forward from its normal shy reaching position and the sheet is even sometimes passed to windward of the mast, to keep the leech tight.

The flat spinnaker is cut from a cloth lighter than that used in a headsail but quite a lot heavier than the normal parachute spinnaker, usually 2 oz. to 3 oz. per sq. yd. This may sound too solid for a dinghy spinnaker, but it must be strong enough to hold the shape in quite strong winds. As with the genoa, if the drive drifts too far aft it will tighten up the leech and thus reduce shy-reaching ability. As this spinnaker is relatively flat there is no great area of cloth floating up in the air as there is with the parachute, ready to collapse at the slightest excuse, so heavy cloth is no disadvantage.

Sailmakers over the years have tried many different methods of making flat spinnakers, with cloths running in all directions—sometimes to seek stability of shape, sometimes to try for the "magic" shape, and alas, sometimes just as a sales gimmick, if you'll pardon the pun. Most popular, and I believe the most successful, is the radial cut, which is difficult to make but can be designed with the drive a little farther aft than in other cuts without fear of its shifting, either in strong winds or as the sail ages. The more normal mitre cut is a good performer, but must be cut from slightly heavier cloth to achieve the same shape stability.

The flat spinnaker, having to be set with the wire luff forward, presents handling problems. It is difficult to gybe. The pole must be thrown around the forestay, still attached to the luff, the boat gybed, pole picked up out of the water and reset on the mast, sheet swapped to the new leeward side—a complicated manoeuvre, fraught with peril. The skiffs have evolved a system all their own to simplify this: the wire jib-luff also serves as a forestay. Coming into the gybe they drop the jib, unclip the halyard, rehoist on the windward side of the spinnaker pole. The boat is then gybed and the sheet swapped over to the new leeward side. An endless sheet, rigged right around the boat, is sometimes used in both types of gybe to make the sheet-swapping operation easier.

These gybing systems sound simple—and *are* simple in light weather—but until you have

This 16-footer shows off the favourite sail of the Australian development classes, the wire-luff flat spinnaker. Pressure from the pole is forcing the mast aft. A preventer is usually rigged to counter this.

Rainbow, a popular Australian two-man scow, carrying a double-luff flat spinnaker with the brace hooked under a shy hook on the gunwale.

tried re-clipping the jib halyard in an open skiff with the breeze piping over 20 knots you have never suffered. Every time the fourth hand goes for'ard the boat ships green water over the bow. If he can't make it you are eventually forced to gybe with spinnaker up and no jib forestay supporting the mast—instant disaster. Throwing the pole around, as done in the two-man dinghies, is easier. But if the throw is misjudged the bow can run over the end of the pole, leaving it on one side of the stem and the spinnaker on the other.

These problems, and the influence of the simple parachute spinnaker from the international classes, have led to the double-luff type of flat spinnaker now commonly used on such classes as the Cherub, Javelin, and Lazy E. It has cross-cut cloths, similar to those of a big-yacht spinnaker, and symmetrical about the centre seam, allowing the spinnaker to be set with either edge as the luff. This makes gybing much less complicated, although still hazardous in strong winds.

SHEETING

The correct sheeting positions for a flat spinnaker can be found by the same method as that used for the genoa, with the boat set up on the beach, fully rigged, and the lead position shifted back and forth until the leech of the spinnaker, when set with pole against the forestay, falls with an even, open slot around the lee side of the main.

The attaching height of the pole on the mast should preferably be at the level of the for'ard hand's shoulder when he is standing in the boat. This gives him good leverage when he is pushing the pole forward for a set.

Pole length, spinnaker luff length, and halyard height should then be juggled so that the pole is as near as possible to parallel to the water. This means that when the brace (wire or rope controlling the position of the pole from the windward side) takes the strain, it is inclined to pull the pole down, tightening the wire luff, rather than allowing the pole to sky. This downward angle of the brace is helped by a fitting called a "shy hook". It has two forms—either a single projection under the gunwale, or in the international classes where the rules forbid sheeting the sails outside the skin, on the deck in the form of a fixed hook. The fitting is attached just in front of the for'ard hand's sitting position so that the windward brace can easily be hooked under it. This not only increases the downward pull on the spinnaker pole but keeps the brace clear of the side-deck, allowing the crew unrestricted movement in and out on trapeze while reaching in a puffy breeze.

PARACHUTES

Easier to set and lower, but more difficult to trim, the more universally used parachute spinnaker is common to the bigger yachts and international dinghy classes such as the Flying Dutchman and 505. The parachute is set off a pole the same length as the base of the fore-triangle, which means that it will only project past the forestay 5 or 6 in. when the pole is raised to the normal position.

Its size is usually governed by luff, foot, leech, and half-height restrictions. So the total area is anything the sailmaker can cram in full-ness within these limits, and this is where the fun starts. The owner and sailmaker must decide on the maximum performance range of the spinnaker, as there are many distinct types

—reaching, running, light-weather, or heavy-weather. The reaching spinnaker is normally flatter, especially in the head, and more dish-shaped than the running spinnaker, allowing the air to flow in and out more easily, which enables it to be carried closer to the wind without too much heeling force. The running spinnaker has much larger shoulders running to its head and is slightly tighter in the leeches, making it more stable and easier to trim for slight changes in wind direction.

A good parachute spinnaker, no matter what the type, should be fairly easy to keep full, especially if it is to be used in rough water. This means that when the luff starts to collapse only a small amount of sheet need be pulled in to flip the leading edge up again—it will sometimes snap up again of its own accord.

A slightly more efficient spinnaker with freer leeches can be made, but this is difficult to keep full and must be trimmed very carefully. If not trimmed before or as the luff starts to collapse, the spinnaker will completely roll in from the luff and large amounts of sheet will have to be pulled in to make it fill again. More speed is usually lost through this than with the slightly tighter-leech spinnaker which stays full.

If class rules restrict you to one spinnaker, you must compromise between the extremes to gain a good all-round performer.

BASIC CUTS

There are many variations to parachute spinnaker design: normal cross-cut, spherical, radial head, tri-radial and Starcut with others in between and they all have fairly specialised uses (see Ocean Racing chapter).

The spherical, invented by Frenchman Herbulot many years ago, was probably the first real parachute. This cut is still very popular in Europe and is widely used in international small-boat classes such as the Flying Dutchman, 505 and Fireball.

The spherical has no seam running vertically down the centre. When it is made the sail is laid-up on a half-diagram, as are most para-

Left. This tri-radial spinnaker combines radial cloths from head and clews with central cross-cut panels. It is versatile, can be used equally well running or reaching.

Far left. Good example of flat parachute spinnaker with good pole height and correct trim.

Centre top and bottom. Compare these two spinnakers being carried on the same reach. The yacht above is using a very effective Starcut —radial cut from heavy cloth to give shape stability. The shallow, dishy shape gives maximum drive for minimum heeling force. The yacht below is using a running spinnaker for the reaching leg. Its light cloth has allowed the spinnaker to become full in the middle, causing the leech to close up and impede the exhaust of air. The sail is being over-sheeted, stretching the foot to try to reduce some of this excessive fullness.

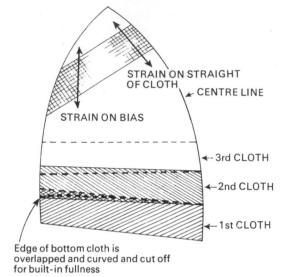

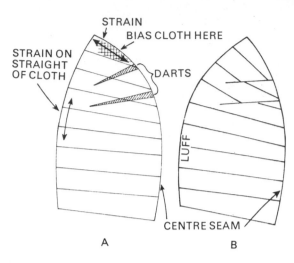

Figure 28. Layout of spherical spinnaker showing cloths at right-angles to centre-line. Cloths increase their angle downwards as they near the head. Bias stretch is increased out towards the leech while strength is gained down the centre of the sail.

Figure 29. Cross-cut spinnaker. All cloths are at right-angles to the luffs. The shaded areas in **A** are cut out, and when the edges are seamed together the head is pulled over and flattened, the shoulders are thrown out, and fullness is built in (**B**). This also makes the centre seam flatter and gives more shape to the luffs.

chute spinnakers, but with the cloth folded at the centre-line. As the cloths run away at right angles to the centre-line, their edges overlap each other towards the leech (Fig. 28). The amount of curve in the centre-line controls the fullness of the spinnaker—the more curve there is, the more overlap of cloth there will be at the seams, allowing more seam taper in the final shaping.

The spherical is relatively quick to make, as there is no centre seam to deal with, and it can be reproduced accurately, provided the seam-tapering is well controlled. It keeps its shape well, as it has the weft of the material running parallel to the centre-line of the spinnaker. This prevents stretch down the centre, which, if it occurs, makes the shape fuller but reduces the effective silhouette area. If a spinnaker that has stretched this way is laid back on the loft floor it will be found that the centre-line curve has increased and the luffs, which previously may have had 2 ft. to 3 ft. of round in them, are nearly straight.

The disadvantages of the spherical are few but fairly serious. A lot of cloth has to be used, as the overlaps are mostly cut to scrap, and this makes the spinnaker fairly expensive. If the

sail is going to stretch, it will do so out towards the edges where all the bias cloth is to be found. The luff and leech tapes used for finishing the sail will not stretch correspondingly, so a big hooking leech and luff will result. This fault can be remedied by removing the tapes and replacing them loosely, but this is a fairly big job that will only temporarily correct the problem.

This cloth-bias problem is the main reason why spherical spinnakers are used only on small craft where the pressures are relatively slight. The degeneration cycle is accelerated in bigger yachts by the spinnaker having to drag 2 to 3 tons of hull through the water.

The radial-head construction method was developed for bigger yachts and ocean racers to replace the stretchier bias cloths in the head of the spinnaker with low-stretch panels of cloth radiating from the head with the thread-line placed along the direction of loading. Normal cross-cut panel construction is used below the head.

The radial-head form of construction is also used to cope with the highly-stressed clew areas of specialised reaching spinnakers for big yachts. Bruce Banks' Starcut was probably the

46

first to radiate panels from clews and head to place the lowest-stretch direction of thread along the stress lines. The tri-radial is really a fuller version of the Starcut. The radial clews help stop the flattish-cut reaching spinnaker from stretching into inefficient fullness when under high, tight-reaching loads.

The cross-cut spinnaker is still favoured for moderate-displacement one-design classes such as the Soling and Etchells 22. The shape is difficult to control accurately enough for radial construction to be used in these very competitive classes.

The cross-cut is constructed with the cloths running at right-angles to the luff and leech into the centre seam.

Each cloth in a cross-cut spinnaker is cut at the centre-line of the half-diagram, and the spinnaker, when seamed up, comes out as two complete halves. Overlaps for seam tapering are allowed as required to give shape to the spinnaker, but towards the head they become more prominent near the centre seam instead of out towards the edges, as they do in the spherical. If not enough seam taper is allowed for, the shape will be too pointed towards the centre, leaving the edges flat and making the spinnaker very unstable when set. To overcome this, American sailmaker Ted Hood designed a variation to the cross-cut spinnaker with broad darts running across at the head, allowing the pointed area towards the middle to be flattened and at the same time adding seam-taper fullness evenly across the spinnaker towards the leech (Fig. 29). This darting also increases the amount of leech curvature as it flattens the centre seam, making all round for a larger, wider-shouldered spinnaker than can normally be obtained. The one drawback is that the bias cloth around the head of the spinnaker is inclined to stretch, lengthening the centre seam and straightening the leeches—the spinnaker becomes fuller, with less area projected to the wind, and performance falls off.

Over the last few years, the radial-head running spinnaker, the tri-radial reacher and the Starcut have come into general use by both off-shore and in-shore racing yachts. The radial construction method cuts out stretchy bias cloth areas and replaces them with narrow radial panels cut in such a way that the thread line of

An excellent example of tri-radial spinnaker on Quarter Tonner. Combination of crosscut panels in centre and radial panels from clews and head enable it to be carried equally well shy reaching or running.

the cloth runs in the same direction as the greatest strain out of the corners of the spinnaker. This keeps stretch to a minimum, preventing the high-strain areas from growing fuller under sailing pressure. This type of construction has also increased the wind range of lightweight spinnakers, especially for off-shore yachts. In light weather at sea the lightweight spinnaker is of great advantage; not only does a very large area of cloth have to support itself in mid-air but it inevitably has to be used in a sloppy left-over sea which has the masthead gyrating in circles. Cloths as light as $\frac{1}{2}$ oz. per sq. yd. have been woven to try to master these conditions. Half-ounce spinnakers still have to be carefully nursed, and used only in winds of 5 to 6 knots as they will distort or blow out very quickly in anything stronger.

Above 5 knots, a $\frac{3}{4}$ oz. spinnaker is probably the most used on big yachts, as it can be held up in quite light airs and is strong enough to hold out until about 20 knots, depending on the weight of the yacht. Remember when choosing cloth weights that a light, planing dinghy in an 18- to 20-knot breeze will be speeding downwind at 10 to 15 knots, so there is only an effective breeze of 5 to 8 knots working on the spinnaker. Conversely, a big, heavy cruising yacht in the same breeze may be doing only 6 knots, putting the spinnaker under 14 knots of pressure.

The most durable spinnaker for general use, and essential in the high-wind range, is the $1\frac{1}{2}$ oz.

Spinnakers are generally made from Rip-stop-based nylon, a very fine-based cloth with a heavier thread running through it in squares for added strength. Care for your spinnakers, repairing promptly tiny holes that can soon become great big holes, and, when drying them, remember that nylon exposed to direct sunlight for long periods will rot and deteriorate.

TRIMMING AND HANDLING

Trimming a spinnaker once it is aloft is a mystical art that has few masters. There are not many yachtsmen who can view a three-dimensional shape suspended in space, appreciate it, and adjust pole and controlling brace and sheet until it reaches the shape that will give maximum performance for that particular point of sailing. It calls for the same inherent skill that allows some people to draw freehand perfect circles and straight lines while the rest of us can manage only egg shapes and dogs' hind legs.

However, for both the naturally talented and the trier, practice will always improve your skill. And you'll always do better if you sit in a position, no matter how uncomfortable, from where it is possible to study the whole of the spinnaker shape. This allows you, when trimming, to notice and adjust the shape differences obtained by your trimming efforts as well as those caused by wind-strength variations and directional changes. Absolute concentration is needed at all times. However, before we deal with the more ethereal side of spinnaker trimming, the mechanics of setting the thing must be outlined. The techniques I am about to outline have been perfected for the intensely competitive Dragon and Soling classes. They hold good for most big yachts and dinghies but may need modifying to suit your own boat.

Despite simplified modern fittings and techniques, spinnakers continue to cause more foul-ups on yachts than anything else. Setting the sail, gybing, and lowering it are not as difficult as many clumsy crews make them look, provided some time has been given to practice, where the problems are carefully analysed beforehand. When racing, there is no time to stop and analyse.

Most standard spinnaker set-ups comprise a pole, uphaul to raise the pole and hold it in a horizontal position, downhaul to stop it from skying, brace to hold the pole back at the required angle to the wind, halyard for hoisting the spinnaker itself, and sheet to control the angle of the spinnaker's trim to the wind. (Fig. 30). The main guiding rule when hoisting is that sheet, brace, and halyard must be outside every other piece of equipment—the spinnaker must then go up clear and set. I bracket clear and set together because it is useless getting the spinnaker into the air if you are unable to get it set and working before a foul-up occurs. To achieve this the sheet and brace must be trimmed as the spinnaker is hoisted, keeping the sail free of twists and avoiding that 30- to 40-second period with the sail flapping around wildly during which clips are apt to undo themselves, sheets to tie themselves in knots, and holes to appear in the cloth.

This comes from crews being too hasty, usually urged on by an impatient skipper roaring "Get it up! Get it up! Get it up!", where his stream of command, after allowing the crew a pause of several seconds for a last-minute visual check before hoisting, should be: "Right.

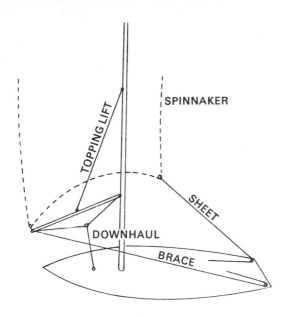

Figure 30. Diagram of simple spinnaker arrangement, showing sheet, brace, uphaul, and downhaul.

Everybody ready? Go!", and the spinnaker shoots up—bang, set—in a sequence so smooth it's like a single action.

With that cautious pause, possible snarl-ups can be spotted before they happen and when they are much easier to remedy, although it means a few seconds lost before the spinnaker leaves the deck. Many crews are so intent on a quick spinnaker hoist that they neglect to trim mainsail and jib to gain maximum initial speed for the new downwind leg, and are liable to lose sight of close opponents who may be taking advantage of the confusion to blanket their wind from astern. That pause for thought on rounding the mark enables the main and jib to be trimmed to optimum for the next leg and for the helmsman to assess the tactical situation.

The best spinnaker systems are evolved through a simple work study to find the best method of using the number of hands available. The system is then tried on the yacht in slow motion so that faults can be found and eliminated. Once the system works smoothly in slow motion, speed will automatically increase. The system must work perfectly in heavy weather. If there are some short cuts to it, use them only when the weather is light. Some fast spinnaker methods have been evolved which work only in light breezes and fail in heavy winds where disaster is liable to become real disaster.

In pre-planning the spinnaker system, the optimum height for the pole should be determined and marked on the mast. To find the height, the spinnaker should be set fairly square in a moderate breeze and the pole lifted on the mast as long as the spinnaker wants to lift itself, with the shoulders opening out to their full height and width. When the pole is lifted higher than this point, the luffs will become excessively curved with the mid-section flatter and distorted and the clew probably hanging down at a lower level than the pole. As a rough check, the tack and clew should be level, but, if the wind is light, be sure you are not misled by a heavy sheet dragging the clew down.

Having found the maximum height, you must realise that the pole must be carried lower as the breeze lightens and the spinnaker tends to droop towards the foot. Lower the pole with it until you are just holding the weight of the brace off the spinnaker so that the luff falls in an even curve and does not hang up on the end of the pole. Fit a light-weather sheet. As soon as there is any sign of the spinnaker lifting to a slight increase in the strength of the breeze, raise the pole to follow it.

The angle of the pole to the boat should initially be a fair bit ahead of what you expect the final setting to be, because it takes some time for the apparent wind to move aft. On most boats, the pole should probably be preset to 35 degrees from the hull centre-line for a square run and hard against the forestay for any other point of downwind sailing. But you must be instantly ready to drag the pole aft, especially for a square set, to keep the spinnaker filling.

SETTING

Basically there are two positions to hoist the spinnaker from—the bow or leeward shroud. In yachts with only small jibs, such as the 5.5 and Soling, you can hoist from a basket attached to the leeward shroud with the brace running around the forestay from the end of the pole and the sheet attached. It is very important with this set-up to have the tack of the spin-

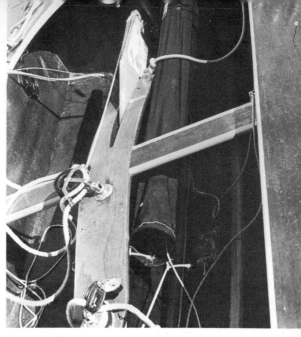

Fireball spinnaker launcher. Launchers are now common to many classes, up to Quarter Ton.

naker being pulled to the pole as the sail is hoisted, otherwise the spinnaker will be sucked into the area of disturbed air behind the mainsail, with the likelihood of wrapping itself into the dreaded wineglass knot. The pole must be pulled aft quickly, in the next instant, to keep the spinnaker filling.

Setting shy, you will also strike trouble in the mainsail's backwind area if the trimmer drags the sheet in very tight initially. The idea is to flick the pole to get the luff filling and ease up the sheet until the whole spinnaker is full. This is why it is good in genoa-rigged yachts to have the headsail on the way down as the spinnaker hits the top.

In boats with genoa working rigs, this leeward set is difficult because of the big headsail overlapping the lee shroud, so the general method is to set from a basket or turtle on the bow, ahead of the forestay. The disadvantage

of this method is that you must have a man on the bow for a short period to set the turtle and hook on brace, sheet, and halyard. This normally is done approaching the weather mark, where the small drop in performance through the extra weight of the man on the bow can lose you more in distance and tactical position than a slightly slower set around the mark. So, especially if you are at close quarters with other boats, it may be better to delay setting up the spinnaker, ready for hoisting, until after the mark is rounded.

On larger yachts, such as ocean racers, the spinnaker may be set from turtles under the genoa, but the genoa must be dropped the instant the spinnaker is hoisted, leaving free air to fill it immediately, and avoiding the danger area behind the mainsail.

Packing a spinnaker in basket or turtle so that it will hoist cleanly can be unnecessarily time-consuming, taking up to ten minutes or so if both luffs and the foot are laboriously sorted out. My own method is this: Take hold of the head; this is normally the easiest to find, as the halyard is still on it or has been the last line detached from it. Run the hands quickly down one luff, gathering the luff tape in loops against the head in the left hand, until you reach the clew. You have found two of the three corners and ensured the spinnaker is not twisted. Hold onto the clew and throw head and sorted luff to one side. From the clew, run the hands quickly along the foot tape to find the other clew. Sit with a clew either side of you and the luff to one side, run the hands back along the foot to its centre and then begin grabbing with both hands the bulk of the cloth, from the bottom, in large handfuls, bundling it into your lap. This way, you'll automatically end up with the three corners clear of the bundle, as they should be, as you poke it into the basket or turtle, and with the spinnaker ready to hoist cleanly without twisting.

There should be some positive holding device on the basket to firmly secure the three corners so that in the period between the brace being released to be hooked onto the sail and hoisting, when the brace usually drags in the water, the spinnaker cannot be pulled out prematurely. The corners can be tied to the basket or turtle with stopping cotton or wool, eyes poking out clear, ready to be hooked on, or, if a basket is being used, shock-chord may be rigged around the top under which a fold of cloth near the corners may be poked. Stopping spinnakers with wool or cotton is a practice that is disappearing from one-design yachts

Far left. Spinnaker packed in a turtle has been set on the bow approaching the mark. As soon as the mark is reached, the pole is raised by the forward hand. After he has done this, he will take the sheet, ready to trim as the spinnaker is hoisted by hand in the cockpit . . .

Centre. The sheet hand, who has preset the brace, hoists the spinnaker; the forward hand is trimming the sheet as the sail goes up . . .

Left. Thanks to the trimming-while-hoisting technique, the spinnaker sets immediately without twisting. Here the sheet has been hauled on hard a fraction too long, causing a slight knockdown.

51

Right and centre. Common fault: leech hangs open in the middle as sailing angle becomes shy. Contrast this with Miles Furniture spinnaker, at similar angle. The head is standing up and the leech is firm.

Far right. Boat well balanced with genoa deliberately undersheeted so that it does not suck in the spinnaker.

and smaller craft these days, but on big yachts and ocean racing yachts it is wise in very hard weather to stop the spinnaker so that the pole angle can be set and everything cleated down firmly before the sail is broken out.

This stopping is normally done with rubber bands, with the aid of a plastic bucket with the bottom cut out. Two ¾ in. square lengths of wood are usually screwed to the bucket, on opposite sides and running down its length, to make the bands easier to slip off with wet, cold hands. First, a hundred or so rubber bands have to be stretched over the outside of the bucket (normally penance for seagoing sins like dropping winch-handles over the side). The bucket is then secured by a couple of lanyards and clips across the yacht. The head of the spinnaker is dragged through it, with one crew member sorting the luffs to ensure there are no twists while another flicks off a rubber band from the small end of the bucket every 3 ft. or 4 ft. along the length of the spinnaker. With this method, a very large spinnaker can be taken down and be made ready for re-setting within three or four minutes. It is very suitable for Starcuts and any other spinnaker that will have to be set on a tight reach in strong winds.

TRIMMING

You have hoisted the spinnaker. You have established the pole height and know how to vary it for different breezes. Now begins the tense task of trimming—to keep the spinnaker full and working to its maximum.

The pole should be kept as far aft as possible. The best angle can normally be judged from the reaction of the area of spinnaker closest to the end of the pole; when the pole is approaching being too far aft, this area will luff in a similar way to the luff of the jib when sailing too close to the wind. The spinnaker will not necessarily collapse on the luff if the pole is too far aft, as it can be held full by having the sheet trimmed too far in. So the ultimate position is gained by bringing the pole to this luffing position, then easing it forward slightly until the luffing symptoms near the pole disappear, and finally easing the sheet until the luff of the spinnaker is just on the verge of folding in.

If you were sailing a constant course in a perfect, unshifting breeze, there would be no need to alter this trim further. But such an ideal set of circumstances hardly ever occurs. The luff of the spinnaker will become unstable as

the wind goes forward in relation to the boat. In my opinion, the first trimming action that should be taken to stop the luff collapsing in a slight "header" is to ease the pole forward and then trim the sheet. This keeps the spinnaker up high and well away from the back of the mainsail. The helmsman can help by pulling the boat away slightly, giving some acceleration, and, on larger yachts where the spinnaker cannot be trimmed in by hand, helping the task of the winchmen in heavier winds.

If the reverse procedure is followed and the sheet trimmed first, the leech of the spinnaker will come in close to the mainsail, checking the exhaust flow of air, slowing the boat and increasing the heeling moment, especially if it is reaching shy.

In light air, the spinnaker trimmer should handle both brace and sheet, if he can, so that he can synchronise the easing of the pole forward and the trimming in of the sheet.

The old adage that the spinnaker pole should be trimmed square to the direction of the wind pennant is no use; different spinnakers respond to different pole angles, and it does not take into account the variations of apparent wind angle to the boat with speed alterations.

In a light, puffy wind a boat on a broad three-quarter or square run can accelerate two or three knots in a puff and carry its way into a very light patch; the apparent wind swings forward of the beam and the pole will have to be eased forward almost to the forestay to keep the spinnaker full. Then, as the boat slows down and the next puff catches it, the pole will have to be pulled aft smartly and the sheet let go at the same time to save the spinnaker from being sucked in behind the mainsail. You see more bad trimming in in this type of weather than in fresher winds, where it is easier to keep the spinnaker constantly working.

A good spinnaker trimmer will be easing the sheet nearly all the time to keep the sail as far as possible from the main, especially shy reaching with the pole hard against the forestay, when the luff of the spinnaker should be constantly on the move, or on the verge of collapsing; otherwise the spinnaker will spend quite a lot of its time overtrimmed. With a good spinnaker you should be able to collapse the leading two or three feet of the luff without its continuing into a general collapse. But, if the spinnaker is being trimmed in this fashion, intense concentration is needed to avoid un-

Spinnaker, genoa and mainsail all in perfect trim.

Good example of why genoa should be dropped, so as to fill spinnaker as soon as it hits the masthead.

Figure 31. Angle of spinnaker pole when square running. Don't trim the pole too far aft when running square. It is better to shy a little and get the main pulling force acting fore-and-aft rather than have the spinnaker tending to pull you over to port.

necessary collapsing.

When running square, the same trimming techniques apply. However, I think many skippers insist on having the pole dragged too far aft. This tends to pull the tack of the spinnaker much further aft than the clew, leaving the main pulling force of the spinnaker angled to windward instead of along the line of the yacht's course. By easing the pole slightly forward, and only trimming in the sheet slightly, tack and clew are positioned more or less at right angles to the hull, allowing the main driving force of the spinnaker to fall directly along it (Fig. 31).

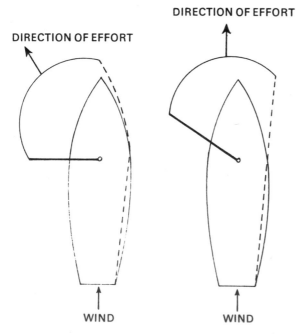

DIRECTION OF EFFORT

DIRECTION OF EFFORT

WIND

WIND

Far right top. Well-trimmed dinghy spinnaker— pole high and sheet tension correct.

Right top. This spinnaker pole, too low for the weight of breeze, is pulling the spinnaker luff tight and causing the leech to collapse.

Right bottom. These spinnakers are being perfectly trimmed for light air. The pole on 18 has been lowered until it is just high enough to keep the weight of cloth from pulling the spinnaker down. Boat 24 has more breeze, which is lifting her spinnaker.

When the spinnaker is being carried very square, it is essential for the trimmer to be able to see the whole of the spinnaker, as on this point of sailing the first signs of a collapse will appear down the leech rather than the luff. This is caused by the turbulent area of air behind the mainsail. The same signs viewed from aft, behind the mainsail, are often mis-interpreted as indicating the spinnaker is set too square. If the pole is eased and the sheet drawn on—the normal reaction—a bad collapse will result. The sheet should be eased first, and the pole squared at the same time.

If the spinnaker is constantly collapsing on the leech, it is obvious that the boat is being sailed too square, or by the lee, and a gybe should be considered.

The practice of carrying headsails under spinnakers has become common on close reaches with three-quarter-rigged boats such as the Dragon, Soling, and Flying Dutchman where the headsail can still do its job. The spinnaker must here be kept as far as possible away from the back of the mainsail and genoa, since at any sign of a collapse it is liable to get sucked into the backwind of both sails and become very difficult to fill again. To keep the spinnaker filling when it is being carried shy in this way, ease the halyard two or three feet from the mast at the head and set the pole a little farther than normally to leeward, enabling the sheet to be eased farther out. Both measures help keep the spinnaker clear of the dangerous backwind area and allow it to exhaust at the leech.

SHEET LEADS

The best spinnaker sheet-lead position on most one-designs is as far aft and towards the side of the boat as possible. This is simply because the sailmaker has designed the spin-naker to set correctly with the sheet in this position. However, on restricted classes spec-ialised reaching spinnakers may be used which can be quite flat and short on the foot; for these the leads may need to be brought for-ward, although still kept as wide as possible. The governing principle is still to keep the leech of the spinnaker away from the mainsail.

On any point of sailing other than dead shy, the spinnaker sheet normally runs under the mainsail boom, which eliminates any possible fore-and-aft adjustment of sheet leads, anyway. But a critical situation is reached on a very shy reach where the spinnaker sheet may either be kept under the boom or allowed to flick out over

Right. The spinnaker sheet has been flicked over the top of the mainboom end to give a better sheeting angle and allow the spinnaker to lift and the shoulders to open to their maxi-mum size.

Far right. Dinghy gybe technique in strong winds is to gybe the boat first and worry about passing the pole through later.

the top of it and cut across the leech of the main. With the sheet over the sail, watch that the foot of the spinnaker is not being dragged bar tight while the leech is falling wide open, with damaging loss of pressure in the sail. Solings and 5.5s favour this type of sheeting for a shy spinnaker, while the Dragon appears to perform better if the sheet is kept under the boom. There's a problem in recovering the sheet from over the boom when dropping the spinnaker in heavy winds—you have to haul the main boom almost amidships before you can pull the sheet over the end of the boom while another crew-man pulls on the recovery line. A recovery line is a light line from the hull to a light ring or block running on the spinnaker sheet, which enables the crew to recover the sheet at all times, even if it is way off to leeward.

For running square in heavy winds on big yachts, a snatch-block is needed to choke down the spinnaker sheet towards the bow to counter the terrifying "death rolling" tendency. This rhythmic rolling, to use the more correct if less spectacular term, is caused by the spinnaker trying to drag the displacement hull through the water faster than it was designed to travel. As yachts are not inclined to plane, unless assisted by big waves, the wind spilling out of

the sides of the spinnaker causes it to oscillate—first rolling the boat to windward and then to leeward as the righting action of the hull drags it back. If this rolling develops with a regular rhythm, the boat will eventually round up and broach or dip the spinnaker pole in the water, with the danger of breaking mast or pole.

By leading the sheet through the forward snatch-block as well as the main lead aft, pulling it down forward and keeping the spinnaker pole further forward than usual, the oscillation of the sail can be kept to a minimum with consequent reduction in rolling. If this starts to become violent, always shy the yacht up a little to settle it down.

GYBING

Gybing the spinnaker is another forbidding task that can be made easy by following simple procedures. The successful gybe is not dependent on a champion for'ard hand, who really plays a minor role in the drama. It is controlled mainly by the crewmen working the brace and sheet and by the timing of the helmsman.

There are two basic gybes—square-to-square and shy-to-shy—and they call for different treatment. Square-to-square is the sim-

plest. Suppose we are on a small yacht, like the Dragon—the for'ard hand stands on the foredeck before the mast, facing the stern. He first takes hold of the sheet, which should be easily reached as it is under the main boom and falls close to the lee shroud. He hooks it in the crook of his arm, reaches with his other arm and trips the brace from the end of the pole. With both hands now free, and the sheet held and under control, he then takes the pole end from the mast and clips it onto the sheet which he has hooked in his arm. The mainsail should start to gybe as the for'ard hand fits the pole across the boat to the new windward side and hooks the pole back onto the mast. Only minor adjustments to sheet and brace are needed during this type of gybe to keep the spinnaker full. The major danger is the helmsman gybing the mainsail before the for'ard hand is ready to poke the pole out on the new windward side. This blankets the spinnaker, causing it to be sucked into the turbulent wind area behind the main. Care must be taken to pull on the new sheet quickly to keep the spinnaker filling on the new windward side.

Shy-to-shy gybes are more difficult, as major adjustments of sheet and brace must be made from the cockpit. I prefer the dip-pole method where the pole is not detached from the mast. Timing is all important here, and if the helmsman is able to make a wide, sweeping turn, the crew's task will be easier. The whole spinnaker can then be squared back as the boat goes into the gybe. The topping lift is eased, and the pole tripped from the brace to let the pole swing down inside the forestay just as the main boom starts to swing across. The old sheet new brace must be eased until the clew of the spinnaker is close enough for the for'ard hand to reattach the pole to the new brace. The topping lift is hauled up again to bring the pole to the right height. As the new brace is eased, the sheet must be drawn on at about the same rate to keep the spinnaker filling. Have the brace plainly marked so the sheet hand can see when the brace is eased far enough for the pole to be reattached. The sheet hand must be standing in a position where he can both trim the sheet with ease and see the spinnaker, for if he oversheets just as the gybe is completed, the spinnaker will be sucked in behind the mainsail

and collapse. The for'ard hand must be certain he has enough brace to reattach the pole and must work quickly to attach it before the mainsail reaches the centre of the gybe. After this point, there is a danger of the spinnaker skying into the air, pulling the brace out of his reach. To minimise this danger, a recovery line should be tightened on the brace before the gybe, keeping it lower.

If the helmsman and sheet hand have done their job, the spinnaker will stay full and working right throughout the gybe.

Some yachtsmen still favour the end-for-end pole transfer for shy-to-shy gybing, but I have always found it difficult to reattach the pole to the mast if the spinnaker is filling, especially if there is any weight in the breeze.

The techniques described here have been developed to perfection on one-design keel yachts like the Dragon and Soling, but basically, with variations to suit the characteristics of the boat, they work for anything carrying a parachute spinnaker—big yachts to small centreboard dinghies.

On big yachts, where the poles are too heavy to manhandle end-for-end, the dip pole technique is used for square-to-square as well as shy-to-shy. On the 12-metres and off-shore yachts racing in short round-the-buoys events, I like the double-sheet-and-brace set-up. Here, a wire brace and rope sheet, made up with a single attaching clip, is hooked onto both corners of the spinnaker. The loose wire brace on the leeward side is dragged forward to the bow and clipped into the pole-end beak as it swings under the forestay, and the pressure winched onto it as the pole is raised again. At the same time, the strain is transferred from wire to rope to become the new sheet on the leeward side, leaving the load off the wire ready for the next gybe.

DROP

What goes up must come down, and even the most exhilarating spinnaker run must come to an end. Slightly overtrim the spinnaker so that it will stay full more easily while the crew prepares for the drop. The main hand must make sure that the spinnaker sheet is cleated.

The recovery line should be drawn in to ensure that the sheet, the only means of recovering the spinnaker, can easily be reached after the spinnaker or brace has been tripped from the end of the pole. The for'ard hand should himself check that this has been done before he trips, otherwise the spinnaker can blow away to leeward, flying wildly between the masthead and corner of the tuck from where it is very difficult to recover.

Having checked that the sheet is cleated and being held by the sheet hand, the for'ard hand trips the brace from the end of the pole, makes sure that the brace is free to run around the forestay—dragging it forward, if necessary, for if the brace fouls, the spinnaker will keep filling and be very difficult to pull into the boat.

As the pole is released, the hand gathering the spinnaker should drag on the sheet and get some downward pressure on the leech of the spinnaker. This will ensure that the spinnaker will flag directly to leeward, without danger of fouling.

The halyard should then be let go by the for'ard hand, who by this stage should be back in the cockpit. He should not let the halyard run freely, but have it pulled through his hands by the sheet hand recovering the spinnaker. This keeps the spinnaker in close behind the mainsail, out of the wind and easy to pull directly into the cockpit. Once the spinnaker is half-way into the boat, the for'ard hand can let the halyard run completely, leaving the sheet-hand to recover the rest of the spinnaker, and turn his attention to the pole. Dropping the pole should be left to last, because in a crisis the boat can be brought on the wind with the pole still hoisted.

In heavy weather it may be necessary to use both crew members to recover the spinnaker. In these conditions, the for'ard hand must be absolutely certain the brace is free to run before he leaves the foredeck, for if the spinnaker lands on the water still filling, it will scoop itself under. And if it does land on the water, both crew hands must recover it quickly, using a quick grabbing action, rather than hauling, to keep it from sinking.

Note: More about spinnakers in Ocean Racing chapter.

The "death rolls", a bad downwind problem for displacement hulls, particularly in smooth water where there are no waves to help them surf beyond hull speed. This 5.5, Barranjoey, *Bill Northam's 1964 Olympic gold medal winner, should have kept the spinnaker sheet under the boom and shifted the sheet lead forward, near the shrouds.*

End-for-end gybing: the leading boat has collapsed her spinnaker through being pulled away too sharply for the mark. KA 137 is positioned for the perfect gybe.

Spars and Rigging

SAILING'S greatest advance in recent years, the flexible rig, has greatly influenced the design and nature of masts, booms, and the rigging needed to hold them in place. For the flexible rig, which allows the mainsail to alter its shape, while sailing, to suit changes in wind strength, depends entirely on these spars bending exactly the right amount at exactly the right time. While it has cut down drastically the number of sails a boat need carry, it has made the quest for perfect spars even more important.

Before selecting or making your mast or boom, ask yourself what you are trying to achieve with the flexible rig. Many yachtsmen are using flexible rigs—some successfully, some unsuccessfully—but not many really know how they work.

The guiding theory is that the rig should maintain enough pressure on the sail between the tip of the mast and the end of the boom to tension the leech of the mainsail, making it stand up and give full power to the sail through light to medium wind strengths, but when any further increase in wind strength threatens to overpower hull and crew, spars should bend automatically, allowing the leech to begin opening, or breathing. The sail can then quickly exhaust the increased airflow it cannot handle, allowing the hull to accelerate. Besides freeing the leech, the bending mast considerably flattens the sail by taking up the line of the luff curve and removing draft from that area. Boom bend, to a lesser extent, also frees the leech and flattens the sail.

The whole process is something like a car changing gear—an automatic car at that. The sails change shape to deal with an increase or decrease in wind strength: flat sail curvature and free leech for high-speed airflow; full curvature and tighter leech for low-speed flow. For each crew weight and hull design there will be a slightly different "gear ratio" expressed in leech pressure.

The modern, well-tuned flexible rig will give

Right. Mast is bent to maximum for fresh wind speed, despite the distortions apparent in the sail cloth. It has been bent past the luff round of the sail, as indicated by the typical downward-running creases.

Far right. These Fireballs' powerful mainsails opening up on the leeches in the fresh breeze are quite flat in the top, cut for the newer style of stiffer mast.

good results in winds up to 20 knots with one mainsail where previously three different mainsails had to be carried for light, medium, and strong winds. It only increases the range in which the mainsail can be used efficiently and doesn't do much for headsails. If anything, headsail shape has become less flexible, as forestays cannot be set up as tightly as they used to be on the older-style stiff masts because the flexible spar will not withstand the compression loads. So, as the wind increases in strength, the mast bends, limiting the tension that can be transmitted to the forestay. The forestay sags and the headsail becomes fuller and you must change it for one that is cut to cope with the increased luff sag. These days it is very seldom, except in extreme wind conditions, for a championship winner to use more than one mainsail in a series. But his single, spar-bend controlled mainsail will be supplemented by two or three jibs. Specialised light- or heavy-weather jibs should be chosen to overlap the best range for the most-used medium-weather headsail. A light-weather headsail may give good performance from 0 to 15 knots but be at its absolute best up to 10 knots. The medium-weather headsail should be good from 10 to 20 knots and at its best around 15 knots. So if you are caught with your light-weather headsail on, you are still competitive in winds up to 15 knots.

While you can get away with one mainsail, complemented by two or three jibs, it is almost impossible to carry a flexible mast that will be perfect in all weathers. You shouldn't need more than one mast, but you will have to decide which breeze range it should be rigged for. If the mast is flexible enough to release the pressure on the sails and keep the boat moving in heavy breezes, it is normally too soft for medium weather because it is inclined to release the pressure on the leech too early, before the boat is in danger of being over-powered. This mast will probably be quite efficient in very light winds, when there is not enough pressure in the sail to bend even a very soft mast. Such a mast can even be an advantage in drifty light weather when it can be prebent with pressure on the vang and chocking at the deck to keep the drive well back, without too much fullness near the mast. This allows the shape of the sail to be maintained without much pressure on the sheet. But for the boat to be a good all-rounder in the predominantly medium winds, the mast must be tuned to be brilliant between 10 and 15 knots and still good enough to earn you a placing in the first six or seven if the breeze falls below 10 or increases above 15 knots.

Right. Typical old style rig, with a mass of wire, spreaders and jumpers to keep the mast straight and stiff. Compare it with the simpler modern rigs pictured throughout this book, which are aimed at controlling bend rather than obtaining telegraph-pole stiffness.

Centre. Even mast bend allows this Australian 14 restricted-class yacht to carry a big mainsail to windward. The sail has been flattened completely towards the head by the mast bend but still carries enough power low down to give plenty of drive.

Far right. Mast bend and luff curve must be carefully matched. The wrinkles from clew to mast on 246 and 218 show that the masts are bending too low down, beyond the luff curve of the sail. The lower area of the sail, with built-in fullness through seam taper, has been over-flattened, causing the tight spot from the soft section of the mast to the clew. These boats will be easy to hold upright but will not point. The leech will also be thrown too wide open. The remedy here is to stiffen the mast by glueing extra wood on the front of it.

Tuned this way, with a special heavy-weather mainsail for extremely strong winds and perhaps a light-weather headsail to complement the standard mainsail in light weather, you will face only two decisions: when to change to the heavy-weather mainsail and when to change to the light-weather jib. And a wrong decision, either way, should not be too disastrous.

Naturally, if you sail in areas where the wind is either predominantly light or strong, you tune the mast mainly for these conditions. The softer mast can be stiffened for medium winds by rigging controls—we'll deal with these in detail later in the chapter—at all times assessing whether the advantage in extra power is out-weighing the weight and windage of the extra rigging. I prefer to have that extra bit of power to call on when the breeze eases from fresh to medium, putting up with the weight and windage of the supplementary rigging in stronger winds.

MASTS

Wood, from the Viking days the traditional material for mast-making, has been superseded by aluminium alloy. The early wooden small-yacht and dinghy masts were big in section, solid, rigid, and heavy. Then came the hollow mast: still large in section and rigid, but much lighter. Yachtsmen began to discover the advantages of bending masts and reduced the wall thickness of the hollow masts to allow them to flex a little. This led to some spectacular dismastings, as the thin walls would compress very easily on the after edge.

So the size of the cross-sections was reduced to allow bend, and the wall-thickness was increased to counter compression failure. Oregon and other timbers harder than the normally used spruce were tried to further reduce compression fractures. But these were also heavier than spruce and added more weight to the masts.

Masts for top-class competition thus continued to be made from spruce because they were light and flexible—they were also expensive and quickly expendable, for if they did not break on an extremely windy day, they gradually became tired, losing their spring and taking on permanent bend after a few months of hard racing.

About this time yachtsmen began looking seriously at aluminium masts. They had been around for some years but were not really suit-

able for smaller boats. They were mostly too stiff, too big and pear-shaped in section with large reinforcing webs at the back of the section that formed the track, making it impossible to taper them to small-enough dimensions to bend at the top.

Designers and some top helmsmen got together to devise round masts, with the sail track outside the section. This allowed the tapering needed towards the top to permit the mast to flex. Some aluminium extrusions maintain strength in their smaller sections by adding internal ribs, normally running laterally, to decrease sideways bend without having to make the mast oval or bigger in section. These thin, flexible aluminium masts don't seem to break with the frequency of wooden masts. But this is probably because we now have a better idea of how to control a bending mast and know just how much bend it will stand before it breaks, rather than because of a strength advantage in the metal.

The real advantage of aluminium is that it is durable and doesn't gradually get the compression fractures through constant use and old age that ended the lives of many great wooden masts. Aluminium mast failures usually result from the breaking of a piece of restraining

rigging. Very flexible masts often rely heavily on intermediate rigging, such as diamonds or spreaders, to stop them breaking under sailing strain.

The broken aluminium mast doesn't crash down in a spectacular shower of splinters. The alloy bends past its elastic limit, making a permanent kink or bend in the mast. This bend may be straightened, if it is not too serious, but you are only giving the mast a reprieve from its inevitable doom, because the alloy has been weakened. If the bend is localised, it is sometimes possible to cut out the kink, fit a sleeve inside, and re-weld the two sections over it—especially if it is at deck level or at the hounds. But there is danger here that the heat from the welding will create a soft spot in the metal.

Unlike wood, aluminium masts are fairly constant and predictable in their behaviour, irrespective of climatic changes, and can be easily replaced. Many a championship has been lost because a "fast" wooden mast smashed just before or during the series and a replacement couldn't be tuned to the same performance straight away. But with aluminium, by carrying a spare of identical section (as you normally would to a major championship) you know that if your favourite mast breaks you

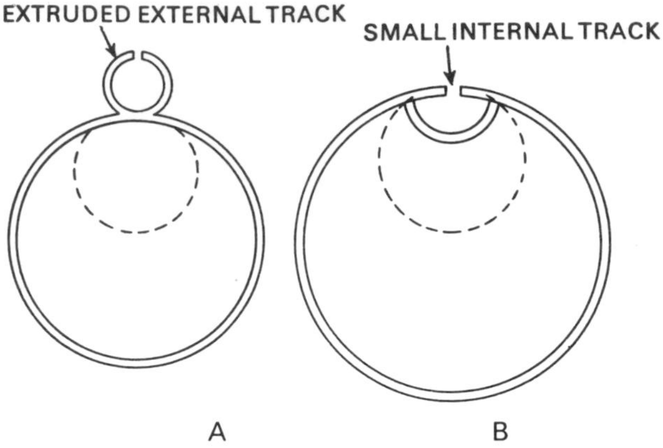

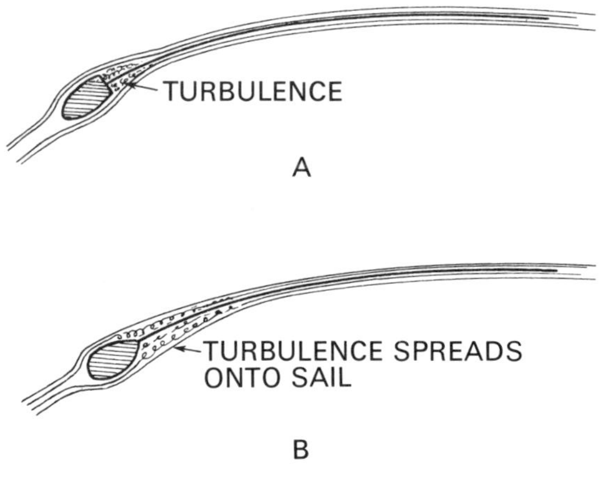

EXTRUDED EXTERNAL TRACK   SMALL INTERNAL TRACK

A   B

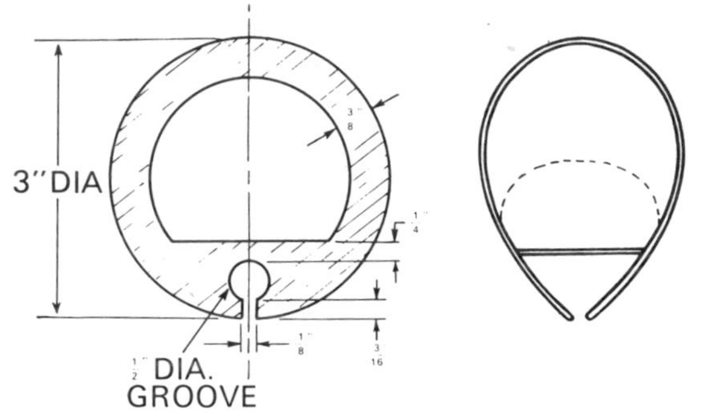

3" DIA

½" DIA.
GROOVE

TURBULENCE

A

TURBULENCE SPREADS
ONTO SAIL

B

Figure 32 (top). Typical modern aluminium round sections. Dotted outline shows extent of tapering when extrusion is not obstructed by large sail-track web.

Figure 33 (centre). A, wooden mast section. B, pear-shaped aluminium mast section with large internal web. Dotted outline shows minimum size to which mast can be tapered.

Figure 34 (bottom). A, turbulence produced by a square-backed mast is kept in close, allowing the maximum undisturbed air flow on the mainsail. B, pear-shaped mast spreads turbulent air flow on the first third of the sail.

only have to re-rig the replacement in the same way to be sailing just as fast the following day.

SECTIONAL SHAPES

The pear-shape cross-section used to be considered the most aerodynamically correct shape for yacht masts, especially when pivoted along the line of curvature of the sail. However, recent experiments in air flow, using wool tufts pushed through the sail, have proved that a pear-shape throws just as much turbulence onto the sail as a round mast-section. A pear-shaped mast that is not pivoted exposes a lot more of its area to the apparent wind and causes about the same amount of turbulence on the windward side and probably more on the leeward side than either a pivoted pear-shape or a round section. It does not appear to make any difference whether or not a round section is pivoted.

Another trend is to the square-backed mast, which has a pear-shaped forward section but is cropped off flat at the back, something like the tail of a fastback car. The eddies of disturbed air coming off this mast tend to hug in close to the back. Undisturbed air, starting quite close to the mast, then flows off evenly on both sides of the sail (Fig. 34).

The smaller-section round mast also offers a big advantage in reducing windage. Try hoisting a 3 in. section mast into its step a in 10 to 15-knot breeze and then repeat the exercise with a 2 in. section mast. The smaller section is dramatically easier to hold upright. The round mast is more flexible fore-and-aft without loss of sideways rigidity than a comparable pear-shape, making the mast easier to control with rigging. The fore-and-aft stiffness of the pear-shape is still used to advantage in some classes to resist the higher sheet pressures needed to stand up tall, narrow sails. But in the direction of the smallest dimension, such a mast becomes most unstable—inclined to buckle out sideways in the middle between the hounds and deck where it is in compression and fall off sideways—in the opposite direction to the buckle in the middle—at the top. It needs restraining intermediate rigging to control this.

Unlike fore-and-aft bend, sideways bend will

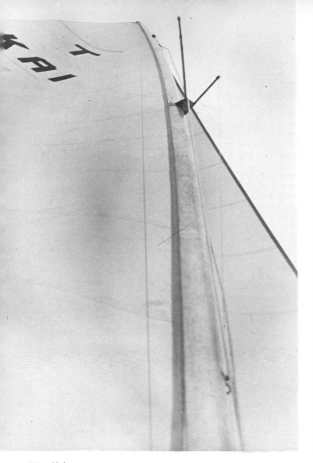 

Flexible mast on a Tempest, with single spreader attached to the shrouds, has adjustable diamonds angled forward to control fore-and-aft as well as sideways bend below the hounds. Note that with average mast bend the sail is still too full with the drive well aft. If the mast is bent further in an attempt to flatten the sail more, the drive will slip further back to the front edge of the battens, causing them to hook badly. The sail should be recut to reduce luff curve.

Tornado catamaran, with very high hounds position, has athwartships diamonds only, as the pear-shaped mast section is strong enough to withstand the fore-and-aft pressures.

affect your pointing ability. But it is a necessary evil on some boats, like Finns, OKs, and Stars, to release more power than the fore-and-aft bend can handle on fresher days, and to open up the slot between jib and main on some high-performance centreboarders like the Flying Dutchman.

ALTERING MAST FLEXIBILITY

Altering the flexibility of a wooden spar is easy —too stiff and you plane off a few shavings; too soft and you glue on some more wood. Altering an aluminium mast's bend is more

difficult, so it pays to be extremely careful selecting the correct section in the first place. Check on what the top performers in the class are using.

There are, however, ways of making an aluminium mast more flexible. The most simple is to cut the sail track with a hacksaw every two, three, or four inches, depending on how much bend you want the mast to have. Individual areas can be made to bend more; to make the top more flexible, make your saw cuts down to the hounds and leave the rest uncut. All this sounds rather drastic, but it does work, by making ineffective only a small part of the compression side of the mast, and doesn't seem

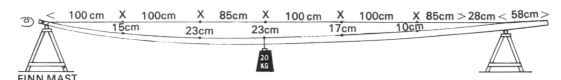

Figure 35. Elvstrom method of measuring mast bend.

Figure 36 (right). Bethwaite method of measuring mast bend.

to weaken it. If you are skilful enough (and game enough) you can tear into the mast with a dreadnought file, but there's the danger of going right through the mast walls. Paul Elvstrom once cut the front right out of the aluminium mast of his Flying Dutchman, deliberately, and just taped over the inch-wide gap. I don't recommend it, but it got results for him when nothing else was available.

In altering a mast, there are two proven methods of measuring bend and reproducing almost exactly the bend characteristics of another mast. The best-known, developed by Elvstrom for his Finn and OK dinghy masts, is by laying the mast horizontally, supported at each end, hanging a weight at one point along it, stretching a string line between the ends, and measuring between mast and string at regular intervals (Fig. 35). The second method, developed in Australia by Frank Bethwaite, works on the principle that the amount of bend in the mast is directly proportional to the amount of pull you place on it. The mast is supported at the base and hounds position, as it would be

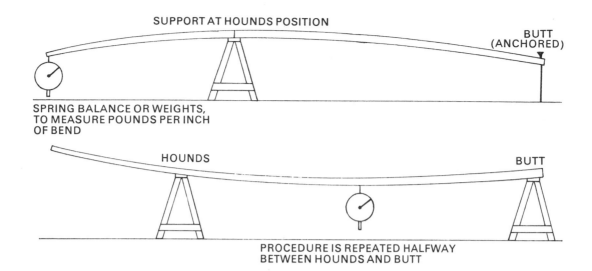

SUPPORT AT HOUNDS POSITION

BUTT
(ANCHORED)

SPRING BALANCE OR WEIGHTS,
TO MEASURE POUNDS PER INCH
OF BEND

HOUNDS

BUTT

PROCEDURE IS REPEATED HALFWAY
BETWEEN HOUNDS AND BUTT

while sailing, then a given pressure applied to the tip of the mast using weights or a spring balance. The mast is classified according to how much weight is needed to deflect it an inch—a Cherub mast needs 7 to 8 lb. an inch, a Northbridge 14, 6 lb. This method gives a direct comparison between masts. This same deflection test is also applied to the lower section of the mast, between the hounds and the deck, as it is important to control this section accurately on masts having set shroud positions (Fig. 36).

RIGGING

Ideas on the amount of rigging needed to hold the mast upright have gone round in a big circle over the past decade. Once, everyone believed the best masts were those that stood straight, so masts were solid wood with plenty of rigging to make certain they could not bend. The sails used to set perfectly without any mast bend to cause distortion. But three or four mainsails had to be carried, all of differing fullness, to cope with light, medium and heavy winds.

Far left. Thunderbird rig with jumpers angled forward, transmitting pressure from the back-stay through to the forestay by restricting fore-and-aft bend. If less mast bend is required for the same amount of forestay pressure, the backstay should be eased, the jumpers tightened and the backstay pressure reapplied. Where class rules allow, jumpers can be led down the forward side of the mast for deck-level adjustment.

Centre. Masthead rig on this Junior Offshore Group boat has a fixed set of crosstrees and a single lower to control sideways flexibility. The inner forestay, running from the spreaders, can induce fore-and-aft mast bend to control the mainsail's draft.

Left. When using minimum-section masts, the excessive pressure from the boom vang applied going to windward should be readjusted before going downwind, otherwise the mast may be forced out sideways, buckling it, when sheets are freed.

Came the revolutionary flexible rig and everyone went overboard for the ultra-light spars, so flexible that they needed quite complicated rigging to stiffen them for light to moderate winds. But it is surprising how much weight and windage you can add to a light spar by hanging extra diamonds and jumpers to the essential main rigging, trapeze wires, and halyards in order to control its bend. Nowadays, the trend is to reducing the rigging again and increasing slightly mast-section thickness.

The simplest rig is the forestay and two main shrouds—these days found normally only on very small or light sailing craft. The first additional complication is the spreader, which is normally fitted halfway between the hounds, where the main shrouds and forestay attach to the mast, and the deck (Fig. 37). Spreaders may be the swinging type, which are hinged on the mast; these give very little support and are good only for holding a mast from bowing to leeward, leaving it free to move fore and aft. A more efficient type is the fixed or limited-swing spreader, which can be set at a predetermined angle either to encourage the mast to bend forward or to restrict it from doing so, as well as stopping it bowing sideways (Fig. 38).

You must remember that the outer end of the strut is being held only by the middle of a tight shroud and there is a limit to the amount of loading it will stand before the shroud is pushed out of line, allowing the mast to do what it likes. So if a lot of sideways support is needed to hold the mast in this area, you must use a diamond stay which starts at the hounds and passes over a strut halfway down the mast then reattaches to the bottom near the mast step (Fig. 39).

A diamond is usually adjustable through a rigging screw or some other device while sailing. Tightening this will keep the bottom of the mast very straight sideways; slackening it will allow some bend. Some fore-and-aft control can also be achieved by angling the diamond struts forward. If more support is needed at the top for windward performance or to support shy spinnaker loadings, the top of the diamond stay can be attached above the hounds. On non-pivoting masts the diamond prevents the boom vang loading on the boom pushing the middle of the mast out to windward when running or reaching, which flattens the mainsail on a point of sailing where it should be full. This fault leads to many broken

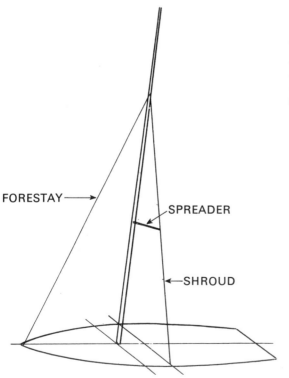

FORESTAY

SPREADER

SHROUD

Figure 37 (left). Simple three-shroud rig with spreaders.

*Figure 38 (below). Fixed or limited swing spreaders may be set at a predetermined angle either to encourage the mast to bend forward or to restrict it from doing so. **A**, to restrict the mast from going forward, spreaders are angled forward of the shroud line; the mast is then pulled back to the dotted line position and the tips of the spreaders attached to the shrouds. **B**, reverse procedure encourages the mast to bend forward.*

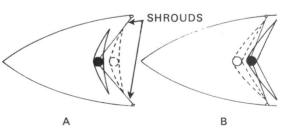

SHROUDS

A

B

masts in strong winds, especially when spinnakers are flown from a point two or three feet
above the main hounds position.

Diamond struts must not be made too short
as this increases compression and puts very
heavy loading on the light rigging wire. They
must be kept as long as possible on boats without spinnakers and short as possible on boats
with spinnakers where they could make
spinnaker-hoisting difficult. On boats setting
spinnakers it is also wise to keep the lower
attachment point of the diamond above the
spinnaker-pole point so that it will not foul the
pole during spinnaker handling.

If a mast is rigged with lower diamonds
angled forward as well as a set of spreaders, it
is wise to join the end of the diamond struts to
the end of the spreaders to stop spinnakers
being caught in the narrow vee between them.

The jumper stay does the same job as the
diamond, except that it is rigged in front of
mast and will only stiffen it in a fore-and-aft
direction. If only the section above the hounds
needs stiffening, the strut should be placed
half-way between the hounds and the top with
the stay attached to the head of the mast and
the hounds. If the mast needs general fore-and-
aft support, the strut will be placed at the
hounds with the top of the stay fixed at the
head of the mast and the lower end brought
down half-way between hounds and deck. Take
care that the middle of the mast is not pulled
forward by the strain transmitted through the
jumper strut. On yachts where this is liable to
happen it is usual to rig a lower shroud opposite
the diamond stay anchor point to counter this
tendency. On smaller dinghy rigs this can be
overcome by taking the lower fixing point
closer to the bottom of the mast (Fig. 40).

A single strut is all that is required on cat-
rigged boats; however, on headsail-type rigs,
twin struts must be used so that jibs and spinnakers can be led into the mast between the
jumper wires to avoid fouling them. The twin
struts can also give some sideways support to
the top of the mast if they are set far enough
apart. With double jumpers you should have
another strut joining them, to prevent them
from spreading apart under load and to keep
spinnakers and halyards from becoming caught
around them.

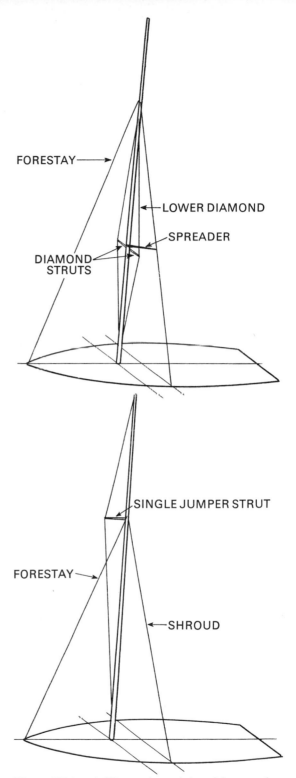

*Figure 39 (top). Three-shroud rig with spreaders
and lower diamond.*

*Figure 40 (bottom). Three-shroud rig with
shrouds low down and single jumper controlling top fore-and-aft mast bend.*

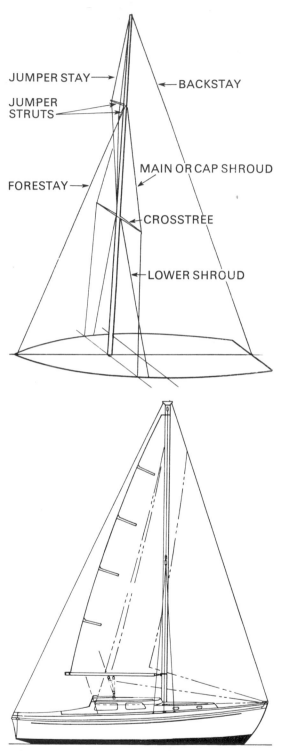

JUMPER STAY

JUMPER
STRUTS

BACKSTAY

MAIN OR CAP SHROUD

FORESTAY

CROSSTREE

LOWER SHROUD

Figure 41 (top). Typical three-quarter yacht rig with jumper stays transferring backstay pressure to forestay (and hence, jib luff).

Figure 42 (bottom). Simple masthead rig on 27 ft. cruiser-racer.

On dinghies, jumpers and diamonds are usually adjustable so that fore-and-aft as well as sideways mast bend can be altered while racing. Most of these extra stays are disappearing from smaller yachts and dinghies with a bigger range of well-designed alloy spars available of minimum weight but still strong enough to require only one set of fixed spreaders for support and control.

Jumper stays play a different role on bigger boats such as Thunderbirds, 5.5s, and Diamonds. On this rig, called the three-quarter rig because the forestay meets the mast approximately three-quarters of the way up from the bottom, the forestay is held tight by the pressure on the backstay which is transmitted through the jumper stays down to the hounds. If the jumpers were not there the backstay would bend back the top of the mast, until it broke, without ever holding the forestay very tight (Fig. 41). If the jumpers are slackened and the backstay tightened, the mast will take on more bend. If you want to tighten the forestay without allowing the mast to bend more, then the jumpers must be tightened and the backstay wound on to the point where the mast is straight again.

Spreaders, or cross-trees as they are often called on larger yachts, push the main shrouds well out of their normal line, giving the shrouds a better angle at which to meet the mast, easing compression and giving much more sideways support to the middle of the spar than would the spreaders of a dinghy which hardly push the shrouds out of line at all. Big-yacht cross-trees are normally fixed, but if the mast is to bend fore and aft, some movement is allowed to let the mast go forward in the middle before the spreader begins to restrict it. Lower stays running from the base of the spreaders oppose the inward loading of the spreader, thus controlling sideways bend in this region. On small cruising rigs there are usually two sets of lowers—one forward and one aft of the mast. On smaller racing boats, one set is usually considered enough.

On some three-quarter rigs the forestay is held tight by runners set the same distance behind the mast as the forestay is forward of it. These are tensioned in direct opposition to the forestay with large Highfield levers or runner winches. Runners are still probably the best method of ensuring a really tight forestay, but you have to put up with the inconvenience of letting off the leeward one and pulling on the windward one through every new tack.

Lower runners are sometimes used in conjunction with the main runners to control the long, unsupported middle section of very flexible masts, such as in the Star class. If runners are used a shock-rubber preventer should be rigged from the runner-wire to the base of the cross-trees, short enough to prevent the runner flicking around the spreader when it is not in use—nasty if a non-observant crew-member then slams the runner on tight.

Figure 43. Diagram showing how the position of the hounds governs the type of mast bend and methods of controlling it. The big problem in jib-headed rigs is to control the area from the hounds to the mast step.

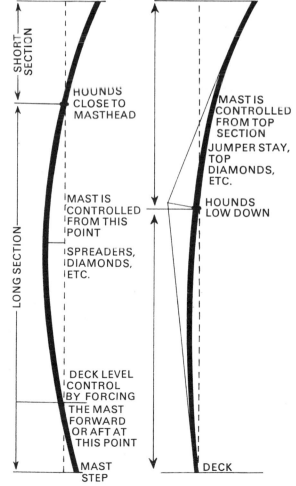

The masthead rig, developed by off-shore racers and now used extensively in the popular small cruiser classes, is basically the same as the three-quarter except that the forestay and shrouds attach to the masthead and the back-stay falls in dead opposition to the forestay to keep it tight (Fig. 42).

When planning your rigging, remember that the area of the mast most prone to uncontrolled bending and therefore most liable to break is below the hounds (Fig. 43). It is normally under heavy compression, especially in rigs carrying big headsails. A well-designed mast-section is just strong enough to stand this constant load, but not normally strong enough to take shock loads such as those imposed by shy spinnaker poles pushing the mast suddenly into a reverse bend, or the big strains on the gooseneck from the boom vang when running square. The danger of breakage is highest in strong, gusty winds when the loadings reach a maximum just before the hull starts to plane, or the bow buries in a sea. A preventer running to the mast from a reasonably wide angle on the foredeck will deal with the pole loads. A diamond stay running from below the hounds is one of the few ways to counteract the vang pressure.

PIVOTING MASTS?

Should the mast be pivoted or fixed in its step? There is little advantage in pivoting a round mast, but considerable advantages in pivoting a pear-shape, especially with a high-ratio rig, and a square-back, to improve airflow onto the main. The disadvantages are found mainly in the rigging, which can make it difficult for the mast to pivot in the correct direction, or far enough, especially if a vang is being used. To help overcome this, the main shrouds and forestay should all be attached to the front edge of the mast with the pivot-point on the mast base also forward of the half-way mark. This allows the mast to pivot without the rigging tending to restrain it.

Spreaders are not as effective on a pivoting mast, since they must be fully swinging to allow the mast to rotate. And care must be taken that the diamonds and jumpers do not foul the

standing rigging as the mast turns—struts must be kept shorter and diamond fixing points kept below the hounds to stop this. On masts that are stepped through the deck, pivoting makes chocking at deck level very complicated. On boats with halyard tails or sail-tension control lines leading back into the cockpit, these must still work when the mast is rotated. A spinnaker pulling on the front edge of a fully pivoting mast will centralise it, and the vang pushing the gooseneck in from the leeward side will complete the job, reversing the angle of pivot when the mast is under a lot of tension and threatening to break it if shock-loaded.

So you can see from all those problems why pivoting masts are normally used only on small-rig boats such as Moths and Northbridge 14s, where the loads are smaller, or on catamaran rigs where the benefits are greater.

OVER-ROTATING MASTS

Catamarans like pivoting pear-shape masts. They are stable craft, always looking for more power instead of ways to discard it in moderate winds, and need the fore-and-aft stiffness of the pear-shape to withstand the heavy sheet pressures needed to support their tall, narrow mainsails. The tendency of pear-shape masts to buckle sideways is even used. The mast pivots beyond the line of the boom, turning the minimum-dimension sidewall toward the leech's pull. When the sail is sheeted on hard it bends the mast against the line of least resistance—the top comes up to windward and the bottom bows out to leeward. This stands the top of the leech up very straight and overcomes the tendency of the upper section of the roach to fall off. This method calls for careful control. The angle of pivot should be readily adjustable. As the wind becomes stronger, the pear shape mast is allowed to pivot further—over-rotate. This exposes the smaller sideways dimension of the mast to the backwards pull of the leech, allowing the sail to flatten without increasing the leech tension. The diamond on the lower section, below the hounds, now becomes important for it will control to a large extent the low-down sail fullness. For maximum performance and power, the sail should

72

Far left. Pivoting wing mast, pictured on Australian C class catamaran Quest III, provides a most efficient and controllable rig. The fullness is controlled basically by increasing the angle of pivot. The trailing edge of the mast is curved so that it takes up approximately one-third of the chord width of the sail and pushes fullness into it when over-pivoted. Shrouds and forestay are taken off the leading edge for easy pivoting. Novel controls are fitted to bend the battens in light wind.

Centre. Boom bend here is too much and does not match the round that has been cut into the foot of the sail. Tightness radiating from the block area is causing the mainsail to "S-bend" higher up. Subsequently, not enough pressure can be applied through the boom to bend the mast sufficiently to achieve correct mainsail fullness.

Left. Boom bend working well for this Star, pulling fullness in the lower area of the sail into a smooth shape and applying pressure to the sail just in from the boom so as to keep the leech flat in this area. Small distortions are not worth worrying about as the overall shape is perfect.

reach its correct depth with the mast pivoted to a point where the major axis of the mast lines up with the angle of entry of the leading edge of the mainsail.

BOOMS

Booms have followed a tighter cycle of revolution and reaction than masts. They used to be stiff, then they became very bendy, went back to medium bend, and now are stiff again. Nobody seems to have the complete answer to whether or not they should bend, and if so how much. Central sheeting has taken over, in most Australian dinghy classes at least, from end-of-boom sheeting, aggravating the problem of boom bend.

I don't recommend bendy booms unless they are used by experts who really know what they are doing. When you have both flexible mast and boom, it is doubly hard to tune the rig as a whole, because it is difficult to determine how much each is contributing.

To be useful a bendy boom must have just the right amount of flexibility to match

perfectly with the sail; if it is too flexible you will lose power in the leech area from the boom bending before the mast does. This flattens all the bottom section of the sail before you have enough wind pressure to bend the mast and flatten out the top—the area you want to discard first in a strong wind.

The boom that bends before the mast does also tend to pull a hard spot into the sail two or three feet in from the outer end of the boom. This makes the leech hang off low down before the full power is achieved. This lay-off can be an advantage later, as the boat becomes overpowered, if it happens at exactly the right moment—when the mast is fully bent but release of more power through easing leech pressure is still desirable. The lay-off will also take the weather helm away at the right moment to get the boat planing to windward if it is inclined that way. But the amount of boom bend has to be exactly right if it is not going to rob the mast of the bend it needs to flatten the top of the sail first. To be good a bendy boom must be a wooden one so that you can persistently plane pieces off or glue pieces on to achieve the perfect bend.

When perfect it is worth having, but the bendy boom is a very dangerous piece of equipment unless you are fully aware of all its problems; it can do you just as much harm as a poor mast. I once had one in a Flying Dutchman that was causing all the same symptoms as an over-soft mast: we were sailing well in light winds, not pointing in medium winds and not getting onto trapeze as soon as our competitors, showing we were gaining less power from the sails. But while our performance was mediocre right through the medium-wind range, we came into our own in winds over 20 knots with the boat moving very fast because the boom bend was leaving the leech of the sail wide open.

So we made another boom, only ¼ in. diameter thicker. The boat immediately pointed four or five degrees higher, going just as fast through the water as before, in those vital medium winds.

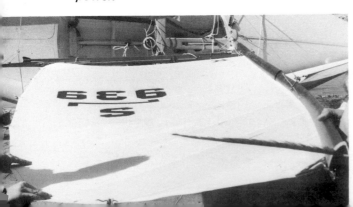

NS14-uses pivoting mast, over-rotated to gain maximum power from small sail area in light winds and to de-power the sail in a controlled manner. The pictures above show the angle of rotation set at 20 degrees rotation angle (of mast in respect to the boom). Sailing, the mast gives perfect control over the leech. The mainsail has a very fine entry and the jib is sheeted close inboard. The pictures below show the heavy air setting, mast rotated even further to 30 degrees, to hold the upper leech open but absolutely flat to feather without flagging while drive in the lower third of the sail still provides power.

Basic Tuning Techniques

WITH off-the-shelf mast and boom sections developed to suit each class, even the average sailor has a good chance of coming up with a race-winning rig just by buying the same spars as those used by the champions and ordering a sail to suit them. But there will always be marginal differences in sail-spar combinations for each crew-weight and hull design. And even assuming you have secured a mast of the correct flexibility and mainsail cut to fit that mast, you still cannot expect to throw them together and win races.

It can happen, in you first race with the new gear, that you find yourself as fast as the top boats in the class. But this would be sheer luck. I have achieved this magical result only twice in twenty-five years of racing. The big trick, and the one that marks the true champion, is knowing how to develop a winning rig out of one that does not click straight away. And there is only one way to do this—through a laborious and time-consuming procedure of trial and error, with success depending on your ability to recognise fault symptoms in your sail-spar combination and remedy them. This procedure, known as tuning, follows the same pattern for nearly every class of boat.

Tuning any boat, it is important to pay a lot of attention to how the boat feels; whether she has weather helm or lee helm and whether these change dramatically with wind strength variation; whether or not the boat moves smoothly through a seaway; whether she accelerates smoothly when hit by stronger gusts or tends to heel excessively in gusts. You must relate all these feelings to tuning alterations to try to estimate whether small changes are improving things.

Once you have appreciated how to fix the things that feel bad with trim alterations, you will be well on the way to being able to sail and trim a boat for maximum speed through varying wind strength and sea conditions during a full-length race. The golden rule is the

boat must want to go in the direction you want her to go. Then you have only to encourage her a little with the rudder. If you have to make her go where she does not want to go, then the tuning or trim is certainly wrong.

Tuning generally begins on the beach as you rig your new mast, sail, or both for the first time. Here, if you really know what you are looking for from previous experience or study of the top performers in the class, you can foreshorten the tuning process by setting up your rig so that it "looks" right. This approach is 90 per cent visual but it is enough to give a few very talented, experienced skippers instant success. However, few yachtsmen are in this class, and even the most experienced eye can still miss some minor fault which can only be uncovered by trial and error on the water.

Before you begin tuning seriously you must establish how fast the boat already goes, in order to determine whether drastic or only minor adjustments are needed. The first indication of a new rig's performance is usually gained in a race, but don't take your finishing place as a direct indication of speed; allow for such other factors as your own steering ability, crew-work, how you used wind shifts, and all the other variables apart from boat speed that can affect the result. If, however, during the race you found that boats near you were going faster, or outpointing you in clear air, you know where to begin trying to improve. If you were very badly left behind, look to drastic measures such as shifting the mast position 6 in., shifting the centreboard or trying a new one, and recutting sails. If the opposition was only fractionally faster, you are faced with only minor adjustments. However, because of the many variations to choose from, these can still involve you in a lot of work.

On the early outings when tuning new gear—either in practice or in a race—you and your crew should be working like computers, gathering every scrap of information from observing the behaviour of sails and spars and comparing them with those of the opposition. Mark reference points on the mainsheet and jib sheets to indicate the pressures on them when the boat was going at her best, and also mark the sheeting angles that give best performance. Carry a notebook or, if your boat is too wet for that, record all your observations in one as soon as you reach shore.

You will return from these early outings probably more disappointed than elated. Resist the temptation to make wholesale alterations. You should not make more than one adjustment at a time which should then be tested afloat before anything else is changed. Each step should be judged on its merits and not confused by a second alteration which could be cancelling out any improvement offered by the first, and even making your boat go slower.

The best way to test your adjustments is with the help of a tuning partner; not necessarily one of the top boats but one about your own level whose crew is keen to improve. Just the two boats should go out. One boat experi-

A lot can be learned on the beach about the effect of controls on the overall shape of the sail. Right top, the heavy distortion wrinkles in the sail, with mast bent to duplicate heavy-air settings, are completely removed, bottom, by Cunningham eye tension.

Far right. By the time you reach the starting line, it's usually too late to correct tuning faults and you'll be quickly passed by well-tuned boats with sails perfectly adjusted for the day. KA 33's jib luff is not taut enough, shown by wrinkling at the hanks. KA 59 has started with insufficient Cunningham eye tension.

76

ments, making one adjustment at a time, while the other acts as a control. As soon as the experimenter is beating the "trial horse" convincingly, the roles are reversed and the slower boat adjusts to increase his speed while the other remains unaltered. To quicken the process you must be frank in exchanging information on the adjustments you have made. Five or six hours of this type of tuning, without interference from other boats, wind shifts, or tactical demands, can improve your speed probably more than a whole season's racing.

In this type of tuning the two boats should sail to windward on one tack, sailing not more than 20 to 30 ft. apart but both with clear wind. They should sail on without tacking until one boat gains the advantage, then stop to allow the boat that has been beaten to make an adjustment and try again. The boat pointing highest to the wind should always start to windward so that it does not immediately climb up into the lee-bow position, throwing disturbed air flow at the sails of the windward yacht, ruining the test. And if the leeward boat while pointing lower is also sailing faster it can eventually reach a point where it is able to tack and cross ahead of the windward boat to prove an overall superiority in the course made good to windward.

If you become greatly superior to your training partner, and you are really dedicated to reaching the very top, you must be callous and discard him for a faster one. The better you become, the less difficult it is to find a training partner. Keep it to two boats. Three or four slow down the process and tend to get in each other's way.

Your tuning should, where possible, be carried out in medium-strength winds where the boat is easiest to sail and therefore the results of adjustments easier to assess.

ASSESSING SAIL SHAPES

After gaining a general idea of the rig's main failings in these initial tuning sessions you can confirm your suspicions with a careful check of

the sail shapes on shore. First, check the head-sail shape and sheeting angle. This is the easiest sail-shape to observe and is not going to be changed greatly through altering the mast bend. The jib must be full enough to achieve good boat speed through the water but not too full or the boat will stop pointing high to windward. (Refer back to Chapter 3 for a full outline of optimum jib shapes.) If the boat has not been pointing high, try sheeting the jib in closer to the centre-line of the hull and check the jib luff for excessive sag.

The sailmaker will have cut a slight hollow in the luff to allow for some sag in the forestay which is almost inevitable, but if the luff is sagging too much, the jib will become very full in the front third as the wind increases, thus increasing the angle of entry and causing loss of pointing ability. This problem is very evident in yarn-tempered jibs where the fullness will not move back into the sail as it will with softer materials.

You will have to put up with some sag, but it must be constant if the sailmaker is to allow for it, not jumping from 3 in. one minute to 1 in. the next, changing the shape of the sail with every oscillation. If it does this, then your forestay must be made tighter. This cannot be done just by tightening the rigging. When you are sailing to windward, the leeward shroud is always slack, leaving the mast supported only by the forestay and the weather shroud. Tightening the rig will only make the leeward shroud less slack than before.

I believe main rigging should be just tight enough to hold the mast steady in light to medium winds, the only wind-range in which the lee shroud will be tight when sailing to windward. If the rig is left too slack there is danger of the mast jumping out of the step when running square in heavy weather. The mainsheet has a bearing on forestay tension in most boats, as any pressure applied to it is putting direct tension on the forestay through sail and mast. Many skippers rely too much on this; it works in medium weather where the sheet pressure is constant, but in heavy winds, when the sheet has to be eased in overpowering puffs, the forestay becomes slack and you are left with a full jib when you need it least.

The way to increase tension permanently on the forestay is to move the main shrouds further aft behind the line of the mast. They should be as far aft as you can secure them without preventing the boom from laying off sufficiently for running downwind. In classes like the Heron, which do not carry spinnakers, the need to let the boom out square for running is so important that you may have to put up with some jib-luff sag and have the jib cut with the correct hollow in the luff to suit this. Some dinghy classes get around this problem by having the shrouds on slides or Highfield levers which ease the leeward shroud so the boom can push it out of the way when running square. Keel yachts—Dragons, Stars, and some 5.5s—use a runner set well aft to maintain forestay tension on the wind.

Many dinghies are now rigged with the jib halyard running down through the mast onto a multi-purchase tackle to allow them to sail with a slack jib luff in light to medium conditions but easily re-apply the tension as the wind strength increases. This means that the luff sag can be controlled to cope with the hollow cut into the jib with the sag kept relatively constant from light to heavy conditions.

Turn now from the jib to inspect the general shape of the mainsail. This is where the reference marks you made on the mainsheet become really valuable. The sheeting pressure where the boat feels best sailing to windward usually remains the same irrespective of how good the sail is. This pressure can now be used ashore as a good reference point for checking the shape of the mainsail. Assuming your boat is a dinghy, lay her on her side on the beach and use the reference marks to pull the mainsheet on to the same position where performance was best while sailing. Lay a straight-edge across the sail from the leech to the luff at right-angles to the mast. Measure the ratio of maximum depth of curvature to width of chord and repeat the procedure at four or five points down the sail (Fig. 44). The ratio of depth to width at all points should be roughly one in ten. This method is obviously impracticable for keel yachts, but their sails can be measured in the same way on a test mast, laid on its side, with boom attached, in the sail loft.

If it is only slightly outside this ratio, you may be able to induce the correct shape by rig

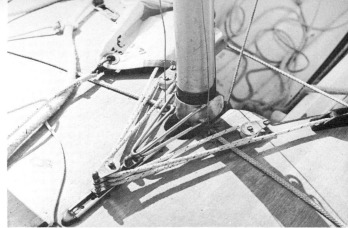

Two methods of controlling mast bend at deck level. In picture on left, lever and roller is controlled by under-deck winch; collar in picture on right runs on slide controlled by multi-purchase tackle.

control. If flatter, the sail is going to be slightly better in heavy breezes and could be made more full for light or medium winds by stiffening the mast slightly with rigging. If fuller than the 10 per cent ratio, you have a sail which will probably be good in light weather but you will have to encourage a little more mast bend to cope with medium to fresh winds.

Here is a basic guide to methods of controlling a mast to vary mainsail shapes:

Sail too flat. Stiffen the mast's flexibility by the following methods: (*a*) lengthen the spreaders to reduce sideways bend; (*b*) angle the spreaders farther forward so that they have to be pulled back to attach to the shrouds; (*c*) have the forestay meet the mast slightly higher than the shrouds (if class restrictions permit); (*d*) have a set of lower diamonds, angled slightly forward. Encourage the sail itself to take on greater curvature by lightening the battens all through, easing luff and foot tensions. Use a stiffer boom. As you stiffen the mast to allow

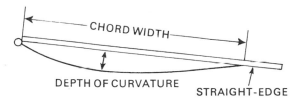

Figure 44. Diagram showing how to measure the ratio of maximum depth of curvature to chord width of a mainsail. This should be approximately 1 : 10. If a pivoting aerofoil or wing mast is used, the straight-edge must be taken to the leading edge of the mast.

the sail to take on more fullness you must ease the mainsheet pressure. If you leave the mainsheet cleated onto the same mark, as the mast is stiffened the tension on the leech will increase but the sail will not become any fuller.

Sail too full. Don't just pull the sheet on harder to flatten it, as this puts too much pressure on the leech, destroying the basic aim of the flexible rig of freeing the leech as wind pressure increases. You must encourage the mast to bend by other means: shorten the spreaders to give the mast more sideways movement; angle the spreaders aft to allow the middle of the mast to move forward more easily; chock the mast forward at deck level; haul the boom vang on harder to increase the bend in the lower section of the mast; shift the blocks farther aft on the boom so that the mainsheet pressure tends to push the boom forward into the mast, making it bend more, low down. By bending the mast forward low down you will make the top automatically bend further aft, pivoting around the hounds. If the class rules allow, the forestay attachment point can be shifted to below the hounds, encouraging the mast to bend by pulling it forward in the middle with forestay load.

After softening the mast, sheet pressure will have to be increased slightly to maintain the same leech tension. The rigging can also be made to deal with a sail that is too full or too flat in either the top or bottom areas. Put top jumpers on a mast where the sail is too flat at the top—stiffening the top of the mast will induce fullness in the sail at the top. But take care that the stiffer top does not cause the bottom section of the mast to bend more, wrecking the set of the sail low down. If the bottom of the sail is too full the mast can be bent more in this area by using more boom vang pressure, chocking the mast forward at the deck, adjusting the spreader angle aft so that the tips must be forced forward to attach to the shrouds, and tightening the spinnaker-pole preventer stay if your boat uses one.

To assist any of these measures, a wooden mast can be softened or stiffened by shaving-off or gluing-on timber, and an aluminium mast can be softened by sawing cuts in the track.

All of these remedies, except the softening or stiffening of the mast itself, tend to bend or restrain the mast mechanically before the sail goes on it. So don't overdo any of them, as they will lessen some of the benefits of an automatically flexible mast and give instead a controlled-bend mast which must be continually adjusted to meet the demands of different wind strengths. You are tuning for medium winds, you must remember, so if you have to bend the mast excessively to get the 10 per cent ratio, you have no automatic flexibility left to reduce power as the winds get stronger and, at the other end of the scale, no adjustment left to increase stiffness for light weather.

These remedies will improve your performance, but the real answer is to have your sailmaker alter the luff curve of the sail—increase it to make the sail fuller, decrease it to flatten the sail.

BALANCE

Any alteration you make in sail shape is apt to change the balance of your boat. So after adjusting your rig and possibly having your mainsail cut to reach the 10 per cent depth-width ratio, you should rebalance the boat so that there is neither excessive weather helm, tending to make the boat round-up into the wind, nor lee helm, making her fall away. Most skippers like to sail with just a fraction of weather helm to give a positive feel on the tiller and keep the boat hunting out the closest course to windward. Too much weather helm means the rudder has to haul over to such an angle to keep the boat on course that it acts as a brake.

Weather helm should not be confused with another fault, weight on the tiller. If the tiller is hard to shift, but stays down the centre-line of the boat most of the time, that's weight on the helm, caused by the rudder blade being angled too far aft or set too far behind the rudder pintles.

Shift the centreboard aft to correct weather helm and forward to correct lee helm. Most dinghy classes have a centreboard slot big enough for the small adjustment necessary to compensate for the slight change in balance caused by normal tuning alterations to the rig. If a pivoting centreboard is demanded by class rules it can still be swung slightly aft to relieve weather helm or kicked forward slightly to cure lee helm.

In small boats, balance can also be adjusted by shifting crew weight slightly fore and aft. Stacking the crew aft gives the stern sections more grip on the water, removing any small degree of weather helm. In the same way, shifting the crew forward will tend to encourage weather helm by giving the forward sections more grip. Balance will alter, too, with variations in wind strength; you must be alert to adjust to them constantly. If the boat is well balanced in medium conditions—tiller moving a little either side of the centre-line with only a slight tendency for the boat to hunt to windward—as the wind drops, you will gradually develop lee helm. This continues until in extremely light breezes, with almost no way on, it is almost impossible to hold the boat on the wind and you can end up drifting around in circles. To counter this, at the first sight of lee helm move the crew a little further forward. This also tends to lift the transom, reducing the drag. You can also heel the boat slightly to leeward, using the curve in the side of the hull to produce slight weather helm. These are all good tricks when winds are variable and the balance of the boat is changing back and forth, as they keep rudder movement to a minimum, reducing drag. They demand a good deal of concentration by the crew. But if any of these tricks have to be used excessively in near-moderate winds, then the centreboard must be moved.

As the wind increases above the medium

range, shift the crew aft, which also tends to lift the bow and induce planing to windward, the race-winning "overdrive" of powerful light boats. Sail the boat as upright as you can, making full use of the bottom lines designed for planing. Once you have found the angle of heel where balance feels good, concentrate on keeping the hull on that exact angle, as any appreciable change will need sudden use of the rudder to maintain course and, nine times out of ten, will drop the boat off the plane.

Varying the rake of the mast aft from the vertical can be used to change the balance of the boat—more rake to increase weather helm, less rake to take it away. How much rake, if any, a mast should carry cannot be dealt with in a generalised way. In any class I like to sail with as much rake as possible while still keeping the balance on the helm neutral. I don't know why, but most boats seem to like going upwind with as much rake as possible.

ADVANCED TUNING

When you are happy about your boat's balance again after the initial alterations to rig and sail,

re-mark the mainsheet for its new optimum pressure. You'll really need three markings, mainsheet pressure being slightly more in fresher breezes, and quite a lot less in light breezes, than that for the range for which you are basically tuning—12 to 15 knots.

In more advanced tuning sessions you must observe how the drive is placed in the mainsail. You have already checked the general fullness of the sail, but is the area of greatest curvature best placed to give maximum efficiency? It should usually be about 45 per cent back from the mast. The best way to check this is to lie on your back in the bottom of the boat, looking up the lee side of the sail. The shape of the cross-sections should show up clearly at each seam. If the drive is too far forward, the luff tension may be too great or the battens (if full length) too flexible near the inner end. Conversely, if it is too far aft, check the effort of more luff tension and having the battens stiffer towards the outer end. Positioning of the drive may also be controlled by bending the mast slightly to reduce fullness near the mast. But if all tensions and batten shapes are correct, and the drive is still not in the right place, the sail should be recut.

This mast is too stiff, which makes the sail too full and leaves the leech standing up bar tight, causing the catamaran to heel excessively, although the crew are swinging their hearts out.

This Heron is going to windward in perfect trim. The hull is as flat as possible on the water without digging in the windward chine. The transom is clearing the water cleanly. The crew are sitting close together to keep the weight as close as possible to the pivot point. The foot of the sail is showing distortions because it has been dragged out along the boom to flatten the sail in this area for the fresh breeze.

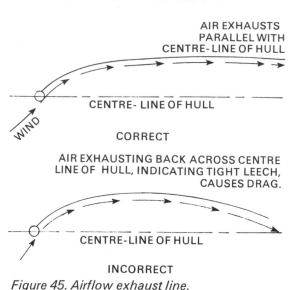

AIR EXHAUSTS
PARALLEL WITH
CENTRE-LINE OF HULL

CENTRE- LINE OF HULL

WIND

CORRECT

AIR EXHAUSTING BACK ACROSS CENTRE
LINE OF HULL, INDICATING TIGHT LEECH,
CAUSES DRAG.

CENTRE-LINE OF HULL

INCORRECT

Figure 45. Airflow exhaust line.

Next, check the leech to see whether it is hooking too far to windward and acting like a brake on the airflow exhausting from the sail. Stand 30 or 40 ft. directly behind the boat, line up the mast with the forestay, and look into the sail with sheeting and boom angle in the sailing-to-windward position. If the leech is too tight, you will be able to see a considerable section of the leeward side of the sail as well as the line of the leech. Air coming off this leech will be flowing across the centre-line of the boat, tending to give it weather helm and choking up performance. If the leech of the sail is free, you should be able to see the horizontal lines of cloth of the windward side terminating in the vertical line of the leech. The air coming out of this sail will be almost parallel to the centre-line of the boat, giving maximum drive in stronger winds or very light winds where there is not enough wind pressure in the sail to make a tight leech stay open and exhaust air easily.

THE SLOT

Still standing behind the boat, but moving a little to leeward, observe the slot between jib leech and mainsail curvature. This, theoretically, should be as constant a width as possible from top to bottom. But usually the leech of the jib is closer to the mainsail at the top. So the leech of the jib should be encouraged to lay off

Good parallel slots between main and headsail shown in a variety of classes. The NS14, top right, has its small jib sheeted close to give high-pointing ability with a narrow but good slot with the close sheeted mainsail. Top centre. This Soling has the head of both the jib and the main twisted off to retain parallel slot. This 470, top far right, also has the head of the jib twisted to match sail, powered up for the chop. The Flying Dutchman, bottom right, has good slot with main sheeted well to windward and flat low down to retain drive without backwinding from jib; twist in the head of the jib matching twisted mainsail. The Flying Dutchman, bottom far right, carries more twist in both jib and mainsail heads, mainsail still centrally sheeted for drive, to handle a stronger wind.

slightly to remain as parallel as possible to the mainsail shape.

It is a common fault with dinghies to have the slot very wide at boom level and almost touching at the top. To cure it, move the sheeting point closer to the centre-line of the hull to close the slot near the bottom of the jib, and sheet the jib with less pressure so that the leech will tend to curve around the main. Sheet pressure here is critical, as half an inch either in or out will be greatly amplified in the distance the upper part of the jib leech is from the mainsail. Sheeting pressure also has to be carefully adjusted to wind-strength variations, especially in the lighter range. In keel yachts, it is easier for the for'ard hand to adjust to new wind strengths as he can view the slot from the leeward gunwale while sailing. On dinghies, however, the for'ard hand must depend mainly on feel as the jib leech is hidden from him by the mainsail.

The top wool tufts on the jib are also an excellent guide to jib-sheet tension. Using the windward tuft that is always easy to see, ease the jib out until the tuft stalls then pull it back on until the tuft is just moving a little. This is normally the fastest trim. The boat is always slow if the windward tuft is flowing solidly. With this much sheet tension, you can bet that the lee side is stalled at least 60 per cent of the time. Experiment with sheeting positions during two-boat training sessions to find the fastest positions. Get off onto a powerboat and inspect the rig from behind under sailing conditions. Call for different sheet tensions on both mainsail and jib to study the effect on both the sail exhaust angles and the slot. Take a series of photographs for future reference and try to photograph some of the faster boats from similar angles for comparison.

Making the jib work at its best in relation to the mainsail is essential to both speed and pointing ability. The angles at which these sails should be sheeted to each other vary for each type of boat and even for slight differences in shape between sails.

Suppose the jib is sheeted too wide in relation to the mainsail; the jib will luff and stall before the mainsail does. But if you sheet the mainsail wider, to correspond with the angle of the jib, you will have speed but not pointing ability, since both sails will be sheeted much too wide.

If the jib is sheeted too close in relation to the mainsail, you will be able to sail very close to the wind before the jib luffs, but the mainsail will stall (flap near the mast) well before the jib. Some of this lifting will be caused by back-wind off the jib, but most of it by the mainsail just being sheeted too wide for the wind. If you try to fix this by easing the jib to give it a better angle to the main, the top half of the jib will end up at a much wider angle than the bottom, giving it only half efficiency.

Compromise can be achieved in either of these two extreme situations, by clever sheet trimming, but your boat will never be going at its best.

Somewhere in between there is an angle where both sails give their maximum at the same time. To find it you need intelligent practice sailing, varying sheeting angles of both jib and main. Trial and error is the only real way, as sheeting angles vary with the shape and fullness of the sails, dimensions and shape of the hull, and the prevailing seas and winds of the area in which you sail.

Light, small boats such as Manly Juniors, Herons, Mirrors, and Sabots cannot sail very close to the wind because of their lack of momentum and tubby shapes—they just bob up and down if you try to sail as close as a bigger boat. To sail faster through the water it is best to sheet main and jib at wider angles; this is even more essential in order to keep them moving smoothly ahead through waves. Boats of similar size such as Moths, Northbridge 14s, and Flying Ants, also light but more easily driven due to their finer hull shapes, can sheet their sails a little closer without losing speed.

Really high-performance-hulled dinghies like Skiffs, Lightweight Sharpies, Flying Dutchmen, Cherubs, and 505s—all capable of planing to windward in stronger winds—need two sets of sheeting angles: one for displacement speed in light winds when they can point high, and the other at a slightly wider angle to promote speed when the breeze is fresh and the hull inclined to plane. You should do all you can to encourage any hull that will plane to windward to do so. The difference between planing speed and displacement speed is so great you can afford to sail freer, with your sails sheeted wider—just how much freer is a subtle point of judgement found the hard way, in racing or intelligent practice.

The fore-and-aft position of the jib-sheet leads is also decided by trial and error. The best position is the one at which the boat goes fastest. But, to find a starting point, lay the jib out on a flat surface, bisect the angle formed by the clew, and draw this line on the sail. After hoisting the jib extend this line to where it hits the deck, and you have a good starting point. Extending the line of the mitre, once the accepted rule-of-thumb method for finding this point, no longer works with mitres being cut at all sorts of angles these days. Some yachts move the jib lead aft on heavy days, which tends to stretch the foot tight, flattening the headsail in the lower section and allowing the leech to free from half-way up the sail. On light days it is a common practice to move the lead a little forward so that the foot of the jib will set to its shape without distortion.

The amount of twist in a jib depends on how hard you sheet it in. If it is pulled in really hard and the leech is still too open, shift the leads further forward. This will transfer some of the load more directly onto the leech, allowing it to close to the correct position. This lead adjustment will also make the bottom part of the jib fuller or flatter for any required twist.

Fullness of sail and the type of cut have such a bearing on sheeting angles that it is not wise to measure those of a competitor who is sailing a little better than you are, even if he is in the same type of boat. His sheeting angles may suit his sails but not yours. This is particularly true with dinghy classes where fuller sails sheeted

It is easy to sheet incorrectly, especially when sailing in light winds and sloppy seas as these Stars are. They are pointing in all directions. Boats 5350 and 4780, which have just rounded the mark, obviously have their sails sheeted in much too hard, probably because they haven't yet found the true breeze. The boat second from right has found the correct angle to the breeze.

slightly wider may give you more power to reach planing speed to windward or just result in a more favourable angle of leech to hull. If you are being constantly beaten by a competitor who is sheeting his sails differently, consider having your sails recut, as his must suit the hull shape better than yours.

Keel yachts generally sail higher to windward than dinghies because of their fine hull shapes and momentum. But even here there are variations in pointing ability, and hence sheeting angles, between classes. A Dragon will not sail as high as a 5.5 because it has a relatively blunt entry and has to be driven with more power to maintain speed, especially in waves.

Unlike a dinghy, which can jump out on top of the water and plane in stronger breezes, a keel yacht cannot exceed her maximum hull speed which is restricted by her length, weight, and design. Therefore the sheeting angles must be arranged so that the yacht will sail as high as she can to windward while still retaining her maximum hull speed in medium winds. Sailing a big yacht fractionally freer will not increase hull speed in average to fresh winds; it will only result in loss of ground to windward. In light winds, where the yacht is below maximum hull speed, a slight increase can be gained by sailing a little freer with eased sheets.

In all types of boat, big and small, light weather calls for sympathetic sail trim. There is not enough pressure from the wind to bend the mast which in heavy weather automatically takes care of many adjustments. If you are too heavy-handed on sheets in light weather the leeches of the sails which previously were blown free by the weight of the wind will all stand up too tight, and will not let out what little wind there is. The jib, normally smaller in area than the main, should have light sheets fitted to it for light breezes so that when the sail is eased the clew will lift and allow the leech to curve out around the main to form an ideal slot. In light weather the for'ard hand should sit to leeward and carefully adjust the sheet pressure for each slight variation in wind strength so as to keep the slot a constant width.

The mainsheet, in light weather, also has to be handled with kid gloves. For a start, it is wise to drop a couple of purchases out of the

mainsheet tackle so it will run with less friction and the crew will be able to feel the pressure on the sail more easily through it. The hawse traveller, especially if it is of the centre-sheeting type, should be moved to windward so that the boom angle can be altered without too much downward pressure on the boom, allowing the leech to breathe even in the lightest winds. As soon as the wind increases a little the traveller should be moved back to the centre and the sail sheeted normally. If you sheet on too hard with the traveller pulled to windward, the boom will come into the centre-line, closing the bottom of the leech drastically and killing boat speed.

Again, it pays to record best light-weather settings of sheets and travellers once you have found them. Once the wind drops you know immediately from your past experience and your markings where to sheet to, and you avoid wasting 5 or 10 minutes of your concentration while experimenting.

SPECIAL SITUATIONS

Once you have your boat tuned to perfection for all-round performance, you should look towards tuning for special situations. If you are going to sail on a course that has flat water you should tune your boat to sail high to windward because it is easier to maintain speed in flat water than in waves. If you are sailing in tidal waters it is also of great advantage to be able to point high to perhaps lee bow the current or claw up a shore out of the tide.

And in any tuning you should never lose sight of the importance of being able to point high as well as sail fast through the water as an aid to tactics. This is particularly valuable in big fleets, where the starts are crowded and it is necessary to be able to point quite high in the first 10 minutes or so after the gun in order to clear your wind. Settings should be known and marked on mainsheets, travellers, jib sheets, and Cunningham eye adjusters so that the boat can be trimmed before the start to sail very high for the first half-lap to windward, even at the expense of a slight loss in speed. Once you have cleared your wind and are in open water you can then alter all settings quickly to their positions for best speed.

DOWNWIND

If you have tuned your boat well for windward work, it should also go well downwind. If possible you should start tuning for downwind performance while the boat is being built, keeping everything to minimum weight—most important in marginal planing winds in which the light boats will get up and go where others will not. Boat balance, sail trim, and steering technique are the next most important factors. When reaching, the boat must have as little weather helm as possible, especially when planing, and no lee helm. Any excessive force applied to the rudder will slow the boat and sometimes stop her planing. Sails must be constantly trimmed to follow wind changes, the helmsman's course over seas, and constant changes in apparent wind due to sharp increases in hull speed (the apparent wind moves forward as speed increases; sails must therefore be trimmed closer). The spinnaker should be as powerful as possible, and it pays to ease off control lines to Cunningham eye and boom out-haul to give the mainsail more fullness when reaching.

CONCLUSION

Always keep an open mind when tuning. Don't believe what others tell you unless they can explain why. I have heard some incredible tuning hints like "Rake your mast 6 in.; it makes your boat go like a rocket in a heavy breeze." He cannot tell you how it works, and, when you try, it doesn't for you. What has probably happened is that in raking his mast the other fellow has accidentally made some other alterations which have improved his performance—he has lowered the clew of his jib, which has the same effect as shifting the jib leads aft, easing the leech and widening the slot; if the mast was supported at deck level, by raking the mast he also has bent the lower section of his mast, flattening the sail; he has altered the height of the boom from the sheeting horse which altered the mainsail's angle of sheeting—any of which should help a boat go faster in a heavy wind. But your boat may already have these adjustments right for a heavy breeze, and raking the mast will just throw them all out. So when you adjust one item in the rig, understand why and make all compensating adjustments to your other equipment before assessing the results.

If you have tried every available option and still don't have boat speed, take a day off, have someone else steer your boat in the race, and tag along in a small powerboat, comparing the appearance of your sails and rig with those of someone who is going well. Remember, the spectator still sees most of the game. A small 12 ft. outboard-powered boat is about ideal, as you can manoeuvre in close without interfering with the racing yachts through wash or windage. Take a camera to record for later comparison the sail shapes of your own boat and those of your faster competitors.

Tuning with Tufts

WOOL tufts, besides assisting the helmsman to steer an accurate course to windward, are a valuable aid to tuning and sail trim. They indicate, visually, the behaviour of the air flow around a sail: when the tuft streams aft steadily, the flow is perfect on that surface of the sail. When it stalls—gyrates or points upward—the flow is turbulent and has become separated from the sail.

Tufts can be used to establish whether sails are too full or too flat and to correct the inter-action of airflow between headsail and mainsail.

I believe tufts have more value in tuning and trimming than in steering, at least in smaller yachts like Solings and in dinghies. While the tufts are a good guide as to whether the helmsman is steering too high or too low a course to windward, the helmsman that steers only by the

tufts, or has a fixation about what they are doing, tends to lose the feel of his boat. While he is gazing upward, mesmerised by the tufts, he tends to forget the much more important "feel" characteristics of the boat such as bal-ance, lee or weather helm. Sometimes it is a faster compromise to sail with the windward mainsail tufts stalled through the sheet being eased or the traveller widened to give com-pletely neutral helm.

The feel of speed of the hull through the water is important—as the wind strength increases, more height to windward can be gained without loss of speed by sailing for short bursts with the windward jib tufts stalled. A constant angle of heel must be maintained, a precept the average helmsman too often neglects, and this is more easily achieved while

looking forward over the bow and relating the angle of the deck to the horizon. The helmsman must also be able to glance at the water ahead for indications of wind shifts and to assess the wave pattern.

If you have developed an obsession with wool tufts, as I did at one stage, I suggest you remove them from your jib for some weeks, re-develop your sense of feel, then replace the tufts, using them as a guide only. I guarantee this experiment will make you a much better helmsman.

Steering a big, heavy unresponsive yacht like an ocean racer by the tufts is good and much more accurate than steering to electronic wind instruments. No matter what the instruments indicate, you can sail only as high as your sails will allow. There is no way of steering a yacht at, say, 30 degrees to the wind, as the instruments tell you theoretically you could, if once you achieve 30 degrees, all the headsail tufts stall, and your speed drops off. You can sail only as high as the sail shape will allow, without a major recut of the sail.

Headsail tufts are valuable aids to steering

Far left. In fresher winds, steering tufts should be used only as a guide and not followed religiously. This boat is in perfect trim with the genoa slightly stalled, as indicated by the just-lifting windward tuft, to keep the boat at the correct angle of heel.

Top left. The traveller has not been used to de-power the rig in a gust. Tufts and ribbons are all working nicely. Bottom left. Full power being extracted from same, very efficient rig.

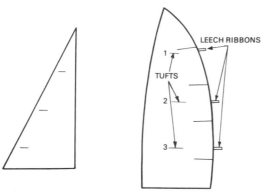

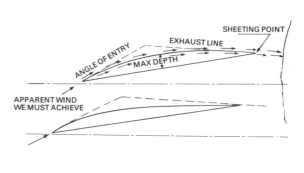

Figure 46. Headsail tufts should be about 6 in. back from the luff for dinghies and 10 in. back for yachts of 30 ft. and more. Mainsail tufts should be placed at the position of maximum draft.

Figure 47. The upper drawing shows the fullest jib that can be used for this apparent wind. The lower drawing shows how a jib with shape further forward has to be slightly flatter to fit the same triangle.

any yacht in the lower wind range where the helmsman tends to lose the feel of his boat. The limit to the zone of loss of natural feel goes up in relation to the size of boat, and the experience of the helmsman. For a Moth or OK dinghy, you can sail by feel once the wind reaches seven or eight knots. In a Dragon or Soling, the feel will be lost under 10 knots; on a 40 ft. ocean racer, the feel may be lost under 10 to 12 knots and then tufts are a great assistance to accurate steering.

The tufts should be 4 to 6 in. long, preferably of fine darning wool, light enough to be responsive in the lightest winds.

In the headsail, the bottom tuft should be located about 4 ft. up from the foot where it is easily taken in by the helmsman's eye as he glances across the bow at the water ahead. The remaining headsail tufts should be spaced at intervals of about 4 to 6 ft., about 6 in. back from the luff for dinghies and 10 in. back for yachts of 30 ft. length and bigger.

TUNING THE HEADSAIL

The headsail leads the yacht to windward and is the starting point in tuning for maximum windward performance. Remember that the sail's fullness must vary to suit the type of boat: A 5.5 or Soling will need flatter sails because they have easily-driven hulls that quickly reach hull speed and in fairly low wind strengths.

This type of boat can therefore be encouraged to sail high to windward without loss of speed. Boats such as the Dragon, Folkboat, Heron and Mirror Dinghy with hulls that are fatter and harder to drive, particularly in any seaway, cannot sail so close to the wind and therefore need fuller sails.

With class boats, it is easy to find how high you should point by watching the rest of the fleet. To succeed, you must sail as high as they do.

The angle of entry of the jib is pre-determined by the type of boat you sail. It must be parallel to the apparent wind and the jib must exhaust nearly parallel to the centreline of the yacht (a small amount of hook back across the centreline at the foot, especially with short—footed jibs is acceptable). Draw in the angle of entry line, the exhaust line to the sheeting point and you have a triangle within which the jib must be shaped to achieve unstalled airflow, indicated by cleanly-streaming tufts on both sides of the sail (Fig. 47).

Theoretically, a sail with maximum fullness further forward produces a higher lift factor than a circular arc-shaped sail. However, the air flow over a sail with fullness forward will stall much more readily. Considering these aerofoil shape sails must be made to work in an air flow that is constantly changing in strength and direction, a more tolerant circular-arc shape must be chosen. It is better to endure a slight loss of lift factor for a sail that will keep the airflow attached for, say, 80 per cent of the time than have a sail that is theoretically more efficient yet retains the flow for possibly only 50 per cent of the time. This can be proven on a boat like a Soling where the fullness in the jib may be easily shifted forward by over-tensioning the halyard. With the sail set in this shape, it is impossible to steer accurately enough to keep the tufts flowing constantly. Ease the halyard slightly and the more circular headsail shape is immediately found to be easier to steer to.

If you are sailing to windward with the tufts indicating smooth flow on both sides of the jib, but pointing too low in relation to your competitors, the jib is possibly too full or the drive too far forward, making the angle of entry too wide. This can be adjusted to a small degree by decreasing the luff tension to lower the angle of entry and move the drive aft. Too much luff sag can also increase the angle of entry and reduce a yacht's pointing ability. The cure, on yachts, is to tighten the forestay. On dinghies, where jib tension depends on mainsheet pressure, crew on trapezes and the distance the shrouds are located aft of the mast, more hollow may have to be cut into the luff of the jib to cure the problem. Re-cutting will always be necessary for headsails made from very hard finish cloths such as yarn-tempered Bainbridge. Reducing luff tension on these headsails does not help as the sheetmetal-like stability of the cloth will not allow the fullness to move back into the sail. Reducing the luff tension until light horizontal wrinkles form behind the luff tape can help in light air. But re-cutting will always be the real solution.

Tuning should preferably be undertaken in a wind strength where the particular yacht is not over-pressed (for example, Dragon 8 to 10 knots, Heron 12 knots). Above these wind strengths, a better sailing result is achieved with sails in a semi-stalled state to relieve pressure and allow the boat to be sailed at her best angle of heel with no loss of speed. So tuning in these wind strengths would lead to a false result unless it is to develop specialised heavy-weather sails.

Follow this sequence to select sheeting position, correct sheet tension and to assess the shape of the jib: Sail to windward, using the

Leeward tufts are flowing perfectly on this Tasar. The mainsail tufts are much closer to the mast than is normal on other boats but still working, due to the efficiency of the aerofoil shape of the over-rotated mast section.

bottom tuft as a guide to accuracy. Increase the sheet pressure until the top, windward tuft just begins to flow.

Now look at the bottom of the jib. If it appears to be stretched very tight, looks flat and is strained along the foot, shift the lead forward until, under the correct sheet pressure with the top windward tuft just working, the bottom of the jib takes up its curved built-in shape with rounded foot not curling or stretched too tightly.

With the top and bottom of the jib balanced

to sheet pressure and lead position, the rest of the wool tufts should all stall on the windward side at the same time when the boat is luffed slightly. All tufts should stream and stall at exactly the same time on both overlapping genoas and high-aspect Soling-type jibs. However the high-aspect sail is much more critical to twist in the head: an $\frac{1}{8}$ in. adjustment on the sheet means the difference between the tuft in the top streaming and stalling. For preference, the top tuft should stall a fraction sooner than the bottom one. It is vital to maintain the twist to prevent the top of the headsail closing up the slot between it and the mainsail, diminishing the flow of air around the back of the mainsail.

If the middle tufts consistently stall first, more hollow must be cut into the luff to flatten this area and align its shape with the top and bottom of the jib. If the boat is sailing high enough, perhaps too high, with the middle stalling first, the top and bottom areas should be made fuller to fall in line with the middle. This will give more speed with only a slight drop in pointing angle. Visually check the constancy of the angle of entry by looking up the lee side of the sail and noting the areas where there is variation, possibly demanding a recut.

The trouble area, especially with high-aspect jibs, is usually in the top half of the sail where the fullness is quickly affected by forestay sag variation. If the top of a high-aspect jib is too full, there is no way the windward tuft can ever be made to work without stalling the flow around the lee side of the sail, killing the speed. So trim to keep the lee side flow working until a recut can be arranged. The same principle should be applied if you are caught out carrying a light-weather headsail in a freshening breeze.

Once the sail is performing to perfection, with all tufts breaking at the same time, the sheet trimmer need only watch the top tufts. He adjusts the sheet pressure until the top windward tuft just starts working. If the jib is oversheeted, the leeward top tuft will stall. It is always preferable to under-sheet a little, as nothing stops a boat more quickly than a jib sheeted in too hard. And if the helmsman is steering religiously to the tufts, an over-sheeted or under-sheeted jib will have him steering either too high or too low.

MAINSAIL

The same principles of degree and position of fullness apply to mainsails as to headsails. Fullness is easier to control through mast bend, but it is much more difficult to make the mainsail tufts work correctly as the sail has the complication of the mast ahead of it. Matching the mainsail's luff curve to the mast bend is critical to achieve the correct fullness all the way up the sail.

Both tufts and leech ribbons should be used. Leech ribbons are a further, very distinctive, visual aid to air flow. They are light pieces of spinnaker cloth or similar material, 1 in. wide by 6 in. long, sewn to the leech opposite the wool tufts. They give a repeat reading to the behaviour of the leeward tuft which, at most times, is very difficult to see through the sail. As soon as the leeward tuft stalls, the leech ribbon will disappear, sucked into turbulent air behind the mainsail with a definite and distinct movement. So, at a glance, skipper and crew under racing pressure can see whether the mainsail is being trimmed correctly.

Do not put tufts all over the mainsail. Too many cannot be taken in at a glance and become difficult to read. Divide the mainsail into four areas, from top to bottom, with a tuft in the middle of each quarter.

The tufts should be placed at the position of maximum draft where they will also be far enough aft to escape the turbulent flow from the mast. The four areas of the sail's shape influencing the tufts will overlap so it can be guaranteed that if all four sets of tufts can be made to work, the whole sail is working efficiently. The sets of tufts are also in the centre of four distinct areas of sail control where fullness may be varied by mast bend, vang tension, outhaul tension or sheet pressure to meet changes in wind and wave conditions. They can be used to indicate the efficiency of each of these areas.

When tuning the mainsail, the boat must be steered very accurately all the time to a properly-tuned headsail. While the mainsail's shape is being altered by the various controls sailing a fraction free or a fraction high of the optimum angle for sailing to windward can lead to absolutely false readings.

APPARENT WIND
ANGLE JIB

APPARENT WIND
ANGLE MAIN

Figure 48. A very full jib will not work with a very flat main. The jib works at a much higher apparent wind angle so both sails cannot be fully efficient.

The mainsail must be made to follow the best pointing angle that has been established for the jib, working in the same apparent wind angle. It is no use having a very full jib with a very flat main or a flat jib with a full main (Fig. 48).

Sail the boat hard on the wind with the jib in the known correct trim and, to begin with, sail by feel, disregarding the mainsail tufts and ribbons until you think the boat is going as fast as it can. Then look at the tufts. It is too easy to make the tufts in a mainsail work falsely by sheeting in too hard or under-sheeting; spoiling perhaps two-thirds of the sail to make one-third work. Do not forget all the things you know from experience that are good speed indicators like the natural, lively feeling of the boat, balance (weather and lee helm), angle of heel, sound of the water.

From this starting point, the tufts will help tune and trim for more speed. The leeward bottom two tufts rarely stall on a boat with a jib. They stream well because they are in the accelerated flow from the jib across the back of the mainsail. However, there is usually a problem making the windward tufts stream in the bottom two-thirds of the mainsail. Many mainsails are just too full in that area. This is not a big drawback for, while there is a slight increase in drag, the flow around the leeward side of the sail which produces the major lift, still works. But if the sail is flattened in its lower area to make the tufts there work, you will go slightly faster. There is an added bonus: Both overlapping and non-overlapping headsails can be sheeted closer to a mainsail that is flatter in the bottom, for improved pointing ability.

If the bottom two windward tufts stall, increase foot tension. Do not hesitate to pull the outhaul really hard. The crease this will cause in the sail along the boom may not look good, but it will not harm windward performance. Boom vang tension can also help, encouraging

Over-trimmed mainsail indicated by leeward top tuft stalling. The leech ribbon at that point is also stalling—the ribbons give a repeat reading of the behaviour of the leeward tufts.

low-down bend in the mast, thus flattening the lower and middle sectors of the sail. Flatten until the windward tuft just lifts if you sail a fraction high or spring the sheet slightly. With this lower tuft just on stall point, you have absolutely maximum fullness in the bottom of the sail.

Fullness is more difficult to adjust in the middle section than in any other part of the mainsail. If the tufts indicate it is too full, the fullness has to be cut out by altering the luff curve. This area of the mast is supported by the hounds and therefore it is hard to alter its bend characteristics.

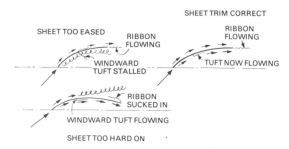

SHEET TRIM CORRECT

SHEET TOO EASED   RIBBON
FLOWING

RIBBON
FLOWING

WINDWARD   TUFT NOW FLOWING
TUFT STALLED

RIBBON
SUCKED IN

WINDWARD TUFT FLOWING

SHEET TOO HARD ON

Figure 49. How the mainsail, in section, behaves at the top wool tuft and ribbon.

Once you have worked on the bottom two-thirds of the mainsail and have the tufts streaming correctly, the top third is basically adjusted by sheet pressure, and this sector is absolutely critical to sheet pressure. It is very easy, through over-sheeting, to stall the leeward side as it does not have the jib's influence (on three-quarter rigged boats) to help promote flow. And some twist is always desirable in this area.

The area of mainsail above the jib's influence must have a wider angle of attack (more twist) than the lower part of the mainsail that has accelerated airflow from the jib passing across it, keeping it unstalled at very fine angles of attack with the boom down the centreline of the hull.

The mainsail should be sheeted in until the top windward tuft begins to stream aft. The adjacent ribbon on the leech should also be flowing. If you oversheet, the leeward tuft will stall and the ribbon disappear behind the leech. Ease the sheet slightly, the top of the sail twists and the ribbon re-appears, indicating flow is restored on the leeward side of the sail. If at that point the windward tuft is not working as well, the top of the sail is too full and should be re-cut. The top of the mast can be softened to allow its natural bend to flatten the sail (Fig. 49).

The whole rig must be tuned so that the tufts on both mainsail and jib work in perfect unison, streaming and stalling at precisely the same time.

Guard against over-dependence on tufts. Sometimes a boat may feel better and actually perform better with certain sheet tensions that make it impossible for the tufts to work. This does not mean the theory is wrong but that the

Mainsail tufts and ribbons indicate efficient flow but stalling after lower tuft on the jib indicates the bottom of the jib is hooking excessively.

sails must be re-cut to allow them to work most efficiently under those sheet tensions that feel good.

Remember that in the lighter wind range you are always looking for power from the rig. So you have to make the sail as full as possible with the windward tufts only just working—if the sheet is eased a fraction, all tufts will immediately lift. It is very difficult to make the top leech ribbon work in very light air without easing and flattening the sail to a ridiculous extent. Under those conditions, if the top ribbon is flicking in and out, you will be achieving the best result.

Ribbons and tufts are extremely valuable when reaching to control boom angle, top twist

Tufts are also important downwind, especially on reaching legs. The sheet on this mainsail needs to be trimmed to get the windward tufts flowing for maximum mainsail efficiency.

from vang tension and sail fullness. Too much boom vang pressure and the top ribbon will immediately stall. The sail can be made much fuller in the bottom and the tufts kept streaming to indicate air flow efficiency as the apparent wind moves aft on a reaching course.

Once the boat is tuned and the tufts are being used only for trim, the skipper should be discouraged from watching them at all in a three-man or even two-man boat. The helmsman should teach the crew to read them and, even if he is working the mainsheet, should have the crew telling him when to adjust it to make the tufts stream. This leaves the helmsman free to concentrate on steering and picking the wind shifts.

Specialised Tuning

EACH CLASS of boat has its own tuning peculiarities. As it is not possible to deal with every class in this book we have selected a representative range of one-design and restricted yachts and dinghies to set down the techniques I have found make them go faster. Many of these techniques may be applied successfully to a wide range of similar boats, but you must understand what you are trying to achieve and not blindly follow fashionable trends. You will often have to compromise to get the most effective use out of the sails you have in your wardrobe.

DRAGON

LENGTH 29 ft. 2 in.
BEAM 6 ft. 4 in.
DRAFT 3 ft. 11 in.
SAIL AREA 235 sq. ft.
WEIGHT 3,747 lb.
DESIGNER Johan Anker

Now that the measurement rules have been tightened, hulls are all much the same. For a while, different builders were supposed to be dropping the bows, or making them finer, or lengthening sterns to make them go faster. The Danish builder Borressen produced hulls that seemed superior, but I think this was mainly due to his building fair hulls and concentrating the weight low in the boat rather than fiddling with rule tolerances. Australia's Billy Barnett and others have been building hulls that are just as good. The finish on the hull, however, is quite important—probably because the Dragon has a lot of wetted area. I have been surprised, after noting a performance drop indicating a foul bottom, to find when the boat has been slipped that there is no weed or obvious growth, only little spots like grains of sand on the bottom. The type of finish doesn't really matter so long as it is smooth and the bottom is free of bumps and dents.

Alloy masts have been allowed in Dragons since 1970. With them, it is much easier to achieve minimum weight and minimum centre of gravity without fear of heavy-weather breakages that plagued the lightest spruce spars of the past.

The plan position for the mast on the boat has not been used for years. The most popular position now is 10 ft. 2 in. from the stem with the fore-triangle being kept maximum size. The caps, lowers, jumpers, and runners control the mast bend.

There are several basic approaches. To achieve forestay control with runners, one of the most popular methods is to have the runners fairly well forward on the boat, controlled by wheel-winches or track slides. The leeward runner is pulled on just before you tack the boat. When you tack, the mast lays over sideways, with the athwartships rigging fairly slack, taking most of the weight on the new windward runner and the forestay, thus tightening the forestay. With this method, you don't have to adjust the runners every time you tack; hence it could be the best method in waters where a lot of short tacking is necessary because of wind shifts or boat traffic. The drawback is that you lose some athwartships control on the mast as the caps and lowers are less effective, especially in light to medium winds, because the runner has most of the sideways load.

At the other extreme is the method I like best—having the runners right aft, almost on the centre-line alongside the backstay, controlled by wheels or Highfield levers. This gives them a direct mechanical pull against the forestay without affecting sideways pressures on the mast. You can still adjust your mast, with the athwartships rigging, to bow to windward below the hounds and clear the genoa slot if you want to, or hold up straight. And you can get the exact tension you require on the forestay for genoa fullness control. The disadvantage is that you have a lot of wire which is liable to tangle unless you are careful, especially when you come off the wind and have the leeward runner going around the back of the sail and across the leech. These runners should be hooked to the backstay by shock rubber at 14 ft. and 10 ft. from the deck to keep the slack runner clear of the mainboom. They have to be let off and pulled on every time you tack, but only 12 to 14 in., just to clear the leech of the sail. When running, they need about 8 ft. of slack to clear the boom.

In between these two extremes is the most often used method—with the runners coming to the deck at about the after end of the cockpit. This does not give you full mechanical advantage on the forestay, but also does not greatly affect the tensions of the athwartships rigging.

The main and lower shrouds need to be fairly loose. Start tuning them with the lowers, adjusting them until they will move about $2\frac{1}{2}$ in. from side to side when you grip them at head height. Then, while under way, keep easing the main shrouds, a couple of turns at a time, until the mast has a slight bend to windward at the spreaders. You may get a shock when you unrig, as this usually leaves the main shrouds very slack, with something like 2 in. to 4 in. of movement at head height. This is not important, but the combination of pressures between the main and lower shrouds is critical. With the runners all the way aft, the rigging can be set up with the caps firm and the lowers adjusted while sailing to windward to keep the mast dead straight.

Mast bend, to suit the sail you are carrying, is controlled below the hounds by the amount of movement you have in the deck hole, which allows the middle of the mast to bend forward as you sheet the sail in. Only $\frac{3}{8}$ in. clearance is allowed all round the mast at the deck under the rules, so if you want more bend low down you have to shift the butt of the mast a little further aft so as to give more clearance at the front of the mast hole. Conversely, if you want less bend you shift the butt forward.

The position of the lower and main shrouds fore-and-aft will also have a bearing on the low bend. To encourage bend, move mains forward. This means that the spreader attached to the

The Dragon class: an out and out racing keel yacht that enjoys extremely close competition.

shroud will not start restricting the forward movement of the spar until more bend is achieved. Moving the lowers forward will also encourage this. But, after taking these steps, a careful watch must be kept on the mast as wind strength increases to see that it does not bend too much and break. To restrict bend, move the same rigging aft.

The jumpers, which mainly control the top of the mast, indirectly control the bottom bend as well. If you have them on very hard the mast will stand up very straight at the head and, as the pressure of the sail is applied to it, the bottom of the mast will be kicked forward. The top bend is completely controlled by the jumpers, which should be set at the widest angle apart to give the mast sideways support and minimum fore-and-aft restriction. For more bend, you ease them, but as you do this the head tends to fall off sideways, so the modern trend is to use fairly tight jumpers with a fairly flat luff curve to the sail near the head. This stands the mast up sideways, helping pointing ability, and bends the mast low down, allowing a full sail to be carried for downwind work. On the wind the main must be flattened enough to prevent the genoa from back-winding it down low, and the top section must be just full enough to stall at the same time as the genoa luff.

Spreaders on the mast must be the minimum length allowed, to enable the genoa leech to be sheeted close. Distance between the genoa and the spreader end can then be an accurate guide to sheet pressure. In winds above 10 knots the sail should be just brushing the end of the spreader. In winds lighter than 10 knots the genoa should be 2 in. to 3 in. away from the spreader end, especially when sheeting inside the gunwale.

The backstay should never be used to bend the mast when going to windward, except in extremely rough conditions. It is there only to restrain the mast while running downwind. On the wind the mast should bend to the pressure of the sail and the sheet. The minute you pull on the backstay as well, you take away the natural spring of the mast from the leech of the sail.

For a big championship, where you expect to encounter all types of weather, your wardrobe should comprise three headsails and two mainsails. One of the mains should be fairly powerful, good for up to 15 knots, and the main for the higher wind-range should be flatter and freer in the leech. You should have a specialised light-weather genoa, a medium genoa versatile enough to be used in any weight of wind, and a heavy-weather genoa.

The Dragon is particularly sensitive to headsail selection for windward work; you haven't a hope if you are caught with a flat genoa on a light day. Mainsail selection is less critical, but when in doubt carry the full one, as in borderline cases the fuller main will give much better reaching speed.

The jib leads should be set up with two control blocks running on the sheet—one attached to an arthwartships traveller on the deck via a piece of wire to make it adjustable up and down, to give fore and aft lead adjustment, and the other a Barber hauler to give in and out adjustment. The inner end of the Barber hauler should be led through two cheek blocks screwed under the coach house on the centre-line (Fig. 50).

The extra length of line from the cockpit to the centre of the coachhouse will allow the Barber hauler block to float up and down freely without interfering with the fore and aft trim. In flat water, and 6 to 8 knots of wind, maximum performance can be achieved with cor-

Figure 50. Dragon jib sheet controls.

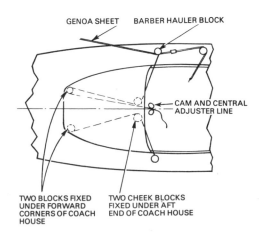

GENOA SHEET   BARBER HAULER BLOCK

CAM AND CENTRAL
ADJUSTER LINE

TWO BLOCKS FIXED
UNDER FORWARD
CORNERS OF COACH
HOUSE

TWO CHEEK BLOCKS
FIXED UNDER AFT
END OF COACH HOUSE

rectly shaped genoas sheeted 18 in. to 20 in. inside the outer skin of the hull. As the wind increases, gradually move the lead out until in strong wind, the jib sheet leads in a direct line to the turning block fixed on the gunwale 3 ft. or 4 ft. behind the aft edge of the coach house. When the genoa is sheeted with the correct twist, the foot should be just touching the shrouds at the deck.

I do not think it matters whether you have end-boom sheeting or centre-boom sheeting as long as the boom is kept on the centreline of the hull with the close-sheeted headsail until the yacht reaches her correct sailing angle. Then ease the boom down as the genoa lead is moved out to depower the rig for stronger winds.

Dragons seem to sail at their best with only a fraction of weather helm. One problem arises when it is blowing very hard. If you are flagging your main, lee helm tends to develop from the headsail dragging the bow away. For this reason, the Dragon seems to perform well in heavy weather with a lot of mast rake which induces a little more weather helm than normal. Usually, the mast is raked between 6 in. and 9 in. off vertical and let forward completely on the backstay for downwind running.

SOLING

LENGTH 26 ft. 9 in.
BEAM 6 ft. 3 in.
DRAFT 4 ft. 3 in.
SAIL AREA 250 sq. ft.
WEIGHT 2,200 lb.
DESIGNER Jan Linge

The Soling belongs to the tender, easily driven keelboat group that respond to dinghy-sailing rather than yacht techniques. Hull shape and ballast ratio are not quite powerful enough for the Soling to carry the amount of sail she has into the above-10-knot wind range without energetic swinging over the side from the crew (including the skipper). If allowed to heel excessively, the boat tends to round up from weather helm induced by the immersed hull shape and also becomes hard to control, as the spade rudder is inclined to stall quickly in extremely rough weather. As it stalls, the boat falls off sideways rather quickly. So in setting up the boat, all the adjustments for sail-shape fullness and sheeting angles must be easily reached from the sitting-out position, so that every ounce of swinging power can be utilised at all times.

Solings provided closest racing of all classes in the 1976 Olympics.

The adjustment lines which should be available both sides of the cockpit include the backstay, with at least an 8:1 purchase for easy variation of tension. This is an important one, for it controls mast bend (hence sail fullness), and also jib-luff tension and jib fullness. Horse traveller control lines for centre- or end-boom sheeting should also be at hand on both sides of the cockpit. I prefer centre sheeting, which allows the end of the boom slight automatic movement to meet increase in wind strengths. It also permits quicker athwartships adjustment in puffy winds, with the traveller eased to keep the boat on her feet going into a gust and pulled to windward again for a high-pointing angle in the lulls. If you use centre sheeting you will have to sheet 4 in. to 5 in. to windward in moderate conditions to keep the end of the boom 3 in. to 4 in. to leeward of the centre-line of the hull at its outer end.

The for'ard hand must be able to reach the Cunningham eye adjustment from both sides of the cockpit in the swinging position. The eye must be pulled down as the mast is bent to keep the drive forward in the sail and the leech free, reducing weather helm to a minimum, and should be released for maximum downwind and reaching speed. The vang should also be easily adjusted with at least a 6:1 purchase tackle. It is worth the trouble to lead this adjustment back to the skipper; besides enabling him to control bottom fullness in the mainsail, it allows him to let the vang go quickly when reaching with a shy spinnaker. This is necessary when the point is reached where the mainsheet has been eased fully but the boom will not go off further because it is restricted by the spinnaker sheet. Easing the vang enables the boom to lift and go out over the sheet. This will also avoid the danger of the boom dragging in the water, causing a broach, if instant easing of the mainsail is not possible.

The most popular position for the mast is the maximum aft permitted by the class rules. This allows the self-tacker track to be fitted far enough aft to allow the jib to be effectively sheeted and adjusted for fore and aft trim using the normal clew board. The most popular masts appear to be Elvstrom, Proctor and Abbott. I do not think it matters as long as the mast is of minimum weight, and has the lowest

centre of gravity and tip weight permitted. It is important that the mainsail luff curve suits the mast bend characteristics.

All competitive boats seem to carry their shrouds through the deck and in line with the mast, with spreaders fixed at right angles to the centreline of the hull. The mast stiffness can be controlled to some extent either by angling the spreaders forward to stiffen or allowing them to come aft, to encourage bend. Some crews have gone to the trouble of fitting tracks for the cap shrouds so that they can be moved back and forth to adjust mast stiffness for different wind and sea conditions. The in-line caps have one other big advantage—they can allow the rake to be altered to place the masthead forward over the bow for running and reaching, or raked well aft for going to windward without losing any sideways support. For maximum windward performance, the rake should be adjusted to place the boom about 10 in. from the deck when the mast is bent to give correct fullness when sheeted in. With the mast set in this way, it should be straight sideways for maximum power from the rig and hence pointing ability.

The amount of backstay used to set the mainsail will have a big bearing on the fullness of the headsail: If a mainsail with a big luff curve is used then a heavy backstay pressure will be used to set it. Therefore, the forestay will be tighter than that reached for a mainsail with a flatter luff curve. A jib to suit a large luff-curve main will therefore need less luff hollow than a jib to suit a flat luff-curve main. This balance is one of the hardest things to achieve with Soling-type rigs.

The best sheeting position for the jib is 16 inches from the centreline of the hull in wind strengths from 0 to 14 knots. The main boom should be sheeted on the centreline. Then, as wind strength increases, the boom should be moved out to reduce power and the backstay pulled on about 1 in. Do not flatten the mainsail too much or travel the boom too wide; this type of trim makes the main look good but will cause low pointing, excessive heeling and hence weather helm in gusts. Except in extreme conditions, the boom should not go farther to leeward than 12 in. with the mainsail trimmed just hard enough to give perfect balance on the helm. In these fresh conditions, with the main

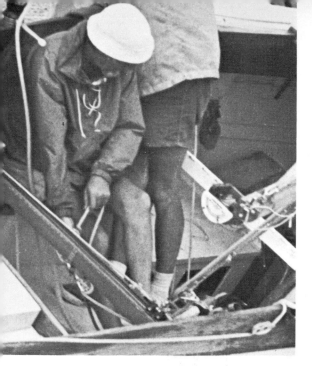

The Thunderbird uses a full-width horse traveller to balance out weather helm, to which the hard-chine plywood 26-footer is prone. The detailed shot shows the mainsheet hand (white hat) easing the traveller out, watching the inclinometer before him which registers the exact angle of heel.

sheeted wider, the jib should also be moved out and the sheet moved forward on the tack plate to flatten the bottom of the jib.

Spinnaker choice has settled to four types: Three-quarter ounce Dynac maximum reacher, three-quarter Stablecote maximum runner, three-quarter Dynac minimax reacher and a small 1.5 Dynac for fresh reaching or running. The softer Stablecote cloth spinnakers have been found faster than Dynac in lighter winds as they are easier to keep alive. Below a certain wind strength, especially if the water is chopped up, the harder-finish Dynac material seems to shake itself empty and hence becomes powerless.

The golden rule with Soling sail trim must be "if in doubt, let it out". Sails so closely sheeted are always easy to stall by over-trimming. In light air, careful attention to wool tufts in the upper jib and mainsail can be of major importance. In strong winds, however, the balance on the helm and the easy motion of the boat through the water are the most important things to look for.

THUNDERBIRD

LENGTH 26 ft.
BEAM 7 ft. 6 in.
DRAFT 4 ft. 9 in.
SAIL AREA 366 sq. ft.
WEIGHT 3,800 lb.
CREW 4
DESIGNER Ben Seaborn

The Thunderbird, a small, 26 ft. hard-chine yacht, has exceptional speed in both fresh and light winds when handled well. Her hull shape and sail plan, however, present rig-tuning problems. As the boat was designed for the lighter winds of Canada, she is rather over-canvassed (for Australian waters at least) with a very large Star-like mainsail as well as a genoa. This makes her heel quickly, in turn inducing large amounts of weather helm as the hard-chine hull shape starts digging in. The aft-set spade rudder stalls easily, making the weather helm harder to counter with the tiller. So in tuning this type of small yacht every effort has to be made to sail the boat upright and have controls to vary the fullness and shape of the mainsail easily.

The mainsail cross measurements are such that if a maximum-sized sail is cut to fit a relatively stiff mast, the roach will be too large and very difficult to support with the length of battens allowed. Therefore the mast should be flexible to keep a lot of the mainsail's half-width measurement in the luff round.

Mast bend can be easily controlled by a six-part tackle on the adjustable backstay which not only bends the mast but applies pressure to the three-quarter-rigged forestay. Under maximum backstay pressure the bend of the upper part of the mast can be varied by tightening the jumpers to reduce bend and easing the jumpers to increase it. Bend in the lower sections of the mast can be controlled with chocks at the deck in a mast hole that is large in the fore-and-aft dimensions. The mast bend should be set so the mainsail can be almost completely flattened in strong winds with plenty of luff tension to keep the drive forward and the leech free. In winds of 15 knots and more the main should be flagged going to windward, being used mainly for balancing weather or lee helm. This can be achieved by cleating the mainsheet and playing its athwartship setting through a full-width horse traveller. As a puff hits, the traveller is eased out to keep the boat on her feet. As the puff eases, the traveller is hauled towards the centre again to keep the boat driving without lee helm through the lull. Sheet tension still has to be varied for different wind strengths and backstay adjustments. Each time this tender yacht heels excessively she will skid half a boat-length sideways, dig in, round up, and stop. It is obviously better to keep the boat standing upright, by easing the main quickly, and thus not lose distance to leeward; then bring it on quickly again to pick up speed. This is even more important when reaching and carrying shy spinnakers.

The sheeting system should be Dragon style, 4 ft. in from the end of the boom, with the boom bendy enough just to grip the sail in this area, allowing the lower leech section, which has a big control on weather helm, to stay well open.

The mast's athwartships rigging should be fairly loose so that the lee shrouds are very slack when going to windward and are pulled inboard by the foot of the genoa when it is sheeted home, thus not interfering with the lead angle. The cap shrouds can have as much as 6 in. of side-to-side movement when the yacht is on the moorings, with the lowers adjusted while sailing to keep the mast straight sideways. When a full mainsail is used the jumpers can be left quite slack so they start taking load when the mast has bent to about a third of its maximum bend. At this point they will start directly loading the forestay as well as helping to flatten the mainsail.

The mast should be set up as near vertical as possible to counter any weather-helm tendencies.

The smaller jib should not be used in winds under 18 to 20 knots.

The jib sheeting track should be in off the gunwale, 5 in. to 8 in., to keep the boat pointing high in strong winds. The boat responds well in a fresher breeze to having the genoa leads shifted aft, allowing the leech of the genoa to lay off around the widely sheeted mainsail.

Cunningham eye, pole topping lift and downhaul, spinnaker halyard, and boom vang adjustments should all be led back and cleated on the after end of the coach-house roof where the crew can easily reach them. The horse traveller can also be made removable to leave the cockpit space free for cruising.

FLYING DUTCHMAN

LENGTH 19 ft. 10¼ in.
BEAM 5 ft. 10½ in.
DRAFT 3 ft. 8 in. (with centreboard down)
SAIL AREA 198 sq. ft.
CREW 2
DESIGNER Uffa van Essen

The Flying Dutchman, when tuned and sailed correctly, is extremely fast, with planing to windward the normal mode of travel. But with this high-performance two-man Olympic dinghy any faults in tuning or boat-handling are immediately apparent, for displacement speed is around 10 per cent slower than planing speed. Watch two FDs together on the wind. If one loses the planing streak, the other will gain six to eight boat-lengths. To keep a Flying Dutchman in the planing groove to windward

Flying Dutchman crew lifts his body in an attempt to keep clear of a wave.

demands intense concentration and expert sail-trimming.

It's a big boat for two men—nearly 20 ft. long, weighing 500 lb., with 200 sq. ft. of sail —and one of the main problems is to find a trapeze hand of the right size to give the power to plane to windward in fresher breezes. The ideal seems to be about 6 ft. 5 in. tall weighing 12½ to 13 stone, which may not be so hard to find, but he must also have the agility of a monkey and a ton of intelligence . . . so good FD crews are rare. Smaller crews can cope in Europe, and there are exceptions to the above generalisation, including the incredible British gold medallists Rodney Pattisson and Iain Macdonald-Smith.

The Dutchman's round-bilge hull has big, flat sections aft and full bilges amidships. This is why she has to be sailed as flat as possible for top speed. The hull has to be strong and stiff to withstand the pounding these flat sections take in strong winds, so it is always difficult to build to minimum weight.

The early single-bottom hulls, drained with self-bailers, were not stiff enough, and with the water sloshing around freely inside did not drain well. The swing was then to the self-draining double-bottom boat with the cockpit sole running from skin to skin and straight through to the tuck. This layout was quite successful and is still popular in Australia, although it has some drawbacks. The sole has to be so low at the tuck, to keep the bilges drained, that water tends to run back into the boat from the open transom in light weather, and the shallow cockpit does not offer a secure working platform for the skipper, who is called on to pull up spinnakers and handle other odd crewing tasks besides steering. To overcome these problems, the "one-and-a-half" boat was invented in Europe. With this layout the double bottom extends only to the centre horse traveller, reverting to a single bottom aft with self-bailers and open ports in the transom to remove large amounts of water quickly after a capsize.

103

To overcome the problems of handling the boat—keeping enough power in the sails to gain planing speed easily in light to medium winds; getting rid of it so that the same sail can be used in stronger winds—the Flying Dutchman rig has become highly adjustable and probably the most advanced of any class.

The genoa has no maximum area restrictions but must fit between the halyard position on the mast, tack at the stem, and with the clew falling within a black mark drawn on the deck. So, to get maximum area, the genoa is pulled right down to the deck with the clew all but fed down the sheet-lead hole. As this makes it impossible to have any fore-and-aft adjustment of the genoa lead, the technique of varying the mast rake while sailing was evolved. The mast is raked to free the leech, and stood up straighter to tighten it, giving the same effect as if the sheet leads had been moved aft or forward. To allow the mast to be raked, the genoa halyard and the shrouds are all adjustable, as they must be taken up compensating amounts to save the rig from becoming too slack.

Masts are normally carried within 2 in. of the maximum aft position allowed, to expose as much of the genoa as possible from behind the mainsail.

The pivot point of the centreboard is normally just far enough forward to allow the board to be fully retracted into the case. Many of the top boats carry the pivot mechanism on a slide on the cockpit floor. This enables them to trim the board farther aft, if necessary, for correct balance in stronger winds.

The genoa, which overlaps as far as the middle of the mainboom, is not easy to control. The slot between genoa leech and main must be exactly right for the wind of the moment. The guiding theory is to have the mast bending sufficiently, particularly low down, to flatten the overlapped area of the mainsail without destroying the shape of the upper part of the sail.

The most popular rig is the Z-spar mast—a small, round section—bendy below the hounds to control the fullness of the bottom of the mainsail and fairly stiff above so that the fullness at the top batten remains fairly stable, varying from 8 per cent to 12 per cent from strong to light winds (Fig. 51). A single fixed-spreader system is used to control the mast with the normal starting point for displacing the shrouds $1\frac{1}{2}$ in. forward and $1\frac{1}{2}$ in. out from a straight line. Be prepared to experiment with this position. Bring the spreader tips aft if the mainsail is too full, lengthen them if pointing is bad and shorten them if the boat is hard to keep flat and lacks acceleration in gusts.

The Diesch brothers of West Germany won the gold medal at the 1976 Olympics using an Elvstrom spar set up with very little fore and aft bend but with enough sideways bend from the mast's flattened top to keep the leech moving and open in strong winds.

The Flying Dutchman used to have a peculiar problem with its centreboard. The restrictions governing width and thickness used to make it difficult to shape without sacrificing stiffness. Glassfibre centreboards are now available that are sufficiently stiff and have good shape.

Kevlar-reinforced glassfibre hulls are rumoured to be faster than those of any other form of construction and may start a new era in FDs. They are now allowed in both general and Olympic competition.

Figure 51. 470 spreader measurements for 'Z' spar.

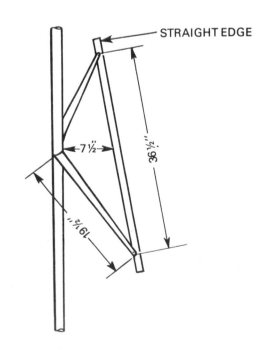

FIREBALL

LENGTH 16 ft. 2 in.
BEAM 4 ft. 7¾ in.
DRAFT 4 ft. (board down)
SAIL AREA 123 sq. ft.
WEIGHT 175 lb.
CREW 2
DESIGNER Peter Milne

The Fireball retains its international popularity. The strictly one-design scow hull can be launched, amateur or professionally built, for a reasonable price. Construction is allowed in plywood or glassfibre, although the glassfibre hull has so far been difficult to build to minimum weight while still retaining stiffness in the flat-sectioned bottom of the hull. Stiff hulls have proved themselves a necessity for speed in these small, quickly planing boats. Some people

are against scow hulls, but I have always found the scow to be very seaworthy, and with the Fireball it gives lively performance with quick-planing ability, upwind and down.

Ease of construction gives the Fireball special appeal to the amateur. As class rules allow the hulls to be brought up to weight with lead correctors, it is wise when building to aim well under the minimum hull weight and use correctors which can be adjusted each year if the hull takes on weight by absorbing moisture into the timber. A well-built hull can this way remain competitive in top-class racing for many years.

The rig is similar in proportion to the Flying Dutchman, without the large overlap in the genoa. The headsail is moderately sized, controlled only by luff length and a diagonal measurement from the luff to the clew. A

A Fireball having damp ride.

maximum-length luff is therefore essential with the leech adjusted so the headsail becomes a deck-sweeper with the clew very close to the sheeting position. This in turn brings the head-sail sheeting position up onto the foredeck, for'ard of the cockpit, where it should be set on an arthwartships track so that the sheeting angle can be varied for different wind strengths. Fairly full headsails seem to be the most effective, sheeted in as close as 12 degrees in light to medium winds on flat water, widened as wind and sea build up. The wider angles, with the full headsail, promote planing to windward in fresh breezes. No fore-and-aft jib-sheet adjustment is available, but this can be effectively overcome by shifting the jib slightly up or down the luff wire, or raking the mast, to vary the tension on the leech. In a short-footed jib of this type, once the correct position is found, very little adjustment will be necessary.

The mast is of quite flexible section, the most popular in Australia being made by de Havilland and Champion, the Champion being about $2\frac{1}{8}$ in. diameter and 0.861 lb. per foot. These masts are round in section with an extruded track on the back edge that allows a fine taper to be achieved towards the top. A moderately bendy boom is used with centre sheeting. The horse has to be set up as close as possible to deck level to gain the most positive boom-angle control as the boom is set fairly high above the deck.

The most popular and effective rig is to set the mast up directly on the jib luff, supported by two shrouds, with one set of spreaders and a set of athwartships diamonds going to the hounds. This allows fore-and-aft bend to be controlled with the spreaders and some sideways control to be gained from the diamonds. With these light-section spars, if restraining diamonds are not used, too much side lay-off in the top of the mast will cause loss of pointing ability in moderate winds.

With the spar at maximum bend, and the diamonds slackened, the mainsail should have just enough fullness to be carried efficiently in the higher wind range. On flexible spars this will ensure a maximum-fullness mainsail for reaching and running. For complete control of mainsail shape, efficient Cunningham eye and boom out-haul adjustments must be carried.

And with the mast stepped through the deck and onto the centreboard case, some form of deck control for mast bend should be fitted. The slot for the mast in the deck should be slightly wedge-shaped, with the wider part of the wedge towards the bow, so that as the mast moves forward in the slot in stronger winds, it will edge to windward as well, thus opening up the slot between headsail and mainsail. To encourage this further the spreaders can be made approximately 2 in. shorter than the natural line of the shroud so that in strong winds pressure from the shroud will tend to pull the middle of the mast to windward. At the same time the diamonds should be slightly slackened. If some kind of gate can be blocked across the slot behind the mast, chocks can then be fitted either in front of the mast or behind it, to restrict or encourage mast bend low down. In very light winds it is often an advantage to be able to chock the mast forward to pre-bend it, giving a clean, dish-shaped sail without the sheet or vang tension normally needed to bend the mast the same amount. The boat can then be sailed with the mainsheet slightly to windward and very little pressure on the leech, allowing the sail to breathe in even the lightest of airs.

The Fireball carries a parachute-type spinnaker, again similar to the FD, with the short international-style pole normally carried in hoops attached to the mainboom so that it does not clutter the cockpit area. Twin spinnaker bags should be fitted to the forward edge of the cockpit so that the kite may be left attached at all times. It is easier to set shy spinnakers from the leeward side and square set from the windward side. Keep this in mind when dropping so that the spinnaker ends up in the right bag for the next set with all sheets and halyards still attached. With this type of spinnaker in small boats, the theory is "what comes down must go up" tangle-free, as long as nothing is touched after a successful drop. Spinnaker launchers have been allowed into the class. As in the FDs, they are proving a worthwhile asset.

Class rules allow both skipper and crew to wear trapeze harnesses provided only one person is on trapeze at a time. So the skipper can quite easily sail the boat from trapeze in such emergencies as when the crew has to be inboard to sort out a spinnaker or tidy up from dropping a shy-set spinnaker at the leeward mark.

The pole is typically rigged with fixed-length topping lift and downhaul held tight to the bottom of the mast by shock rubber when not in use. The attachment point, halfway along the spinnaker pole, is in the form of a double-sided plastic cleat which enables the topping lift to be picked up as the pole is pushed out before attaching to the mast. On the lift there are normally four or five attaching points to vary pole heights for different wind strengths and points of sailing. For shy spinnaker, with the pole close to the forestay, gunwale hooks are used just for'ard of the shrouds to keep the angle of pull downwards on the brace as well as to restrain the brace close to the deck and out of the way of the trapezing for'ard hand.

16 FT. SKIFF

LENGTH 16 ft.
BEAM 5 ft. 6 in. to 5 ft.
SAIL AREA 220 sq. ft.
CREW 4
RESTRICTED DESIGN

This class, unique to Australia, comes from the same strain as the Sydney Harbour 18 ft. skiff. It enjoys less publicity than its heavily canvassed big brother but enormous popularity with nearly 500 boats sailing throughout Australia, mainly in New South Wales. It still has similar restrictions to those laid down in its year of origin, 1908, but within them it has progressed from a gaff-rigged, heavy displacement craft to a sloop-rigged high-performance planing machine.

The restrictions, quite open and encouraging plenty of experimentation, are: Length overall, maximum 16 ft; beam, maximum 5 ft. 6 in., minimum 5 ft.; depth amidships, maximum 22 in., minimum 18 in.; transom width, maximum 3 ft. 9 in. No decking is allowed and the sheer line must be a continuous concave curve from the for'ard thwart to the transom. Built-in buoyancy is allowed but must not extend aft more than 6 ft. from the stem nor forward more than 3 ft. from the transom and

Ted McDavitt's Aeolus *battles hard wind and big sea on the Swan River, Perth. The upper leech of the main is twisting off effectively to lose power.*

at no point may it be less than 8 in. below the gunwale.

The maximum working sail area is 220 sq. ft., which may be split up between main and jib in any ratio, with a maximum mainsail area of 175 sq. ft.

These completely open shells, ideally crewed by four light but strong young men, provide thrilling sailing for both crews and spectators—fleets of more than a hundred are not unusual in interclub events. And it's a 16 ft. skiff tradition that a race is never cancelled because of a strong wind, so when a gale is blowing all roads lead to the 16 ft. skiff course to view the inevitable and spectacular capsizes.

The design has developed over the years to a point where the hulls are surprisingly similar—fine entry, long waterline, with the lines broadening to flat planing surfaces and maximum waterline beam aft; achieved either by hard bilges or hard-chine after sections. Hulls may still be tailored for specialised conditions, such as strong winds and rough water, to be expected at major championships.

The most efficient rig I have found sets a 25 ft. luff, 8 ft. foot, 160 sq. ft. mainsail on a finely-tapered 3¼ in. section aluminium mast showing 27 ft. 6 in. above gunwale height. A high-aspect, 60 sq. ft. jib makes up the balance of the maximum working sail area. The jib is set on a short bowsprit to reduce overlap, giving every square foot of sail area maximum efficiency.

Best position for the hounds is 19 ft. above deck with a set of spreaders to the shrouds, half-way between the hounds and deck. An adjustable diamond is also carried, attaching 20 ft. 6 in. above deck level and 12 in. below the spinnaker take-off point. This effectively controls masthead lay-off and sideways bend below the hounds.

The 120 sq. ft. flat-cut spinnaker, although small, is quite difficult to handle as it is set on poles of unrestricted length and is carried on very close reaches—in fact, almost to windward. A basic 13 ft. pole is normally used with 3 ft. or 4 ft. extensions which are fitted as the spinnaker is being poled out to keep it well clear of the working sails for broad reaches and square running. The spinnaker pole extension has also been found useful for belabouring sluggard crewmen, and rapping the knuckles of piratical competitors trying to pull their way, hand over hand, along the gunwales in jams around marks.

With no restrictions on the number of sails, or size combinations, a complete wardrobe becomes extensive and expensive.

The maximum rig of 160 sq. ft. main and 60 sq. ft. jib is carried in wind strengths up to 20 knots. The first change down above that wind speed is to a 155 sq. ft. flat mainsail and a 60 sq. ft. jib with a little more overlap. This rig is normally carried on days where there is some doubt about how hard it will blow; it can handle 25 knots and still retain near maximum area should the breeze drop to around 18.

When the wind is really blowing, a smaller mast is stepped with, say, a 150 sq. ft. main

retaining maximum foot length but with shorter luff and smaller roach. A 50 sq. ft. jib is set, brought into the stemhead, to keep the boat in balance under this total 200 sq. ft. rig, and the large dagger centreboard, normally nearly 6 ft. long with an area of about 8¼ sq. ft., is replaced by a smaller one.

This unusual open 16-footer, together with its little sister, the 12 ft. skiff—which carries about the same sized rig as the 16 with both forward hand and skipper on trapezes—has produced some of the best boat-handlers I have ever seen. If you don't like swimming, you just have to be good.

470

LENGTH 4.7 m.
BEAM 1.8 m.
DEPTH 76 mm.
WEIGHT 118 kg.
SAIL AREA 145 sq. m.

The 470 has become very competitive and specialised since it gained the status of the Olympic two-man dinghy class. The conservative sail area means that at least there is an international class that two small yachtsmen can sail competitively. The ideal crew weight is between 20 and 22 stone. While heavier crews do well in stronger winds, they are at a distinct disadvantage in marginal planing conditions and lighter winds.

Hulls must be as stiff as possible and definitely down to minimum weight. The "Z" spar mast seems the most popular. This section, unlike many others, is swaged down into the taper rather than being welded. This produces a small but rather stiff top section while the bottom is allowed to bend fore and aft as required. The top section, being stiff, keeps the fullness between 12 and 8 per cent from light to quite strong winds while the lower fullness can be accurately controlled by chocking at the deck as well as intelligent use of the fixed spreaders. The mast has minimum clearance at the deck to stop all sideways movement while chocks are used in front of the mast to help control low-down bend.

I would suggest as a starting point that the rake should be 21 ft. 10½ in. measured with a tape shackled to the main halyard while it is

470 class provides close racing—and a path into the Olympics for younger sailors.

locked in the halyard lock, to the top outside face of the transom at the centreline.

The spreaders should be halfway between the deck and the hounds with the spreader length 19½ in. measured from the side of the mast to the shroud attachment point.

Then, to adjust the angle, put a straight edge across the two shrouds where they attach at the spreader tips. Bring the tips aft until a measurement of 7½ in. is achieved from this straight-edge to the back of the mast track. The tips should then be 36½ in. apart. This will obviously vary for different types of sail. However, it was good enough to win a bronze medal for the Australian crew in 1976 using sails made in the Sydney Elvstrom loft.

For general tuning purposes, here are some guidelines: Alter the fore and aft position of the spreaders until the correct fullness is achieved in the mainsail. This fullness should be the maximum for 8 to 12 knot winds (windward wool tufts just starting to flow). Then, if the boat is under-powered—that is pointing low with the crew unable to get on the trapeze until after the opposition—lengthen the spreaders. If the boat is slow to accelerate in gusts and difficult to hold up in stronger conditions, points high but goes slowly, shorten the spreaders.

The jib should have a flat entry and be quite full for average winds. Up to 15 knots, it should be sheeted 3 in. inside the side tank and far enough forward to leave the built-in fullness in the sail undistorted. When sheeted close and forward like this, the jib must not be pulled on too hard. The crew must use the top windward wool tuft of the jib for guidance. If he keeps it registering a semi-stalled position, the correct

twist-off in the head of the jib will be achieved. This allows the skipper some latitude to steer high and low without stalling the leeward side of the jib. However, as the main boom is travelled down for stronger winds, the jib should be moved out to the edge of the side tank and a little aft to flatten the bottom of the jib. This type of powerful jib setting will give good neutral balance on the tiller even in strong winds as long as the boat is sailed dead flat. For best windward performance, the centreboard should be fully down.

FINN

    LENGTH 14 ft. $9\frac{1}{4}$ in.
    BEAM 4 ft. $7\frac{1}{2}$ in.
    DRAFT 2 ft. 9 in. (plate down)
    SAIL AREA 107 sq. ft.
    WEIGHT 319 lb.
    DESIGNER Rickard Sarby

OK DINGHY

    LENGTH 13 ft. $1\frac{1}{2}$ in.
    BEAM 4 ft. $7\frac{1}{2}$ in.
    DRAFT 3 ft. 6 in. (board down)
    SAIL AREA 90 sq. ft.
    WEIGHT 158 lb.
    DESIGNER Knud Olsen

After the rig complexities associated with most of the classes we have discussed already in this chapter, the unstayed masts of the Finn and OK should seem refreshingly simple. But, speaking as one who has spent many hours knee-deep in shavings and covered in sweat in the tuning of both, I can assure you that this is not necessarily so. For, without the controls of normal rigging, the mast itself must be made to bend exactly to suit both the sail and the swinging power of the helmsman. Some of the world's best boat-tuners have found the task of gaining winning speed out of these two inter-national single-handers beyond them and have gone back to the "bird-cages" of rigging wire in other classes.

The two hulls are widely dissimilar; the round-bilge Olympic Finn is longer, much heavier, and carries more sail than the hard-chine OK. The Finn calls for more swinging power. The OK is more responsive, quicker to accelerate from a tack, but also easier to stop, and hence sensitive to trim and helming tech-nique. But both have evolved towards the same rig theory.

Originally with the Finn, which is the older class, masts were stiff as telegraph poles and needed giants or super-fit medium-sized men to be able to keep the boat upright at all.

Then Paul Elvstrom came along with a flexible mast that revolutionised Finn sailing and enabled quite light helmsmen to compete with the goliaths just by bending the mast more. As Paul proceeded to win four Olympic gold medals in the class, he naturally called the tune.

Then, from the time of Elvstrom's retirement from the class, the wheel turned and stiffer masts came back—but with a subtle difference invented by young Brazilian professor of mineralogy, Joerg Bruder. The Bruder mast was stiff fore-and-aft and sideways except for the top two metres which flicks off sideways under load to open the leech. Sails cut for the old-style bendy mast were cut with no roach and with the entire area saved from the roach put into the luff to compensate for the mast bend. And the amount of bend needed to flatten the sail forced the effective drive too far aft, no matter how hard you pulled on the Cunningham eye. The Bruder type, having less bend, enabled the drive to be kept forward, in turn leaving the leech free, exhausting air-flow effectively and opening from the top first, under load, progressively easing the pressure from the point where it is creating most heeling moment.

As with many other classes, the wooden masts gave way eventually to aluminium and between the 1972 and 1976 Olympics, one aluminium mast, the Needlespar 3M gained complete dominance over all other types in Finns and also gained popularity in OKs. The Needlespar 3M roughly duplicates the behaviour of the later Bruder which began its sideways flexing motion low down the mast to depower the rig associated with a stiffer upper section that gave the sail more leech tension.

A fairly universal type of sail evolved to suit the mast—medium camber with a lot of luff round that when sheeted down hard became very flat off the luff, enabling high pointing. The Musto loft in England led the way with this type of sail. A later development, by North, was to build-in twist into the sail. This type of sail is flatter than earlier Finn sails and fairly tight leeched. It is easy to use because, as it is flatter, it does not stall quickly and as the wind eases, the tight leech closes quickly and automatically.

The Finn sails at its best with the boom close to the deck. A typical mast rake in 1976, measured from the tip of the mast to the transom was 22 ft. 4 in.

Both Finns and OKs carry mid-boom sheeting. As a rough guide, Finns seem to go best in light to moderate winds with the end of the boom up to 2 in. inside the gunwale line. As the wind strength increases, sheet progressively

111

wider to hold the boat on her feet—a lighter helmsman will probably end up on a heavy day with the end of the boom 6 in. to 8 in. outside the gunwale, and the traveller at the outer point on the horse.

Booms are usually as stiff as possible within class rules, although light skippers may still do better with a more flexible boom.

Vangs, of the lever, drum-winch or multi-purchase wire variety, have superseded the old and simple wooden wedge. With the heavily raked stiff mast they are almost essential on the Finn to enable the boom to be released so the helmsman can get under it while tacking or gybing.

All sail adjustments should be led to where they can be reached from the swinging position on either side of the cockpit. Coming inboard from the hiking position to make an adjustment will certainly cost you a boat-length on a competitor. Some helmsmen have eliminated the boom out-haul from their list of strings to pull, but I feel it is still useful to have it to allow the sail to take on extra draft for reaching.

Both the Finn and OK are extremely demanding physically. In both classes, top helmsmen work hard on their fitness, and on designing their cockpits and toe-straps for maximum comfort. Angled side-decks, presenting a flat support for the back of the calf, are preferred to any sort of round moulding. The capping gunwale is also flattened off as even a minimum area of support for the back of the thighs is preferable to the regular round beading.

The straps should be wide enough to give full support to the instep. Safety belting is good, but should be padded. The New Zealanders have the best idea—greenhide, which becomes soft, pliable and moulds to the instep as it gets wet, with a strip of Terylene cloth sewn down the middle to stop it stretching too far.

Swinging straps should be adjustable until the position is found for maximum comfort and efficiency. For most people this brings the knees out of the centre of the side-deck with the legs angled and the body drooped in the shape of a W, level or preferably below the gunwale line.

Padding is essential over the calves and thighs. If you're not sailing with pads, you're

not hiking hard enough. Most helmsmen make up special padded pants, hitched up by braces (belts just won't hold them up against the constant swinging action), and lighter helmsmen especially wear a padded "weight" jacket, jumpers or sweatshirts to make up weight. If you are fit enough it's possible to swing an extra 35 lb. through a load of wet jumpers.

Elvstrom proved fitness was an essential and used to train for hours swinging from a bench, built to roughly the same width as the side-deck of his Finn. Most of the top-liners in both classes follow some regular training programme. By using a swinging bench, and swinging through the limited range that is normal in a boat, loading yourself with weights to build endurance as the body gets used to the idea, it is possible to make a full race without sitting in for a breather—well, I said it was possible. Racing a Finn or an OK in any breeze over 12 knots is hard work, and if you haven't tuned your body to take it, you've wasted all the tuning time you put into the rig.

One of the most useful inventions to come from the Finn class is the JC strap (named after its inventor, John Christianson). This is simply a length of shock rubber attached to each side of the boom about 3 ft. aft of the mast, running freely through a pulley on the bow. When you ease the sheet for running, it pulls the boom and holds it out against the sheet. It is invaluable on a light day when the boom has a tendency, especially in waves, to swing back towards the centre-line.

HERON

LENGTH 11 ft. 3 in.
BEAM 4 ft. 6 in.
DRAFT 2 ft. 9 in. (board down)
SAIL AREA 70 sq. ft.
WEIGHT 145 lb.
CREW 2
DESIGNER Jack Holt

The Heron is a short, beamy, blunt-bowed, hard-chine family trainer that has become a very keen racing class as well. Despite my unflattering description, I think it is an excellent class for both roles. The original trainer concept makes Herons slightly under canvassed, so to race them really competitively an all-up crew weight of 17 to 20 stone is optimum. This can be made up of one adult and a small child or perhaps two youngsters of almost equal weight. But it is essential to keep the weight down and concentrated as close to the middle of the hull as possible when going to windward.

This type of hull is always prone to weather helm, so the mast should be as far forward and the centreboard as far aft as the class rules permit. But it is even more important to sail the boat flat as soon as there is enough breeze to encourage weather helm, minimising helm load caused by loss of balance as well as the hull shape.

The centreboard should have the maximum amount showing under the hull when lowered, it should be of maximum thickness allowed to make it inflexible, and also fit snugly in the centrecase when lowered, ensuring it does not bend from side to side when sailing to windward.

The spars should be as light and as flexible as possible while still strong enough for hard weather. A 2 in. diameter oregon mast should be flexible enough. I prefer this timber to spruce, which is lighter, because it is strong enough to withstand the compression and sideways pressures imposed by the boom vang when running. The gaff should be of spruce to minimum sizes allowed, being of parallel section from the jaws to about 4 ft. 6 in. from the top, where it is tapered off to a minimum diameter. Leave the gaff larger for about 9 in. on either side of the halyard attaching point to allow for the slot to be cut through to take the main halyard without weakening the spar.

Jib and mainsail halyard should be wire, to within 6 in. of the fixing cleats, where they can be laced down with a rope tail or hooked directly onto a Highfield lever. The gaff should be pulled up hard against the mast to allow the mast to take an even bend, just like a single-piece wooden spar. Then, to flatten the mainsail in heavy weather, a spacer such as a rubber doorstop can be threaded onto the main halyard between the mast and the gaff to give a pre-bent effect before the spar takes its normal bend.

The gaff end of the main halyard should terminate in a loop about 7 in. long so that there is a double wire running over the mast-

The simple Heron class is still one of the most popular—both for beginners and for drop-outs from high-performance sailing who have fun in them with wives or families. There is no spinnaker, so the jib is poled out with a jib stick for running. This boat has simple English style end-boom sheeting.

head sheave and into the gaff to take the gaff pin. This cuts down the risk of halyard breakage, likely at this point owing to the small but constant amount of working movement of the gaff.

The jib should have a wire luff, the separate forestay being left quite slack, with a piece of shock rubber at the lower end to keep it from flopping around as well as the normal lacing to support the mast should the halyard carry away. With this set-up, all strain is imposed directly on the jib luff-wire to keep it constantly tight when going to windward.

Rigging should not be pulled drum tight, just firmly enough to keep the rig from shaking around when standing on the beach. The mast at this stage should be vertical to the boat's waterline. With the rigging set up this way, the leeward shroud will be quite slack when sailing to windward, allowing the jib to be sheeted outside the stay and 4 in. to 5 in. inboard from the hull skin, without the stay interfering with the sheeting angle.

The mainsail boom should have an effective vang of 3:1 or 4:1 purchase with an easily adjustable tackle. This should be pulled on hard to bend the mast, flatten the mainsail and hold it flat in strong winds, especially when the sheet is eased for strong puffs. The sheet has to be eased in gusty winds as there is no horse traveller for main-boom angle adjustment. This sheeting system, enforced by the class rules, is still quite effective and seems at its best when the sheet is pulled on just hard enough to make the leeward part of the sheeting system at the horse stand vertical. Any closer angle than this seems to stall the boat. This is not a high-pointing hull shape and must be kept moving through the water. Most practical sheeting method is to have the mainsheet led down through a block under the aft thwart to preferably a ratchet block attached to the after end of the fin case where it can be more easily handled while swinging from the amidships position.

The fullest possible mainsail should be used, as it can be easily flattened for windward work with flexible spars, leaving the fullness to be

This popular little child's trainer still offers fertile ground for tuning techniques.

used to advantage when reaching or running. An adjustable boom out-haul should be used and slackened off 3 in. to 4 in. when reaching. Luff tension should also be released downwind by letting the gooseneck up to a higher setting and reapplying boom vang pressure.

The lower part of the mainsail can also be made fuller or flatter by adjusting the fixing position of the tack at the gooseneck. This is made possible as the distance between the boom bands is 2 in. longer than the maximum length allowed for the foot of the mainsail. So if the tack is set 2 in. away from the mast, the sail above it laced forward against the mast and then allowed to come away again to go into the gaff groove, 2 in. of luff curve has been removed to make the sail flatter.

SABOT

LENGTH 8 ft.
BEAM 3 ft. 9 in.
DRAFT 2 ft.
SAIL AREA 31 sq. ft.
WEIGHT 50 lb.
CREW 1 or 2
ONE-DESIGN

The Sabot is one of the tiny, 8 ft. cat-rigged trainer dinghies raced very keenly by children and coached even more keenly by adults—with some parents it is like racing model yachts with son or daughter as jockey, and some of these youngsters are extremely good jockeys. I have done a lot of work with this class and found its restrictions encourage a bendy rig which gives the junior sailor a good appreciation of the problems he will face with more complicated rigs later in his sailing life.

There is little difference in hull performance, provided the boat is kept light and within restriction tolerances. But the sail, measured within a restricting silhouette, can have as much as 4 in. of luff round without penalty, provided this built-in fullness measures within the silhouette. To cope with this amount of round, the mast, to set the little 10 ft. 7 in. luff mainsail has to bend about 3 in. to 3½ in. before the sail becomes over-sheeted. The mast is restricted to 13 ft. 6 in. maximum length, with a minimum diameter of 2 in. near the deck, tapering to $1\frac{1}{4}$ in. at the top, and made of solid timber. These restrictions make the mast nearly the same size in section as an 18 ft. 6 in. Moth mast, and stiff for such a small sail. To get the required bend, a composite mast is best with an oregon track, about $\frac{7}{8}$ in. thick on the compression side, and a western red cedar lamination on the front. The cedar is both light and weak, bringing the mast up to minimum dimension without making it too stiff.

With the mast supported at each end, and a 26 lb. weight hanging on it at the hounds position, the mast should bend about 4 in. maximum deflection from a tight string line. Then, if the mast is stepped on the keel to give the maximum length for bending, it can be effectively controlled by the vang and sheet pressure. With the vang on for fresh winds, the sail will be flattened and held flat as the sheet is eased to release pressure in the sail for strong gusts.

The slot where the mast comes through the deck should be minimum width to restrict any sideways movement from the mast at this point. But it should allow free fore-and-aft mast movement.

The boom blocks should be 3 ft. 5 in. from the back of the mast with the horse along the rear edge of the thwart. This keeps the horse as far aft as possible and as close to the boom as possible, enabling the boom to be sheeted into the correct angle without too much downward pressure.

Always remember that these tiny sails should not be pulled on too hard. The last fall of the mainsheet system should go through either a swivel, or preferably a ratchet block fixed to the keel, to make a convenient sheeting angle to the hand of the helmsman. To judge the correct boom angle, observe the relation of the end of the boom to the corner of the transom. In strong winds it can be as wide as 2 in. outside the corner, while in lighter breezes, and especially in flat water, it can come in as close as 9 in. inside the corner. But take care if the sheeting is too close, especially when using a fullish mainsail, as this short, light hull will not drive through the water but bob up and down in the one spot.

By using the flexible rig the leech retains some movement to adjust automatically for wind-strength variation, whereas with the stiffer mast the sheet must be constantly adjusted to keep the boat at the correct sailing angle. Luff and foot tensions are critical with the small sail, and adjustments of as little as $\frac{1}{2}$ in. can either improve or destroy the shape.

Weight distribution is also critical in these little boats, and the youngsters always tend to sit too far aft. Remember, it is always easier to push a small amount of water than to drag a large area along with the transom. Keep moving forward until the bow is just not shoving too much into the waves.

Sailing a Sabot is just as demanding on a little fellow as a Finn is for a grown-up. So make sure he has comfortable swinging straps and an efficient tiller extension.

CATAMARANS

Catamarans, once regarded as freaks, have now won world wide recognition as fast, demanding, high-performance sailing craft. The speed of a catamaran is quite different in nature from that of a fast planing monohull. It slips through the water with very little fuss, giving an uncanny, soft ride where a planing dinghy bounces along, giving the impression of much more speed without really having it.

Its great initial stability has appealed to beginners, and in Australia started many people sailing. But the stable platform becomes as difficult to control as a high-powered racing car in strong winds. Once the windward hull lifts clear of the water—flying a hull is the term—they are easy to capsize, and once capsized are very awkward to right.

Like most racing machines, the angle of heel is very critical. The weather hull, where possible, must be kept just kissing the surface of the water, reducing the overall wetted area. Too much heel tends to force the leeward hull down, leading to nose-diving tendencies.

Catamarans are incredibly fast when sailed skilfully, but with only a little less skill they can be quite slow. This big difference in potential speed makes them quite tricky to tune as well as sail. They normally have flatter sails than most conventional classes as their hulls are easily driven and their great speed to windward means the apparent wind is stronger and well forward.

The most common rig is based on the over-rotating pear-section mast which leads to a quite complicated but effective mast-bend system. The mast is rotated to beyond the angle of the boom. The leech then pulls the top of the mast to windward which in turn holds up the leech very straight, giving the rig tremendous power in light to moderate winds. This sideways bowing to windward above the hounds is normally restricted by diamonds going either to the hounds or a little above, for if the top of the mast comes too far to windward the rig can be completely stalled. As the wind becomes stronger the diamonds are adjusted very tightly to keep the mast straight while still having full pivot.

Battens are stiffer than usual to keep the leech flat as well as to help control overall shape. Glassfibre is best; rigidity can be obtained without too much bulk in the pocket.

This flat rig is difficult to make full for reaching and working in very light winds. One solution is to lead a leech line through the outer ends of the battens to apply inward pressure directly to each batten when needed.

The wing mast, fabricated from light wood veneers or a combination cloth and wood framework like an aeroplane wing, is a refine-ment of the over-rotating rig. In B and C catamaran classes, where rigs are completely

This is what catamaran sailing is all about. They are incredibly fast when sailed skilfully, as is this Kitty Cat 12-footer.

free, it has proved itself far superior aero-dynamically while still being easy to adjust through the pivoting principle to alter sail power for varying wind strengths.

Tuning for Ocean Racing

OCEAN racing, with its long nights at sea, often in miserable conditions, hard bashes to windward and terrifying rides downwind, is probably the craziest form of yacht racing. However, in my association with this marathon aspect of the sport over the past ten years, I have found owners and crewmen clamouring to join in—the companionship, challenge and affinity with the sea give ocean racing special rewards. The competition is fierce and the best offshore yachtsmen sail their boats with the same dedication to preparation and relentless concentration as the best round-the-buoys inshore sailors.

The design of an offshore yacht must be honestly evaluated before considering ways of improving speed with rig and sails. Most modern-design offshore yachts, with large sail plans and high freeboard are inclined to be tender and require more careful sail-size selection and sail trim. Fortunately, however, with rudders hung well aft, most of them are easier to steer and more fun to sail than their predecessors—the International Offshore Rule Mark Two boats.

Those older boats were usually heavier and lacked sail area. It is unwise to become involved, especially financially, in trying to make an older design into a world-beater by increasing the size of the rig, re-shaping the hull and then taking other measures to reduce rating.

This type of modification rarely, if ever, works and invariably costs piles of money. From my experience, the handicap rating for a bigger rig increases at a greater pace than it can be reduced by hull modification with the net result that performance will improve but still not be good enough for the yacht to sail competitively at its new rating.

With an older boat, it is better to look for its strong points—it may be an excellent boat for running, or heavy-weather reaching—and learn to capitalise fully on these good qualities when the weather conditions suit them. When wind and wave are unfavourable, appreciate you cannot win unless luck takes a hand, relax and enjoy the sailing and the company.

New designs may also have deficiencies in certain conditions on certain points of sailing. On all yachts, you must learn to sail what you have to the maximum in all conditions.

POINTING ABILITY

The tuning approach is much the same for all off-shore yachts. All of them, sailing to windward, have a maximum hull speed, governed by the waterline length, that is impossible to exceed. A yacht can be sailed at a broader angle to the wind for more speed but then its VMG (velocity made good to the windward mark) will be lower. The primary aim is to attain the maximum theoretical speed in as low a wind speed as possible and maintain it from there on. Most modern offshore racers should reach this speed in 16 to 19 mph of apparent wind. Below this wind strength, light-weather headsails must be carefully selected and trimmed to achieve the best possible VMG. This is not always the same as the highest boat speed as the pointing angle must also be considered. A yacht doing seven knots at 32 degrees apparent wind angle will have the same VMG as one making 6.5 knots to windward at 20 degrees apparent (Fig. 52).

A study of these VMG figures shows that in different sea conditions and for different hull shapes, different speed and apparent wind angles must be aimed for. Basically, if the water is flat, it is possible to sail a boat very high without too much loss of speed to attain a very favourable VMG. In these conditions, flatter headsails can be used and both headsail and mainsail can be sheeted at closer angles as there are no waves, requiring power to be penetrated. This close sheeting must be carefully handled.

NEW COURSE IN DEGREES OFF WIND LINE OR RHUMB LINE	PRESENT COURSE IN DEGREES OFF WIND LINE OR RHUMB LINE: 0	5	10	15	20	25	30	35	40	45	50	55	60	
0		100	99	97	94	91	87	82	77	71	64	57	50	0
5	100		99	97	94	91	87	82	77	71	65	58	50	5
10	102	101		98	95	92	88	83	78	72	65	58	51	10
15	104	103	102		97	94	90	85	79	73	67	59	52	15
20	106	106	105	103		96	92	87	82	75	68	61	53	20
25	110	110	109	107	104		96	90	85	78	71	63	55	25
30	115	115	114	112	109	105		95	88	82	74	66	58	30
35	122	122	120	118	115	111	106		94	86	78	70	61	35
40	131	130	129	126	123	118	113	107		92	84	75	65	40
45	141	141	139	137	133	128	122	116	108		91	81	71	45
50	156	155	153	150	146	141	135	127	119	110		89	78	50
55	174	174	172	168	164	158	151	143	134	123	112		87	55
60	200	199	197	193	188	181	173	164	153	141	128	114		60
	0	5	10	15	20	25	30	35	40	45	50	55	60	NEW COURSE IN DEGREES OFF WIND LINE OR RHUMB LINE
	PRESENT COURSE IN DEGREES OFF WIND LINE OR RHUMB LINE													

Numbers in the body of the table are percentages of present speed required to break even

Figure 52. VMG chart.

Although a closely-sheeted rig is highly efficient, because it is working at a high angle of attack, it is also working very close to the stall point. It can be compared to a glider climbing at a steep angle. If the angle becomes too steep, the glider stalls and falls out of the sky. When the rig stalls, the yacht's speed drops off and is very hard to restore unless the boat is pulled away a little and the sails eased out. Once the flow is re-established over the sails and speed climbs, then the sails can be squeezed in again.

The yacht must be steered very accurately when pointing high in light winds as the rig will stall if the apparent wind angle is varied too much by either steering too high or too low. Close sheeting is also risky when the wind is shifting suddenly, making it difficult for the helmsman to follow the new wind angles accurately.

In light wind with rough water, pointing high and sheeting close is also difficult as the rig is moving around too much. The pitching action of the mast will alter the apparent wind speed and angles erratically: when the mast pitches forward, the apparent wind momentarily goes right forward and when the mast is moving aft again, the apparent wind moves back towards the beam. To cope with this difficult situation, sheet wider and sail slightly lower for the most favourable VMG.

To facilitate the constant trim changes that must be made to keep a boat moving in these light, sloppy conditions, I prefer the headsail to be cut with the clew at least 2 ft. above the deck so that a Barber hauler can be used to move the sheeting angle from the 10 degree track into about 7 degrees. This allows the angle to be widened or closed easily as required. The Barber hauler should be clipped on near the clew and led at right angles across the hull to the weather side. This enables the sheet to be eased slightly and the Barber hauler trimmed on without interfering with the fore-and-aft trim of the sail. If the breeze is steady and the boat easy to steer, then the headsail can be sheeted to an inside sheeting track without the Barber hauler.

Genoas intended for close sheeting can be quite deep but must be flat low down in the after 40 per cent of the sail and flat in the back third of the top half of the leech. Sails that have been used a lot are generally not shaped like this and will rob the boat of speed and acceleration if sheeted too close. In the 1975 Admiral's Cup, we had a sail on *Bumblebee 3* that we cut fairly full to pull her through the sloppy seas off Sydney Heads in winds of 12 knots to 18 knots. In the flatter waters of England, in trials before the series, we found we could not point high enough with this sail and when we tried to close-sheet, the boat was slow. We altered 16 seams to flatten the sail in these after areas and recut the luff to flatten the head slightly. Then we were able to sheet very close and trim harder for very high pointing angles, good speed and good acceleration in gusts. Gust response, a well-known requirement in dinghy tuning, is also important on big yachts and sometimes hard to find. When the sails are correctly shaped and tuned, a yacht sailing into a stronger wind gust will accelerate and naturally climb slightly to windward without too much help from the crew. If the sails are not exhausting correctly, a yacht sailing into the same gust will heel excessively for a sharp increase in weather helm and screw up into the wind. It will feel powerful but will not accelerate fully, even if helped by vigorous use of the traveller.

LIGHT TO MEDIUM WINDS

Light Genoas
Selection of a headsail inventory, apart from the money available, depends on the size of the boat. This governs to some extent how many sails can be carried aboard, still leaving room for the people, and the restrictions on the number of sails that may be carried will also have to be considered.

However, all boats need a drifter, of about 130 per cent overlap with a high-cut clew, about 5ft. above the deck level, enabling it to be sheeted well aft. For boats up to 30 ft. overall, the drifter should be made of 2 oz. cloth; for yachts up to 50 ft. it should be of 3 oz. cloth. It should be quite full because at low wind speeds, say 0 to 5 knots apparent, it will be necessary to sail the boat at wide apparent wind angles of around 35 degrees and as low as 40 degrees if the water is rough. The high clew will enable the sail to lay open, keeping the slot wide with the drifter's leech well clear of the mainsail which will also be sheeted a little wider to handle the broader apparent wind angles. In light air, you invariably end up close reaching to achieve initial speed and apparent wind flow before coming closer to the wind and changing to the light number one genoa as the wind builds.

The higher clew is also a big advantage when the yacht is rolling around in a left-over swell. As the rig rolls to windward, moving the apparent wind around to the beam, the high clew allows the sail to breathe out into reaching trim, giving the boat some forward motion. The high clew, and the fact that the drifter is not full size, allow it to flap over the spreaders without too much interference.

The idea is to use this sail to build up some boat speed and hence increase the apparent wind to say 4 or 5 knots. As the wind steadies around that speed, a light number one genoa can then be changed to. This change is extremely important and must be made without any loss of boat speed, otherwise the apparent wind-speed will fall and not be sufficient to make effective use of the light number one.

Yachts using hanks to secure headsails to the forestay must fly the drifter without hanks on its own luff wire. A genoa can be hanked on, hoisted and set before the drifter is taken off. With a twin-grooved headstay, the drifter will be hoisted in a luff groove and the change to a number one will be the normal one for a twin-grooved headstay. Always make this change slowly with a minimum of crew movement. Crew moving to the windward side will stop even a big boat in these very light conditions. Keep the crew on the leeward rail to encourage the boat to heel, helping the headsail to fall into its designed shape.

The light number one for boats up to 35 ft. overall should be made from 2 oz. cloth, for boats up to 45 ft. of 3 oz. and over 45 ft. from 4·5 oz. cloth. The sail should be flat enough to enable the boat to be sailed to windward at 28 degrees in flat water in winds from 8 to 12 knots with full backstay pressure and moderate luff tension. To gain more power to drive through choppy water, such as that raised by wind against tide or in a left-over sea in lighter wind, the backstay must be eased to create more fullness in the luff and the halyard eased to allow this extra drive to move back into the genoa. If either adjustment is made without

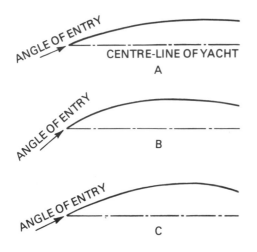

ANGLE OF ENTRY

CENTRE-LINE OF YACHT

A

ANGLE OF ENTRY

B

ANGLE OF ENTRY

C

*Figure 53. **A**, full backstay tension and medium halyard tension for good angle of entry for high pointing. **B**, with backstay eased and no halyard adjustment, the angle of entry is bad and the boat will point low. **C**, with backstay and halyard eased, the angle of entry is better because the drive is further aft.*

the other, the headsail shape will be inefficient with the drive too far forward for good pointing (Fig. 53).

This is the correct way to handle the increase and decrease of power in all number one genoas and should be used to retain the correct shape and fullness from the bottom of their wind range to the top. Fore-and-aft sheeting positions should also be carefully watched throughout the wind range. As the wind increases and the stretch-luff halyard is taken up and the backstay tightened, the sheeting position will need to be moved aft to keep the bottom third of the sail flatter to de-power it. How far aft can be gauged by sheeting the sail home to the correct distance from the main spreaders (found by experience to be best for that boat and sail), and then checking the tension along the foot. If the yacht is being steered in a semi-feathered state, with windward wool tufts lifting most of the time to keep it at the best angle of heel, the bottom third of the sail should be as flat as possible. To achieve this, the lead is moved aft until the foot shows creases along the deck with just enough bend in

the foot to go around the shrouds close to the deck.

If the lead is too far aft, too much tension creasing will show before the leech of the sail is closed to its correct position. In this situation the foot will be heavily tensioned around the shrouds. If more sheet pressure is applied to close the leech further, the sail will be in danger of being torn apart at the foot seams. The position should always be set at mid halyard tension. Then, if the sail is at the bottom end of its range, the crew automatically positions the lead one hole forward.

Once sheeting positions are established, they should be plainly marked on the deck alongside the track in numbers large enough to be read at night. This numbering system is much better than having small numbers stamped on the track. These are always difficult to remember and therefore have to be charted and looked for at each headsail change.

In fading breeze, follow a reverse procedure. I feel most sailors at this lower end of a genoa's range tend to sheet too far forward, sometimes to the point where the middle of the foot hangs outside the rail. I feel the foot of the sail should just touch the lifelines and no more, otherwise the bottom third of the genoa will become too bent and actually hook back towards the centreline of the boat, stalling air flow from the leech as well as pushing the exhausting air into the mainsail. Sheeting full and over the rail may look more powerful but I have always found it to be slower. If close sheeting is used, then the foot must be kept reasonably straight to avoid leech stall and exhausting air into the mainsail (Fig. 54 (a)).

A genoa that is good for close sheeting and still powerful enough in the foot needs to have fullness built in low and forward while the aft 40 per cent of the sail is kept flat for a good exhaust angle when the sheet is sprung (Fig. 54 (b)).

A correctly cut headsail, properly sheeted, should have all the wool tufts flowing correctly. It is foolish to sheet incorrectly to correct bad faults in a genoa. The sail must be recut. However, sheeting can help to improve a sail's weaknesses near the extreme limits at either end of its wind range. These small sheeting compromises can only be found by experiment-

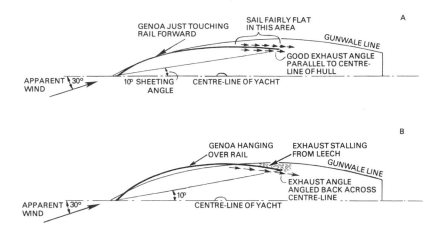

Figure 54. **A**, *correct fore and aft sheeting for light air to give maximum fullness.* **B**, *genoa sheeted too far forward in light air is too hooked towards leech.*

ing and watching the effect they have on boat speed and pointing ability. In light air, it is sometimes better to sail a boat with the genoa eased a little and the bottom leeward tufts stalled. Here, you are disturbing the efficiency of a small area of the sail low down to get more power from the major area high up.

Similarly, you can carry a heavy number one genoa to a much higher than normal wind strength in flat water without loss of boat speed or excessive heeling angle by feathering the boat through the gusts. Pointing angles of 25 degrees can be achieved without loss of hull speed when there is no sea to slow the boat down. Here, you would be sailing with all windward tufts stalled and the sails just extracting enough power from the wind to maintain full hull speed. To do this successfully, a good feel for the yacht and accurate steering by the helmsman are essential. If the yacht is steered a fraction free, it will heel too much and hull speed will drop. Sailed too close to the wind and the yacht's speed will also drop with the fall-off in power from the sails.

LEECH LINES

Leech lines in big-yacht genoas and mainsails are important to control leech flutter. There are many different types of flutter with one thing in common: they annoy the hell out of everyone aboard. If this is the only problem,

then careful adjustment of the leech line is the answer. Many yachtsmen associate leech flutter with loose leeches and sometimes this is so. However, it is possible to have a tight leech shape that still flutters (Fig. 55).

If there is enough flutter to make the whole genoa shake, especially in wind below 10 knots apparent, then too much leech line tension will have to be used to control it. This will cause a large hook in the leech. A hook as big as a bent index finger is acceptable on boats of say 30 ft. overall and bigger. But this amount would be worth a sail recut on a yacht the size of a

Figure 55.

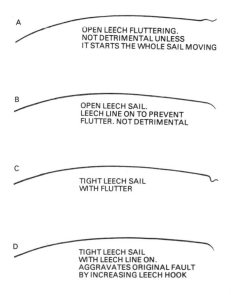

121

Dragon. Look at the shape of the sail just ahead of the leech line. In older sails particularly, the small hook on the edge directly caused by the leech line will become an extension of a deeper distortion running 9 or 10 in. into the sail—and this is serious.

MEDIUM TO STRONG WINDS

Number One Genoa

The cut of the heavy number one genoa will vary according to the type of boat. For all yachts, I think the number one heavy should be of nearly the same fullness as the light number one but made from much heavier material so that it will hold its shape and respond correctly to halyard tension controls. The cloth weight will vary according to the size of the yacht. I would suggest 6·5 to 7 oz. for Half Ton, 7 to 8 oz. for One Ton, 8 to 9 oz. for Two Ton.

Most yachts sail very well near the top of the light number one genoa's wind range, usually around 12 to 15 mph—the smaller the boat, the higher into the range can the light number one be carried. Unfortunately, at this point with the halyard fully up and the genoa leads moved aft, the sail will continue to grow fuller

in the harder gusts, the shape moving aft and the depth increasing.

This rather than sail area is the main reason for the yacht being overpowered.

Most modern ocean racers can carry the number one heavy genoa to 19 or 20 knots apparent and if the water is very flat, perhaps to 25 knots. The flat water allows the boat to keep maximum hull speed while the over-abundance of pressure from the rig allows the boat to be sailed exceedingly high in a feathered condition. *Bumblebee 3*, a 53-footer, would sail this way at 25 degrees to the wind with full hull speed.

As the sea becomes rougher, the yacht must be steered on a much more erratic course to pick the easiest path through the waves and if it is being sailed in a semi-feathered fashion under too much sail, it will get knocked down every time the helmsman comes away to drive through a sea or to pick up speed after going high over the top of a big wave. The intermittent excessive heeling causes excessive weather helm for a few seconds before the boat straightens up and the helm becomes neutral again. This kills the hull speed and causes the helmsman to steer a zig-zag course. It is a misconception that more sail area is needed to drive through a seaway, but I do agree that

Right. On this light displacement Farr Half-Tonner, a reefing headsail and flattening reef is used to advantage at the top of the wind speed range to de-power the number one genoa and full mainsail.

Far right. In a freshening breeze, crew weight is being used to maximum advantage on the windward rail. The first reef has already been used to de-power the mainsail. The reefing headsail would be next used in the power step down.

heavy-weather headsails can be too flat.

Number Two Headsail

The selection of a number two headsail as the first change down from a number one is critical as this change is probably the one most used. I feel the number two does not need to have a great drop in area: perhaps something like 15 per cent in Half Tonners to Two Tonners.

The main objective is to cut down the overlap as much as possible so that the slot is wider between genoa and mainsail. I think the luff should be shortened a little also to widen the slot at the head of the genoa.

Mainsail

The mainsail should now be considered as we go through the natural progression of sail reduction. Its reefing should be considered in conjunction with headsail reduction to retain correct balance on the helm.

Most modern mainsails have a fair amount of fullness built in by seam taper in the lower third to give maximum power on the wind in lighter air as well as off the wind. To remove this fullness, as the wind freshens, a flattening reef should be provided about 18 in. above the normal clew position. The reefing line for this first reduction in power should tack down on

the boom an inch or so outside the black band position. This folds in the bottom seam that has most of the fullness cut into it and allows the flattening reef cringle to be pulled out to the black band. The extra tension along the foot also helps to flatten the bottom third of the main in the same way that a genoa can be flattened by shifting the leads further aft. The flattening reef has benefits other than flattening the sail and reducing power. It reduces the backwinding effect from the headsail, allowing the mainboom traveller to be carried further to leeward.

In larger yachts, where the mainsail has been cut with a drooping boom, a flattening reef tackle need only be put in at the leech. In smaller yachts, where the leech does not stretch down under heavy-weather loadings, it is wise to pull down the luff about the same amount to keep the boom level. Power can be increased or decreased for small variations in wind strengths by adjusting the flattening reef in and out by small amounts.

Number Three Genoa

The next reduction depends largely on the type of boat. If weather helm is a problem, I would reduce the mainsail area by reefing it, especially if reaching. This choice would also

Heavily-reefed main, short-footed jib combination working well in a heavy breeze.

depend on how much reduction in area you had in the change from the number one to the number two genoa. If it were a small reduction, as I suggest it should be, I would like to go to the number three genoa, thus reducing the overlap even further. (Another 23 per cent in area on Half to Two Ton size boats, in 9 oz. cloth.)

If the mainsail has a good open leech, the helm will stay in balance and can be readily adjusted with the traveller. Power can further be varied in the rig by inserting or shaking out the first full reef in the mainsail. It is important that the main works constantly in this stronger wind range when sailing to windward. If it is backwinding too much or flagging, the balance will go from strong weather helm to neutral as the boat is worked through the seaway, thus intermittently filling and emptying the mainsail.

Balance

The most important thing in steering a yacht is appreciating the balance of the helm. This varies with the angle of heel and the mainsail trim. As the wind lightens, the main traveller should be trimmed into the centreline or above it until the boom itself is on the centreline of the hull. As the wind lightens further, you will start to feel lee helm. Move all the crew weight to leeward, to heel the boat as this is the only way correct helm balance can then be maintained.

The heavy-weather end of the scale is even more important. All yachts have a maximum angle of heel, normally around 30 degrees, where they sail at their best. As they approach this angle or if this angle is exceeded, weather helm increases rapidly. Therefore, the helmsman must be largely responsible for calling adjustments to sail trim. His skill at this will have a large bearing on the yacht's performance. Once a yacht gets into this stronger wind range, the helmsman should sail the boat by feel, on the angle of heel in conjunction with the boat speed. If this feel is perfected, the sail-change decisions become a lot easier to make at both the top and the bottom of the range of each sail combination.

Through the fluctuating wind strengths within the range of each rig combination, even in the stronger 25 to 40 knot wind range if the correct rig is being carried, the helmsman must be thinking of the angle of heel, and hence the balance, together with maximum hull speed. He must think power-up or power-down. To power up, first close the mainsail traveller to the centre; next, ease the genoa halyard tension and move the genoa leads forward a little: then reduce the forestay tension to make the headsail fuller. If boat speed cannot be maintained, a sail change up must be made.

For power down—assuming you have maximum forestay tension, correct halyard tension and lead positions fully aft—first move the mainsail traveller to leeward; then widen the sheeting angle of the genoa if possible. The helmsman must do the rest by feathering the boat to keep the angle of heel correct without dropping the hull speed. As the wind continues to increase, it will become impossible to maintain that speed. If the helmsman pulls away slightly, the extra angle of heel will keep the speed down and if he feathers more to stand the boat upright, the lack of power will cause a loss of speed as the boat punches into the waves. And this is the point where sail area must be reduced.

Then you must start all over again at the bottom end of the next sail combination fully-powered.

Skinny-rib Jib

The skinny-rib jib is a nearly full luff-length headsail with very little overlap. It is a tall, narrow sail like a Soling jib. While this sail technically claims good qualifications, it also has many problems. It is designed to the theory that the longer the luff, the greater the efficiency of the sail. Applying another theory that the wider the chord the wind is bent across, the greater the power produced, we end up with a long-luffed sail extracting a lot of small amounts of power with very little drag. This rig was originally developed as a simplification of the heavy-weather cutter rig used with great success off the Australian coast. Changing to cutter rig was always difficult as yankee and staysail were set to gain enough area to take over from the number two genoa. This made the change slow and involved twice the number of crewmen running around the foredeck for twice the amount of time it took to make a single sail-for-sail change. Modern, lightweight boats do not like heavy-footed crew activity.

Cutter rig and skinny-rib jib both have had the advantage that the lack of overlap cuts down interaction with the mainsail, thus keeping the helm balanced correctly in rough water.

The problem I have found with both rigs is they will not handle a decrease in wind strength as well as a slightly lower ratio wider sail, the leads of which can be moved forward a little and sheet eased to power it up. The tall, narrow sail must be sheeted more in a line down the leech to control the twist and so easing the sheet tends to de-power it and the chord depth is more difficult to control. Because of the narrow chord-width forestay sag, or lack of it, dramatically increases or decreases the depth of the jib. If it is to be at all successful, this type of sail must be trimmed expertly, varying sheeting angle and tension to correct the slot effect.

I think the skinny-rib is a good type of sail in an increasing, steady breeze if expertly handled. It needs constant recutting to maintain the correct shape as the long leech is hard to control. The cutter rig is still an excellent concept; especially on long, heavy windward legs and reaching in fresh winds. The higher clew of the yankee, 7 ft. to 8 ft. above the deck, lengthens the foot and shortens the leech, making the sail much easier to control. Shifting the sheet leads aft tends to flatten the sail up to half way while the same sort of adjustment on a skinny-rib jib will affect only the bottom 6 ft. to 8 ft.

THE TWIN-GROOVED HEADSTAY

The twin-grooved headsay is the answer to changing headsails without losing speed. It provides a quick and beautifully simple way of changing sails once its pitfalls and problems are appreciated.

Any genoa will look better set in a grooved stay because hank creases are eliminated along with the hanks. The sail will also be more adjustable in the lower wind range as halyard tension can be eased to the required minimum without fear of the luff sagging between the hanks. However, care must be taken to ensure enough luff tension is applied in stronger conditions. Yachtsmen have become used to gauging luff tension from the small creases appearing on the luff at the hank points and from the sag between the hanks. When faced with a genoa set in the groove, that always looks smoother after initial tension has been applied, they are inclined to sail into stronger winds with the halyard tension too low.

To overcome this problem, it is essential to mark halyards accurately, especially for genoas with luff length shorter than maximum. I suggest stretching up the sail while the yacht is in the marina in windless condition. First just stretch the luff sufficiently to remove the wrinkles in the luff tape and mark the halyard position. Then, stretch the sail further until a tight tension crease appears on the luff just abaft the forestay. Mark this position and note how much the sail has stretched.

Repeat this procedure for all headsails. The amount of stretch will vary depending on the type of cloth and hardness of the surface finish. The softer the cloth, the more the sail will need to be stretched to keep the drive in the correct position when sailing. The harder the cloth, the less stretch will be needed.

The amount of stretch will also vary with the size of the sail. Discuss the degree of stretch with your sailmaker to ensure it remains within safe limits. With powerful winches and no marks on the halyard, it is possible to tear the head out of a genoa without even filling it with wind.

THE TWIN STAY CHANGE

For twin-stay headsail changing, you must have two genoa halyards and two tack fittings—the horn type are the most simple and effective. Use shock rubber retainers to hook over the horns to stop the tack falling off the horn while the headsail is lying on the foredeck.

The outside set inside peel is the most effective method of changing: The new sail lies easily on the lee rail and will slide up behind the sail already set without too much interference. Usually, it is quicker to pull the new sail up than to take the old sail down and so

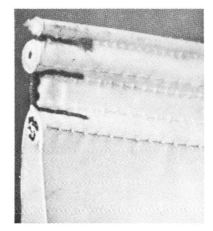

Far left top. A twin-grooved headstay: It is important in strong winds to ensure that the luff of the genoa is held forward in the bow as the sail is hoisted. A sea breaking into the headsail could cause it to break out of the headstay groove.

Centre top. Genoas are flaked down into full-length turtles.

Left. Luff tape is bunched at the head of the turtle, ready for hoisting, secured by a light line passed through eyelets behind the luff of the sail.

Far left bottom. Care must be taken to enter the sail into the pre-feeder device which must be deep enough to engage the second, larger luff rope thus protecting from jamming the finer luff rope that enters the groove.

Centre bottom. For short-hoist headsails, needing wire strops to the halyard, a short piece of feeder tape is attached to the strop to take some of the strain from the head of the sail. The spring tension device on the headfoil must be fully encased by plastic tubing and tape to protect spinnakers from damage.

Left. Shows the small forward luff rope, all that is necessary to hold the sail in the groove, while the second and larger luff rope is essential to obtain the necessary stretch and recovery in the luff for stretchy-luff genoas.

the flow on the leeward side of the sail, the most important for sailing efficiency, will be disrupted for the minimum length of time.

Obviously, the bigger the boat the more difficult will be this hoisting operation. On Half Ton and smaller yachts, one man can pull up the new sail by hand, tailing off on the halyard winch. Another crewman should stand by with a handle to tension the last foot or so to the correct marks. The tailer cleats off the new halyard; the man with the handle uncleats the old halyard as soon as the new headsail is sheeted home. The old sheet is released and the new headsail is sheeted home. The old halyard is released and the old sail is peeled from inside the new one. One crewman will be needed in the bow to pull down on the luff and another half way along the foot pulling the sail forward, to break the suction between new and old sails, and down on to the foredeck. For the few moments that the two sails are up and sheeted, they will laminate together as one, through suction, and so the foot man's job is an important one. The bigger the boat, the bigger the suction problem, through both hoisting and lowering.

On *Bumblebee 3*, with headsails 70 ft. long on the luff, the halyard was taken around the normal halyard winch and then to a coffee grinder. The sail had to be ground up most of the way, especially if the sails were wet from rain, fog, and to a lesser extent spray in heavy weather. Sometimes five crewmen were needed to drag the old sail off. If the suction pressure was too great for them to break by hand, a short luff by the helmsman to shake both sails was usually enough to start the old sail on its way down.

While setting up for a change, great care must be taken to ensure that the halyards do not become crossed. Keep the port halyard for the port groove; starboard halyard for the starboard groove. With the halyard in use under full load and the halyard on the sail going up also under heavy load, a cross will almost certainly badly damage one or both halyards.

Double turning blocks and two cars on each genoa track must be available. Sheeting positions for each sail must be known accurately and marked. I prefer a mark on the deck with the number of the sail painted alongside it, so that there is none of the delay that can be experienced looking for smaller numbers stamped on tracks or checking a chart on the bulkhead for the correct position.

There are many methods for changing the sheet, choice depending basically on what winches and deck gear are available. On *Bumblebee 3* we used a changing sheet. Suppose we were changing to a shorter-footed genoa: the second car was slipped onto the track in front of the one in use and positioned just forward of the exact sheeting position. The sail change was made with the new sheet led through the second car, onto a backup winch and sheeted home. With the load then taken off the main genoa sheet, the first car was moved forward to the exact position for the new sail, the regular genoa sheet bent onto the new sail and the load taken back onto the main genoa winch.

On smaller yachts, where spare winches are sometimes hard to find and the loads are lighter, a clam cleat or sheet jammer on the direct line of the sheet from the turning block to the winch can be used. Press down the old sheet under load and jamb it off, releasing the winch for the new sail's sheet.

I do not like the tack change, where the sail is changed while the yacht is going through a tack. The tack becomes a bad tack and the change becomes less efficient. The procedure is: The new sail is started up its groove and the yacht is put into a slow tack. While the yacht is going across the wind, the new sail must be pulled the rest of the way up and sheeted home while the old sail must be dragged down as it comes across to the new lee side. While that sounds easy, only one small mistake is needed and you end up on the new tack with two headsails—one half up and the other half down.

The helmsman is important to the success of a normal twin-groove headstay change without loss of boat speed. The secret is to block the crew completely from view and mind. If the boat has instruments, look down at them and sail precisely 30 degrees or whatever is the optimum pointing angle for the boat and do not look up until the change is completed. If the helmsman does watch the crew, his attention is inevitably distracted and he ends up sailing head to wind or 10 to 15 degrees too low, losing some of the gains of an efficient twinstay change.

Crew movement should be kept to a minimum for successful changing, especially in fine-entry modern designed yachts where one man in the bow will alter the whole trim. Normally there is no great rush. When a change is imminent, one man can take the halyard forward, get the new sail on deck, hook on the tack, enter the luff in the groove and bend on a sheet handed forward to him from the middle of the boat. So one person only need go forward of the mast, except for the few moments needed to pull off the old sail.

In heavy weather, the helmsman's part in the change becomes more important. He must be careful not to put the bow under any big waves as the headsail is loose on the foredeck, without the normal hanks to keep the luff secured to the forestay. In fact it is vulnerable as soon as it comes out of the turtle, and still when it is half hoisted. A big wave can wash the middle of the sail back along the foredeck, tearing the luff out of the feeders and track. It is often wise in rough weather for the helmsman to feather, slowing the boat a little to allow the bow to rise over each wave rather than smashing through them at full speed.

Modern offshore deck layout distributes the manpower around the deck, and although no one is gathered at one spot, no one is too far away to back up another crewman in an emergency. Similarly, almost any sheet or halyard can be led to any winch in an emergency.

A point is reached in really bad weather, depending on the expertise of the crew, where it is too dangerous to have an unattached headsail on deck at all because the danger of it going overboard is too great. Then, you must revert to a bare-headed sail change keeping the new sail in its turtle until the old one is completely removed from the deck. Really good netting rigged from the toe rail to the middle guard rail helps solve a lot of these problems.

With the old hank system, once the sail was hanked to the forestay there was no great danger. With grooved headstay systems, once part of the foot gets over the side, it will quickly drag the rest of the sail after it, particularly if the hand forward has his attention momentarily elsewhere, as he does when attaching the halyard.

The worse the weather, the greater the danger of fouling up the change. In heavy rain or fog, the two sails can stick together so badly that the crew just cannot get the old sail down. It does not matter so much how long a change

takes, but it can be serious when changing down.

In these conditions where sails sticking together can cause major drama, a point is reached where a normal sail-down, sail-up change should be decided upon. This can be done with very little loss of time if the new sail is started up its groove when the old sail is halfway down.

It is better to accept a brief loss of performance than risk having a sail washed over the side or even having four or five crewmen on the foredeck for three to four minutes battling to get the old sail unstuck and dragged down.

Fortunately, twin-stay changes can be made in most conditions. On *Bumblebee 3*, over a season's racing, with something like 300 headsail changes, only three or four had to be done bare-headed and two of these were in the 1974 Sydney–Hobart race, in the middle of Bass Strait with the wind 45 to 50 knots and really big seas.

The other race where we had problems was

in the 1975 Fastnet where, changing from the number one to the number two in a thick, wet fog, both sails became so firmly locked together that both had to be dropped to the deck to be separated.

Of the different types of grooved stays and foils available, I prefer the twin grooves facing aft in an alloy extrusion that clips over the forestay, as in the Hood Gemini.

The twin aft grooves seem to cause much less friction both up and down than the Stearn Twinstay type—a solid alloy extrusion with a groove on the front and back of the section. The Stearn type is, however, lighter as the extrusion itself is the forestay, eliminating the extra weight of the stainless steel rod or wire. The Twinstay is set up with ball-bearing swivels at the top and the bottom, allowing the forward groove to revolve to the aft position as soon as the new sail fills. As important as the type of stay extrusion itself is the design of the feeders supplied with it to introduce the luff tape on the sail into the groove. In smaller yachts like Half Tonners, a feeder fitting neatly over the bottom of the extrusion is all that is necessary. However, on larger craft, a separate feeder hanging on a strop from the forestay must also be used to guide the sail roughly into the second feeder. If anything is going to go wrong with hoisting the sail, it will show up as the tape goes through this preliminary feeder.

To minimise the risk of hoisting problems, the sail should be flaked up with the luff rope level at one end and the bundled sail extended along the deck with the clew aft. The sail is then picked up at a point two-thirds of its length towards the clew and folded forward until this point is level with the luff rope, still leaving the clew facing aft. The whole sail is then zipped into a long, sausage-like turtle and is stowed with the head and tack eyes poking out of one end and the clew eye out of the other.

To close the turtle, the zipper is joined at the forward end and zipped shut with the slide that completely leaves the zipper at the after end: this end of the zipper is arranged so that one side is about 4 in. shorter than the other. The slide runs onto the longer side, which is fitted with a stop to make the slide captive.

As the sail is hoisted, the zipper automatically

bursts open. Normally, three sail ties are sewn to the turtle and tied around it to prevent the turtle opening prematurely down below, or on deck, attached to the tack, waiting to be hoisted.

Do not forget to tie the turtle itself to something. Turtles are more expensive than winch handles and just as easy to lose. The turtle is probably not as necessary on smaller boats, however flaking the sail is a must, with the bundled sail secured with one sail tie just behind the luff rope.

This preparation is not really that difficult, requiring little more time and effort than stuffing a sail into a bag. If it is done properly, the only remaining cause of a foul-up during a hoist is if the sail catches on a projection such as a foredeck cleat. This will inevitably cause the sail to rip out of its feeders. So it is essential that those hauling up the halyard or tailing a halyard winch are in a position to watch the progress of the sail into the feeders so a foul-up can be detected before the sail is damaged.

REACHING AND RUNNING SAILS

As the course enables a freeing away from close-hauled, an array of sailbags present their contents for reaching and running.

A high-cut reacher should be the first sail considered. It is full size, 150 per cent of the J fore-triangle measurement, with the clew cut 7 ft. or 8 ft. off the deck. This allows the clew to move further out from the lee side of the mainsail of orthodox cut and also improves the exhaust angle of the bottom half of the sail. The sheet is led well aft, near the stern quarter blocks, to facilitate this.

Some will argue that a genoa will perform the same task. If a reacher is cut too flat, the difference in performance will not be noticeable with the only advantage that the high-cut sail will not be pounded by waves thrown into the bottom of it from the lee bow when reaching in heavy conditions. However if the reacher is cut extremely full, as it must be to handle the much-increased apparent wind angle, then the extra speed will make it a worthwhile sail. In light weather, the reacher will work only in a very narrow wind range—say from 35 degrees to 45 degrees or 50 degrees, depending on the type of Starcut you have aboard. As the wind increases, to the point where a Starcut will overpower the yacht, the reacher will give better performance than the Starcut to apparent wind angles as far aft as 90 degrees to 100 degrees.

A "Big Boy" staysail can be set inside a reacher to make a double-head reaching rig, or set under a spinnaker. It is usually cut about 130 per cent of J instead of the normal 150 per cent, with overlap, of the full-size genoa. The Rule says that when the sail is tacked down on the centreline and pulled fully aft, it must not reach further aft than would a 150 per cent genoa set off the forestay. This maximum aft position must be established on the foredeck and then the sail can be tacked anywhere forward of this point. The Big Boy must be cut from the lightest of cloth as it is basically a light weather sail. Some typical cloth weights are: Half Tonner, 1·5 oz.; Threequarter Tonner, 2 oz.; One Tonner, 3 oz. The geometry of a Big Boy is similar to that of a reacher. It is high cut so it may be sheeted well aft, allowing the leech to exhaust correctly and produce the correct slot effect. The first chance to use this sail comes between 45 degrees to 55 degrees apparent, when it is set inside the high-cut reacher.

To slot a big staysail such as this successfully inside a reacher or starcut spinnaker, the breeze must be fairly steady and the water flat. The motion of a yacht in a seaway will cause both sails to breathe in and out and the interference between the sails then results in a loss of power rather than an increase. The slots between the staysail and the mainsail will be narrow and therefore must be perfect. The only way to see if they are correct is from as far aft as possible, leaning out to leeward so that mainsail, staysail and reacher leeches can all be seen. From this position, the correct athwartship position can be found to place the staysail leech exactly halfway between the mainsail and reacher. A Barber hauler of some type may have to be used to achieve this precisely. Twist can then be adjusted with sheet pressure and the relative depths in the bottom half of the staysail can be adjusted by varying the fore and aft position of the staysail sheet leads. With this

Starcut is effective at broader reaching angles in fresh winds.

rig, trim must be accurate. If one sail is trimmed without the other, they will immediately suffer from interference. Once the correct sheeting positions are found, they should be marked, with position 'A' for the tack on the foredeck sheeting to position 'A' back on the genoa tracks.

As the apparent wind moves aft, the reacher should be changed for a Starcut with the staysail kept under it. Make sure that as soon as the spinnaker hits the masthead that the reacher sheet is thrown off and the halyard dropped. At the same time, the staysail is eased well off into a semi-luffing trim. This will allow the spinnaker to fill quickly, minimising the

chance of a twist. Concentrate on the spinnaker trim until it is perfect before attempting to re-trim the staysail. If the staysail is trimmed while the spinnaker is still being settled down, it will almost certainly cause the spinnaker to collapse.

In the final trimming of the staysail, it is always wise to keep the head a little under-trimmed at these close reaching angles to minimise the chance of a spinnaker collapse. If there is a collapse, the staysail sheet should be thrown completely off, making it easier to get the spinnaker filling again. The slots should be carefully checked and adjusted from right aft.

The Starcut range would normally be 45 degrees to 60 or 70 degrees before the change should be made to a tri-radial spinnaker, assuming we are seeking ultimate performance in about 10 knots of apparent wind where boats of all sizes can easily carry these rigs.

The tri-radial is a specialised reaching spinnaker and theoretically will be out-performed by a full, normal radial-head spin-naker as soon as the wind moves to 10 or 15 degrees abaft the beam. As the apparent wind angles move aft, the Big Boy is progressively eased out. As soon as the breeze gets abaft the beam, the tack should be shifted from the centreline of the boat out onto the weather rail and re-sheeted to fit the leech in the centre of the gap between the mainsail and the spinnaker.

As the yacht squares further away to the wind, the Big Boy will lose efficiency, have less and less pull on the sheet until at around 135 degree apparent wind angle it should be replaced by a shooter. The shooter (or blooper) is cut to IOR headsail restrictions with an LP measurement 150 per cent of the foretriangle. The depth from half the luff to the centre of the foot must be 55 per cent of the leech measure-ment. One of the main restrictions is on luff length—when the sail is tacked down on the genoa fitting, the luff must stretch tight when the halyard is fully up.

The sail is cut with a gigantic hollow in the luff and almost equal foot and leech lengths. This design allows the sail, when set with 6 ft. or 8 ft. of halyard let go, to fly well outside the spinnaker sheet and the leech of the mainsail. The shooter works like an extension of the leech of the spinnaker and balances the force exerted by the spinnaker on the opposite side of the boat for more speed and improved steer-ing control.

To trim the shooter, ease the halyard until the foot of the sail is just above the water. Then, the hollow cut into the luff allows the sail to set for maximum efficiency. The shooter is sheeted to the normal spinnaker quarter blocks.

The angles given earlier, remember, are for 10 knots of apparent wind. In lighter breeze, the golden rule is as soon as any staysail is not pulling on the sheet or filling effectively most

Far left. Flat Starcut spinnaker used on very tight reach keeps the boat to windward at a low angle of heel while the full-cut spinnaker on the yacht to leeward causes her to broach persistently and the spinnaker to collapse.

Top left. Excellent example of a full, radial head running spinnaker and shooter in combination. The high-clew position of the shooter allows it to fly freely with the sheet over the top of the main boom and the sail well away from the lee side of the spinnaker.

Bottom left. A fuller, radial-head spinnaker being used in light air to give full power at this tight reaching angle. As the wind increases, the boat would heel too much at this angle of sailing and a flatter Starcut spinnaker would be necessary.

of the time, pull it down. If it is not working efficiently it will first tend to interfere with the bigger and more effective sail, the spinnaker, and secondly it will obstruct the trimmer's view of the whole spinnaker, making it more difficult for him to assess the correct pole trim and sheet trim—critical to good light-weather performance. This complete view of the spinnaker is also important in appreciating the stability of the spinnaker, enabling the trimmer to call the change to the $\frac{1}{2}$ oz. spinnaker at the correct moment. In light air, the sea conditions have a large influence on what downwind sails can be set. For instance in flat water a Starcut, which is normally the heaviest-cloth spinnaker, can be carried very effectively whereas if the water is lumpy with a left-over slop, the Starcut will flop in and out, doing more harm than good. In these conditions, better progress will be made with a very light drifter.

As the winds become stronger than 10 knots apparent, the apparent wind in which each sail is effective moves further and further aft. In the 10-knot breeze as the wind moved aft, fuller and fuller spinnakers were used to produce more power. Now, the choice of sail is similar to that for headsails: if the boat is overpowered, no matter what the apparent wind, change to a flatter spinnaker. For example, if you are carrying a Starcut at 80 degrees in 18 knots of wind and begin heeling excessively with a lot of weather helm, you probably would be faster with the reacher and a Big Boy set under it rather than persist with the Starcut.

If you were carrying the tri-radial at 100 degrees with the same symptoms, you should change to the Starcut . . . and so on.

If the breeze is fluctuating up and down, a Big Boy can be set under the spinnaker to increase or decrease power, hoisting and dropping the sail as required.

This all sounds very basic but any time there is a strong wind, you see boats carrying spinnakers that are too powerful. Remember, it is much quicker to sail from A to B in a straight line than in a series of broaches.

SPINNAKER PEEL

Changing a $\frac{1}{2}$ oz. spinnaker for a $\frac{3}{4}$ oz. or $\frac{3}{4}$ oz. for a $1\frac{1}{2}$ oz. without loss of speed has become just as important as the twin-groove headsail change. So the spinnaker "peel", hoisting the new spinnaker and setting it inside the old, must be part of the repertoire of every ocean racing crew. It is a fairly simple operation providing certain precautions are taken and procedures adhered to. The boat must be equipped with two spinnaker halyards, a spare spinnaker changing sheet and a peeling strop. The peeling strop is a piece of line about 5 ft. long with a snap clip on one end and a loop in the other. In preparing for a peel, the strop is attached to one of the genoa tack points by the loop, the clip end is lifted up and a hitch taken around the forestay to prevent the tack of the new spinnaker blowing away to leeward out of the reach of the forward hand when the new spinnaker is hoisted.

The new spinnaker is made ready with the changing sheet attached and led through an aft turning block—a temporary block is good enough as normally the regular sheet will be re-attached once the peel is completed.

Attach the halyard, making sure it is clear and not running over the top of the halyard already in use as this is the quickest way of chopping through expensive halyards. Attach the tack of the new spinnaker to the clip on the peeling strop.

If the course is square running, it is wise to shy the boat up a little to enable the new spinnaker to be filled as soon as it is hoisted. The pole will also be positioned more forward, ready for the brace transfer.

Now hoist the new spinnaker, sheet in and fill it. As soon as it is drawing, ease the pole forward and lower it, as in a spinnaker drop, fire the brace clip to release the old spinnaker, then ease the brace completely. It is best to throw the brace right off the winch so there is no possible restriction to the forward hand. He must be able to pull enough slack through the pole end to attach the brace to the new spinnaker now flying from the strop. As soon as the brace is attached to the new spinnaker, the brace turns are put back on the winch, the clip on the peeling strop is fired and the pole lifted and pulled aft into normal trim. It is important for the helmsman to follow the progress of the operation carefully so that he can steer a course to keep the spinnaker setting during the change.

The old spinnaker is just left flagging out over the stern, attached by the halyard (still up) and the sheet (cleated off) until the new spinnaker is correctly trimmed. All hands, if necessary, are then available to haul it down. If the takedown is difficult, the helmsman should square the boat away, bringing the wind further aft for a few moments. This makes the takedown much easier. A lot of crews make the mistake of trying to take off the old spinnaker immediately it is fired from the pole. This not only divides the work force available for trimming but inevitably covers the winches and the people doing the job with vast quantities of spinnaker material. If it is felt the old spinnaker is flogging too much while the new one is being finally trimmed, a spare hand, can tighten the old sheet to straighten the luff, reducing the flogging action.

Careful, continual attention must be paid to the halyards. The first spinnaker set should always be made on the leeward halyard. Then after the first peel, the leeward halyard can be taken forward and be clear for another inside peel. After the second peel using the leeward halyard for the hoist, the old windward halyard will become crossed as the spinnaker floats aft for the drop and will be of no further use until it is cleared. It must then be taken completely around the outside of the spinnaker

Forward spinnaker drop: left, crew is preparing to drop tri-radial which has genoa set inside it in readiness for the windward leg to follow. Right, crew drags in spinnaker forward, a relatively easy job with spinnaker collapsed in the lee of the genoa.

now setting. This is a difficult task and I think the only way is to strap the spinnaker in and collapse it, at the same time swinging the crossed halyard, with a weight attached to it, out to leeward and pull it forward from the pulpit with a light retrieving line. Even then, you need some luck.

Another way, which we used on *Bumblebee 3*, was just to pull the offending halyard to the masthead, then send somebody up on a genoa halyard to bring it down again on the correct side. A third alternative is to make the next spinnaker change in the old way—dropping one sail, changing halyard, brace sheet, and rehoisting—uncrossing the halyards in the process, setting on the leeward one again ready

for two more spinnaker peels.

We had still another method on *Bumblebee 3* that should only be tried on big boats in good weather and sea conditions. While running square or threequarter, a crew member used to climb up the pole kicker (foreguy) and onto the end of the pole with the tack of the new spinnaker tied to his waist. Once there, he would lash the tack to the end of the pole with a sail-tie. As soon as the new spinnaker was set, he would fire the old spinnaker and transfer the brace clip into the new tack cringle. This method was perfect at broad apparent wind angles. The pole did not have to be sent forward making the new spinnaker very easy to set. For this method to be legal (crew must not

Forward takedown would have been preferable. Crew will have a harder time now, dragging in spinnaker aft and the boat is losing speed on new, close-to-the-wind leg.

be outside the life rails), the crew member had to be attached to the deck by a lifeline. He also had to have very strong arms to be able to climb onto the top of the pole from the kicker. If this is ever tried, make sure that the pole topping lift, kicker and brace are all tight and securely cleated off. No, we never came back short-handed!

FORWARD SPINNAKER DROP

The forward drop is particularly useful when the wind is strong, the spinnakers are large, or where the spinnaker is being carried ahead of

the beam. In all these circumstances there is a big chance with the normal spinnaker drop that the spinnaker will be caught in the accelerated air from the genoa mainsail slot, making it extremely difficult for the crew to gather it in aft.

The forward drop brings the spinnaker in under the foot of the genoa onto the foredeck. Not only does it keep the sail out of the dangerous slot area but keeps yards of vulnerable light spinnaker cloth clear of genoa lead blocks, winches and crew busy trimming in sails for the next windward leg.

Start the drop by taking the lazy rope sheet from the windward side, around the front of the forestay. As the pole is eased forward and lowered, the bow man takes in the slack on the lazy sheet and makes it fast to a foredeck cleat. Brace and sheet are then cast off simultaneously, the spinnaker instantly collapses but the luff is held forward by the lazy sheet made up to the foredeck cleat, allowing the spinnaker to be gathered in under the headsail foot as the halyard is let go.

For square running drops, the normal method, behind the mainsail, is quite safe. However, the smart crew will always make the lazy brace fast on a cleat around the mast. This eliminates any possibility of the spinnaker, if it is torn from the crew's grasp, of becoming a "paying off" pennant from the masthead.

If double braces and sheets are not being used, then a static line snapped onto the sheet and made fast will do the same job. When dropping aft, always make sure that the trimmer cleats off the sheet as soon as the drop is started. Then, if the spinnaker gets away from the crew, in the initial stages of gathering it in, it will still be securely attached through the quarter blocks to the stern. The boat can then be pulled away square and the spinnaker easily

recovered. This should be a normal precaution but the system mentioned above is the best.

STEPPING AND TUNING A MASTHEAD RIG

Stepping and tuning a masthead rig is not the complicated operation many yachtsmen believe it to be. It is mainly an understanding of simple geometry. Before looking at the problem, several basics must be understood: Cap shrouds prevent the top of the mast from falling over sideways; lowers stop the middle of the mast falling to leeward; the cross trees or spreaders, as they are more commonly called, are there to give the cap shrouds a better angle of attack to the top of the mast. On a 30-footer with single spreader rig, if the cap shroud went straight from the chainplate to the masthead, it would make an angle with the mast of about 6 degrees. The minimum acceptable angle to give the required sideways support at the masthead is 10 degrees. The spreader must therefore push the shroud out at the mid-point of the mast until this angle is achieved. You will

Figure 56. **A,** mast must be straight from step to masthead with deck gaps even before full tension is applied to any rigging. Now tighten caps with spanner with even number of turns on each. **B,** then if mast appears like this under sailing load ease windward lower or tighten cap shroud. Always make even number of turns on lower screws to ensure bottom panel of mast stays in the centre of deck hole. Adjust any irregularities out of the mast finally with even number of turns on cap shrouds. **C,** if mast appears thus, ease weather cap shroud and tighten lower. **D,** if the four points circled are in line, but either panel is bent, there is nothing to do except fit upper intermediates (dotted line) or convert to double spreaders.

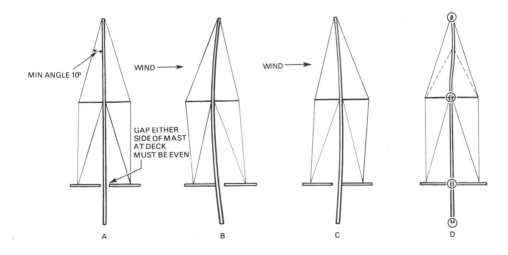

notice that on many catamarans and trimarans that the spreader is seldom used. The chainplates on these beamy boats are far enough apart for the 10 degree angle to be achieved easily (Fig. 56).

The spreader exerts an inward push on the mast. This has to be opposed by a lower stay attached just below the spreader base. The double-spreader rig is simply two sets of single-spreader rigs, one on top of the other and if looked at in this way is no more difficult to set up than the single-spreader concept. It makes little difference to tuning or stepping the mast whether or not it is stepped on deck or on the keel. A mast stepped through the deck does have one more point of support and therefore is a little more controllable.

Before the mast is lifted into the boat, the first step is to stretch the two lowers and two caps down the mast. Place the rigging screws together on the centreline and adjust them until they are nearly fully undone and exactly the same length.

Now lift the mast into the boat, attach the forestay, backstay, cap and lowers, set the mast to its designed rake and tighten the forestay and backstay hand tight on their rigging screws. Most yachts seem to sail best with the mast just aft of vertical. The best way to check this is to stand 50 or 60 yards away and sight the mast against the edge of some tall building. You can use plumb lines, but the building, I find, is the quickest.

Now tighten the lowers until they are just firm. Count the turns on each screw so that the stays will remain the same length. Take the slack out of the cap shrouds. The bottom panel of the mast, from the first spreaders down to the keel step should now be straight and vertical in the athwartships plane.

Before further tightening the shrouds and putting the mast under compression, check the sideways clearance of the mast where it passes through the deck. Fill these spaces with timber chocks until there is just enough clearance (say $\frac{1}{16}$ in. each side) to allow the mast to move fore-and-aft. The faces of the packing pieces should be parallel to the yacht's centreline so that if the mast needs to be bent fore-and-aft the mast can move at the deck as far as necessary without being deflected sideways by curvature in

the deckhole. I hope some designers and boat-builders read this as I have spent many wasted hours trying to fit spacers into oval mast holes, thinking how much easier it would have been had the hole been square. Why not just pack it with hard rubber? First, I do not think you need any sideways movement at the deck as the shrouds are not going to permit the mast to move sideways at the first spreader. Secondly, if you insist on doing it that way, the gap along either side of the mast must be made even before any packing is attempted, otherwise an uneven pressure will be applied, causing the bottom mast panel to take on an "S" shape when it is loaded.

Now tighten the caps down quite firmly, using a spanner on the rigging screws. The caps need to be much firmer than the lowers as they are longer and therefore will stretch more when under full sailing load. Tighten the backstay and forestay to the required tension. For twin-spreader rig, the upper intermediate stay going to the base of the top spreader should be only hand tight.

If forward and aft lowers are being used, the forward lowers should be tighter than the aft lowers to help hold the mast straight in a fore-and-aft direction. At this stage it is wise to inspect the mast step to ensure that the complete base area of the mast is taking the compression load. If the rake is causing the mast to stand only on the front or back, or if the section has not been cut off dead square, one side or the other of the section may be taking all the load. This can cause the mast to bend one way or the other, making it bear heavily against one side of the deck hole. The fault can be cured by filing the base of the mast or by shimming under the mast step. Some riggers always fit a block of timber about $\frac{3}{4}$ in. thick under the mast plug. The base crushes into it, and thus these small differences are evened out.

The mast is finally adjusted under full sailing load. A breeze around 10 to 12 knots is ideal. Come hard on the wind, then sight up the sail track to see how the mast reacts. Remember, with a single spreader rig, there are only two points that can be moved to make the mast straight sideways—the top and the middle. If the head is falling off to leeward, tack the boat to remove the load and take up two turns on the cap shroud. Tack back and sight again. If it still appears to be falling off, ease the lowers two turns. This will allow the middle of the mast to move to leeward, making the whole mast straighter. Keep tacking and adjusting until the mast is straight on both tacks. It is dangerous to keep tightening the caps only from tack to tack as the mast will be put under too much compression. This can make it unstable in the fore-and-aft direction or even drive the mast down into the step, and cause structural damage to the hull.

Now look at the fore-and-aft bend. If you are using fore-and-aft lowers and the mast is bending aft in the middle, ease the aft lowers, allowing the mast to move to leeward in the middle, then tighten the forward lowers until the mast is straight sideways again. The extra load on the forward lowers will pull the mast forward in the middle as well as straightening it sideways. Do the reverse if the bend is too much forward.

If the lowers are rigged in line with the caps, the sub-forestay must be tightened or loosened to adjust fore-and-aft bend. The parallel side packing in the deck hole now shows its importance as the mast can be chocked at the back to help stop the mast from wanting to bend aft in the middle, or it can be chocked in front to control forward bend, or it can be given room to move forward and back to make bend control with the substay easier without affecting sideways support of the mast at the deck.

With the double-spreader rig, the procedure is not much more difficult except that you must send a man aloft to adjust the upper intermediates at the first spreader. Adjust the masthead and the lower spreader as with the single spreader rig, lining up these two points and then send a man aloft to tighten or ease the upper intermediate until the third point, the top spreader, also comes into line. Remember, be careful to put on and take off the same number of turns on each lower, then you know you are holding the mast in the middle of the hole at deck level as it was originally placed in the boat. It is not necessary to count the turns on the rest of the rigging as all you are trying to do there is line up the top of the mast, on both tacks, with the bottom section.

With double-spreader rigs, it is sometimes necessary to provide some fore-and-aft support to the middle of the long, unsupported section between the lower spreader and the head. An inner forestay and runners are fitted for this purpose, coming from near the top spreaders. They are not highly-loaded. Their main purpose is to stop the mast from pumping backwards and forwards in heavy wind and sea conditions. The inner forestay must be taken off and brought back to the mast during each tack and the windward runner re-tensioned. A strict watch should be kept on any mast in heavy weather after each tack to check that the sub-forestay, inner forestay and runner tensions are correct. It is quite safe to bend a masthead rig up to one or one-and-a-half diameters of the mast as long as the mast remains stable. If it is pumping forward and back each time the yacht hits the sea, it will not be long before it jumps over the side. Finally, make doubly sure all rigging screws are securely locked.

It is wise to send somebody up the mast every couple of weeks to check for wear and damage. Check all nuts, split pins, rigging screw lock nuts, spreader bases and end fittings, shackles, halyards, blocks and welds. A careful inspection can quite often discover a fatigued fitting, or loose nut that will eventually cause a dismasting.

Fittings

WITH a tremendous range of advanced stainless-steel, alloy, and moulded plastic fittings available, there is no excuse these days for gear breakages or ineffieciency. Weight-saving must always be a strong consideration—as Uffa Fox once said, "the only place for weight is in a steamroller"—but do not skimp strength to save weight on such fittings vital to seaworthiness as rudder gudgeons, hounds fittings, chainplates, and tiller.

Use the correct fastenings, which the boat shops will supply for the fittings you buy, and make sure you are fixing into something that is strong enough to take the load. Wherever possible, bolts should be used with the head on the fitting and the nut and washer under the deck. This type of fastening can be pulled up tight, the excess bolt cut off, and the thread tapped over with a hammer to ensure that the nut does not shake loose. Fittings that are bolt-ed can also be removed and replaced for re-painting as many times as necessary without losing any of their holding power where screws, similarly treated, tend to become loose.

There is often no need to go to the very expensive stainless steel bolts; for most deck fittings a $\frac{3}{16}$ in. brass metal thread screw, with nut, is sufficient and much stronger than a wood screw. Stainless steel should be used where heavy loads are applied, such as at the hounds and chainplates.

The most useful fastening is a roundhead metal thread screw, which has the thread all the way up and can be used with varying thicknesses of timber. The round head is quite smooth and will not tear sails, clothes, or skin.

Stainless steel studs are also now available in varying lengths. They are threaded at both ends and are excellent for use through masts where shroud plates and trapeze plates are attached on both sides of the spar.

The wood screw is still probably the most valuable fastening in boat building, but ap-proach it warily when fixing thin metal fittings; approximately 33 per cent of the screw is bare shank. This does not compare with the holding power of, say, a self-tapper, which is 100 per cent thread.

Most amateurs sidestep the need to drill two holes into a piece of wood to take a wood screw —one the same size as the shank or bare section of the screw, the other the same size as the core of the threaded section. If only one hole is drilled—or worse, none at all—the tapered form of the screw will cause a split in the timber, forcing it away from the threaded section. A quick way to select the correct drill is to hold the screw up in one hand with the drill directly in front of it. Sight with one eye, and if you see the thread protruding from behind the drill, this or perhaps one size

Figure 57. Six commonly used fastenings shown fixing $\frac{1}{16}$ in. plate to 2 in. timber. Round-head metal thread screw and hexagonal-head bolt give best holding power. The self-tapper is the best of the screw fastenings.

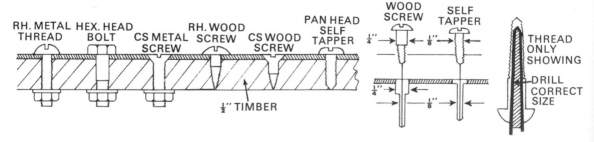

smaller is the correct drill. For the shank hole, choose a drill the same size as the shank near the head.

Only one drill need be used for the easy-to-handle stainless self-tapper—slightly smaller than the core diameter. For this reason, the self-tapping screw, threaded right to the head and available flat-head countersunk as well as round-head, has become the yachtsman's favourite.

Plan the layout of the deck fittings for maximum efficiency and crew comfort. The main aim should be to make your crew's work as easy as possible. I have heard fitting discussions go like this:

Crew: "We need a cleat for this spinnaker halyard."

Skipper: "There's a good strong stringer under this section of the floor—screw it there."

And from that day onwards every time the crew finishes pulling up the spinnaker the cleat is behind him and most times on the leeward side, making a quick, easy job into a very difficult and time-consuming one. This cleat should have been placed by putting the crew into the boat, checking his position when pulling up the spinnaker (on both tacks), and then fastening the cleat in front of him where he can see it, in line with the direction in which he is pulling, and as close as possible to being on the same level as his hands. Thus, when the spinnaker is up, he does not have to change the direction of his pull or move his hands very far to the cleat.

Choose the correct fitting to do the job as simply as possible. Avoid shackles, extra bits of lashing and extension plates, which all add up to extra cost and detract from the efficiency and the neatness of the finished job.

We'll now follow through the procedure of initially rigging a simple sailing dinghy.

STEPPING THE MAST

One of the first big tasks in fitting out a new boat is stepping the mast. Dinghy-class chainplates are usually positioned 15 in. to 16 in. abaft the mast to give fore-and-aft support while allowing the boom to go out as square as possible for running. The chainplates should

fasten directly through the skin and not be bent around the outer capping gunwale which they will tend to crush and perhaps lift off (Fig. 58). The chainplate should be slotted through the capping gunwale and bolted through the skin into a backing piece inside the hull which distributes the strain over a wide area. A simple block clip, bolted through the gunwale, is acceptable for smaller dinghies such as Sabots, Manly Juniors, and Mirrors. Stainless metal threads should be used to fasten chainplates.

Before installing the hounds fittings, the correct height above the deck must be found. In many classes this is variable and the best position is not always the one shown on the plan.

Before the mast is built, find this position, either from a sailmaker or one of the top performers in the class, so that a solid section may be included in the spar.

For example, the Moth hounds position is completely free but stays are normally carried approximately 10 ft. 6 in. above deck level on an 18 ft. mast if the three stays come from the one point. Where a low forestay is used (which I personally prefer) shrouds are approximately at 10 ft. 6 in. to 11 ft. and the forestay as low as 8 ft. 6 in. The Quickcat is another class which is allowed variation. The popular position seems to be 14 ft. The Cherub hounds height varies from 13 ft. to 14 ft. The trend is downwards, with most of the top performers using 13 ft. It is very important to get the hounds position correct, as this will govern the type of bend that your mast will take on.

Hounds fittings available for dinghies normally are formed to fit a 3 in. diameter, but can be sprung around most slightly larger or smaller

Figure 58. Method of attaching chainplate.

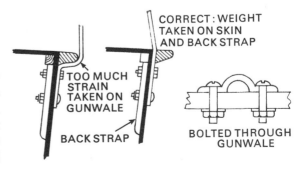

CORRECT: WEIGHT TAKEN ON SKIN AND BACK STRAP

TOO MUCH STRAIN TAKEN ON GUNWALE

BACK STRAP

BOLTED THROUGH GUNWALE

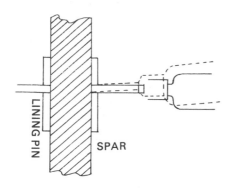

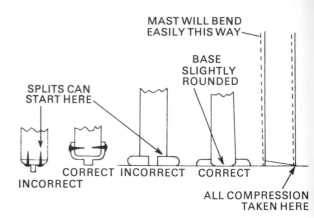

Figure 59. Using a guide pin for drilling through mast for hounds fitting.

Figure 60. Mast heel should cap the butt and not go into the end grain where it may split. The load should be taken up evenly.

sections. Screw the fitting in flat against the front of the mast before drilling the cross-bolt hole. Always drill this hole from one side half-way through, then from the other. A guide pin in the opposite side from the drill, to sight up on, is always a good idea (Fig. 59). If you sight the sideways direction yourself, have somebody at the end of the mast sight the horizontal level and you will find that the hole always meets in the middle. Shroud plates and trapeze plates can also hang off this bolt—shrouds always inside, as they carry the most weight. If they are not against the mast they tend to bend the bolt inside the mast.

With alloy spars, many crews prefer internal shroud fixings. A normal cross bolt is fitted. Smaller holes, just a little bigger than the diameter of the wire are drilled through about $1\frac{1}{2}$ in. below the cross bolt. These holes need to be angled or slotted slightly to allow the wire to take up the correct line to the chainplates. A length of wire is threaded through these holes until it appears out the bottom of the spar. This enables the end to be spliced around a thimble. When both shrouds are spliced in this way, they are then pulled up inside the spar and the loops manipulated into a position where the cross bolt can be passed through them. Positioning these loops onto the cross bolt can be a tricky operation but it is well worth the trouble. The smooth appearance, besides reducing windage slightly, gives a great psychological advantage in the boat park.

MAST HEELS

The mast heel fitting should cap the mast butt and not just screw into the end-grain. This eliminates the chance of splitting the mast when heavy side loadings are applied by the vang and boom. See that the heel takes the load evenly and not all on one edge which puts most of the compression on one side of the mast and makes it hard to bend in one direction and very easy to bend in the other (Fig. 60). These fittings can always be screwed into place, as most of the loading is downward.

Thought should be given to the vang fitting at this stage, for if it is not already built into the mast step, quite often it is wise to fix it securely around the base of the mast. A very simple method is to have a large loop in one end of the wire vang led around the fore side of the heel fitting on the base of the mast. Another method is to use an ordinary block hanger round the base of the mast with the end holes picking up the side fixings for a heel fitting. This fitting must be strong, as it will take some very severe strains.

MASTHEAD FITTINGS

If a sheave is used for the masthead halyard fittings, it should be large enough in diameter to protrude each side of the mast, in order to keep the halyard from chafing the for'ard side,

Figure 61. Sheave used for masthead halyard fittings.

and, on the aft side, to lead the halyard out slightly from the mast so that it falls over the hole in the headboard. This stops the sail being pulled in too tight to the mast at the head, which sometimes causes distortion (Fig. 61). This problem is especially prevalent on mainsails with slides instead of internal luff grooves, as the sail stands well out from the back edge of the spar and, if pulled in, will cause bad distortion creases to run downwards from the head.

A neat method of inserting the cross-pin in a wooden mast is to use a metal thread screw of the appropriate size. Cut the head off, saw a slot for a screwdriver and drill the hole through the mast $\frac{1}{64}$ in. smaller than the screw size. Screw in the metal thread—with some varnish on it to hold it fast—till the slotted side is flush; the other side can then be cut off and filed smooth. This leaves the top of the masthead quite snag-free and offering minimum wind resistance—you never know, you may get your spinnaker caught up there. Keep the clearance alongside the sheave to a minimum and get a sheave with a groove as deep as possible (while still protruding each side of the mast) to prevent the halyard going down beside the sheave.

HALYARD LOCKS

With smaller, flexible masts a mast lock is a must to remove the compression from the fine top sections. The stop should be fitted to the halyard first, the sail shackled on and run up the groove to the black band, and the lock screwed onto the front of the mast.

The stop should be arranged on the halyard to allow the lock to be positioned approximately 12 in. down from the top of the mast. If the lock is too close to the top it may be difficult to get the stop in and out of the lock—especially if it has to be done at sea. With the sheave a short wire length can be used, the talurit metal on the eye splice notching into the lock and the rest of the halyard being light cord.

Another much-used and very simple system is to lace the head of the sail to a hole through the top of the mast. The disadvantages are that the boat must be laid over to rig and unrig, which is very inconvenient in crowded rigging areas, and that it is impossible to lower away when caught in a sudden squall.

GOOSENECKS

Next step in rigging a simple dinghy mast is to fit the gooseneck. Measure down from the top black band the regulation distance and mark the position of the lower black band. If black bands are not being used, you must judge the point to which your sail must be stretched. Approximately 4 in. of track should be allowed above this point so that the boom can slide up to ease luff tension in light weather. The rest of the track is left below the band position to allow the sail to be brought down bodily closer to the deck for heavy weather.

This track has to stand very heavy sideloading from the boom vang and therefore must be securely screwed, using large self-tappers or monel screws. It is a good idea to instruct the sparmaker to inlay a piece of hardwood into the mast in this area to give the screws a good timber base to bite into. The track must also have a good flat surface to bed down on to eliminate any movement.

Goosenecks with an internal track have a wider track surface and a lower centre of strain than those with an external track, and are much easier to keep in place (Fig. 62). The external track is all right for small trainers, but for the Flying Dutchman, Sharpie, and 505 the flat internal track is much more desirable. On larger dinghies and small yachts where alloy masts will be used, it is common practice to pop rivet the gooseneck track into place. If you have trouble holding the track in place, as you may have on any size boat, it is wise to weld the track to stainless steel straps extending around the mast. If screws or rivets pull out, don't keep replacing them with bigger fastenings, as eventually you will drill enough holes to break the mast.

SHROUDS AND FORESTAY

Two shrouds and a forestay wire should now be fitted. These can be cut roughly to length and spliced, with one end directly on to the hounds fitting, around thimbles. A thimble can be easily opened out by laying it on a flat surface and tapping it lightly with a hammer at the large end. This enables it to be threaded through tang holes with ease. To close the gap again before splicing, squeeze the thimble, gripping it with the jaws of a pair of multi-grips across the widest part. Splice directly to the fittings, saving shackles and keeping the hounds area snag-free.

The hull should now be chocked up and levelled in both fore-and-aft and athwartships directions. Fit stay-adjusters to the chainplates and preadjust them first to their mid-position. Fit thimbles in the top holes ready for the wire to be threaded through.

With someone holding the mast, thread the

SLIDE LOW   **SLIDE HIGH**

WIDE BASE   **NARROW BASE**

Figure 62. Internal and external gooseneck tracks.

forestay wire around its thimble which you have already attached to the boat, and adjust the wire with the mast laying back on it until the mast is a little forward of the required rake—allowing about $\frac{1}{4}$ in. short on the forestay length for settling-in stretch. Complete this splice or lash it up very tightly around the thimble, leaving the extra wire to be cut off by the splicer. It is wise to mark the centre of the thimble and the position of the wire with paint to make sure there is no slip between your setting and the final splice.

The mast can now be laid back against the forestay (or jib luff if it is being used as a forestay) to fit the shrouds.

Thread one shroud and, with a weight hanging on the main halyard to act as a plumb-line, adjust its length until the plumb halyard indicates that the mast is vertical athwartships. Lash off and mark as with the forestay. Remove

Rigging terminals. From left to right: a talurit copper sleeve-and-thimble arrangement with copper and alloy sleeves alongside, a machine rolled swage with eye terminal and separate eye and forked terminals. Dinghy types favour the talurit splices whereas the rolled swage is ideal for professionally rigged yachts.

Right. Stay adjuster of punched strip, still about the cheapest kind.

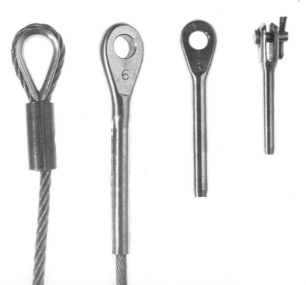

Boom vangs with multi-purchase rope tackle on a Sharpie (left) and fewer-purchase, less stretch wire tackle on a Heron (right).

the mast, splice up the shroud, and then make the other the same length. It always pays to make the shrouds, as you did the forestay, $\frac{1}{4}$ in. shorter to allow for settle-down and stretch.

The mast can now be stepped and strained up.

There are several types of shroud end and stay adjusters. The best (and most expensive) is the roll-swaged end, available in spade or fork terminal, which attaches direct to the chainplates, with screw adjustment. However, the old-fashioned rigging screws, less expensive, still do the job. They are quite snag-free when covered by plastic tube, and no shackles are required to join wire to the fitting or fitting to chainplates.

Disadvantages are that they don't take kindly to sideways bending or re-straightening, must be greased frequently to stop freezing up, and can come undone if not securely locked.

Vernier stay-adjusters are also very good and a lot cheaper, but care must be taken to get shrouds the same length and a shackle must be used between the fitting and the chainplate.

Two pieces of punched strip form a cheap and effective adjuster, except that adjustments can only be made in multiples of $\frac{5}{8}$ in. and bolts used are always a bad snag point unless cut and filed off very carefully.

Don't forget the oldest and cheapest method —lashing, still used on trainers. Its only other real virtue is that it can be cut with a knife if the mast has to be unstepped in a hurry after a mishap. The lashing must be inspected regularly for wear.

BOOM FITTINGS

Make the boom fit the gooseneck and not the gooseneck fit the boom. Goosenecks are available in different sizes with several strap spacings. Choose one slightly smaller than your boom width and then taper the end of your boom starting approximately 18 in. from the end on both sides until it slides in between the two straps, spreading them slightly.

Draw the straps against the flat sides you have planed on the spar and bolt through, using brass metal threads of $\frac{1}{4}$ in. diameter. Never re-bend the straps to fit the boom. With stainless steel this is asking for trouble.

VANG

The vang fitting should be sited about 3 ft. back along the boom. A block hanger with a $\frac{3}{16}$ in. stainless steel stud through the boom is usually strong enough, with perhaps a couple of small self-tappers once the correct angle is found to stop the strap chewing hunks out of the boom.

The amount of purchase necessary depends on the size of the mainsail and the degree to which the vang is to be used. For boats the size of the Heron, and smaller, the standard 3:1 ratio allows you to stand the leech up downwind while still having enough power to bend the mast and flatten the sail going to windward on heavy days. For more powerful rigs, the next step is to double that by adding a

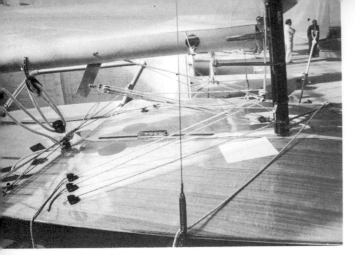

Lever and tackle system used on Moth. Levers provide a simple but powerful mechanical advantage in vang system.

block to the boom and rigging the initial 2:1 in wire and the normal 3:1 in rope. Always use as much wire as possible to minimise stretch. This 6:1 system should be sufficient for boats up to 14 ft. long.

Large-diameter sheave block mainsheet system with swivel ratchet block.

Remember, you only need enough purchase to allow adjustments to be made easily by hand at any time. It is useless to ease the vang slightly downwind to give the main a little more fullness in light weather only to find when the wind freshens in again that the vang cannot be pulled on until you get back on the wind.

Where high loading is to be expected, keep most of the reduction between the boom and the foot of the mast, leaving very little load on the final cleat position which is normally anchored to a more frail part of the boat—decking or cockpit floor.

BLOCKS

Dispense with shackles by selecting the blocks to suit hangers on your boom. Large-diameter sheave blocks are a recent useful innovation for reducing friction in sheeting systems. While they make fine trimming under load very easy,

Simplest end-sheeting system of all, used here on a Mirror.

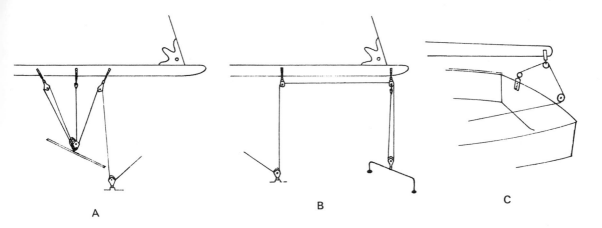

Figure 63 (above). Sheeting systems. *A,* centre-sheeting system; *B,* end-sheeting system; *C,* English system as used on Herons and Mirrors.

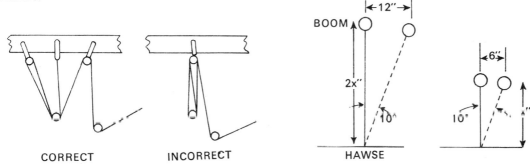

CORRECT   INCORRECT

Figure 64. Spacing blocks on the boom.

Figure 65. Effect of distance of boom from horse on control of boom angle. A boom twice as far from the horse as another will lay off twice as far with the same side loading.

the sheet is harder to hold. A swivel ratchet block should be added to overcome this problem, and the overall improvement is significant. The Elvstrom block that ratchets only one way, allowing the rope to slip smoothly over the sheave on release, is the best. The type with the ratchet that clicks both in and out tends to make sheet trimming very jerky. The latest Elvstrom block can also be made to freewheel for light winds.

A swivel block should never be used on the boom, as the falls run close together and one turn of a swivel block could jam the whole system.

Centre-boom sheeting is the most commonly used system on modern racers with short boom and high sail plan. With this system the blocks should be no farther forward than half the length of the boom; I think it preferable to carry them about 60 per cent of the length of the boom from the mast. This gives a little more control over the boom with the sheet. The blocks on the boom should be spaced at least 6 in. apart to distribute the load, and for this reason it is always better to use two single blocks from two points rather than one double. Spacing the blocks also helps to keep the falls of the sheeting system farther apart, making it harder for them to tangle (Fig. 64).

Advantages of centre sheeting are that a flexible boom can be used to flatten the bottom of the sail, the boom will lay away sideways to ease the power of the sail in heavy winds, and you use less rope. But sheet pressure is critical.

147

If the sheet is eased 1 in. the boom end will probably move out about 3 in. It helps to sew some coloured thread into the sheet near some fixed point so you know exactly how hard the sail is sheeted.

The end-sheeting system is also commonly used. It gives a better mechanical advantage and therefore uses fewer blocks. The sheet can be brought back along the boom and dropped into the cockpit at any convenient position. Sheeting pressures are less critical—for 6 in. of sheet let go, the boom will go out only 3 in. This, I feel, is the best system for beginners. Another end-sheeting system, used in some English classes such as the Herons and the Mirrors, dispenses with a horse traveller. The main advantage of this system is that there is no mainsheet for'ard of the skipper; the rest of the cockpit is thus kept clear. Care must be taken not to sheet too hard with this system, or the boom may come over the centre of the boat and kill the speed.

With all except this third system, a horse has to be used. Rear horses have to be raised high enough to allow the tiller to operate freely underneath. And they must have adjustable stops to allow the angle of the boom to be altered. The most common types are (a) the solid stainless steel rod, bent towel-rail fashion, invariably liable to be knocked around and used as lifting handles by landlubbers; (b) wire strop, simple and inexpensive but not as efficient as the solid horse because the block tends to move toward the centre apex, making angle adjustment difficult; and (c) track and slide raised over the tiller—the best system.

Centre-sheeting horses create fewer problems. The main aim is to keep the horse as close as possible to the boom to gain better control of the boom angle without having too much strain on the sheet. The farther the boom is away from the horse, the more downward pressure is required to keep the boom from laying off to leeward when the wind fills the sail (Fig. 65).

The most popular horse track is the channel-shaped alloy extrusion fitted with a roller traveller, which makes smooth, fine adjustments possible under full sheeting pressures. For easy one-handed operation it is still wise to fit a 2:1 purchase.

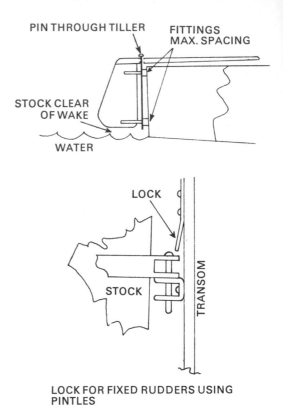

Figure 66. Attachment of rudder fittings.

The last lead of the sheet should always go through a swivel block on the cockpit floor placed opposite the centre-line of your body when swinging on windward legs. This allows you a straight pull on the sheet when hanging out and is an aid to swinging.

The boom blocks should be evenly spaced directly above the horse when the boom is trimmed at normal windward-sailing angle.

RUDDER FITTINGS

Rudder stock fittings are available in several strap spacings—$\frac{3}{4}$ in. or 1 in. for one-piece fixed rudders and $1\frac{1}{2}$ in. to 2 in. for swing-up-blade rudders, which have a much wider stock. Make sure when making your rudder that the stock ends up the exact width to allow the fittings to slip straight on. The fittings should never be bent to fit the stock, and it is a waste of effort to recess them into the stock as this will weaken the unit.

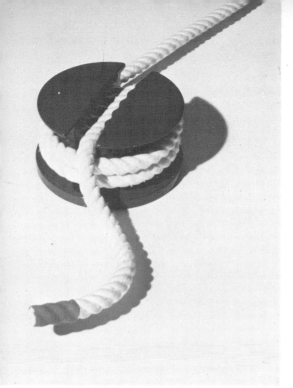

Left, a clam bollard. Right, different types of clamcleat: with lead, double-sided, and without lead.

The stock should be long enough to clear the top of the transom by $\frac{1}{4}$ in., so that the tiller will clear the deck, and fall short of the bottom skin by at least 1 in., so that the under edge of the stock will not drag in the wake (Fig. 66).

Fasten the fittings on with metal thread screws. Keep the top and bottom fittings as far apart as possible so that the leverage caused by the blade on the water is spread.

If a through-pin system is being used, assemble the transom gudgeons between the lugs on the rudder fittings, ensuring there will be no up-and-down movement of the rudder while sailing and the pin will be in line. Hold up the stock against the transom in the correct position, mark one of the top holes, drill and bolt fitting through it. Then drill and fit the remaining metal threads, making sure the pin holes still line up.

With a fixed rudder, pintles must be used so the rudder can be easily fitted while the boat is under way. With this system the rudder will float off in a capsize unless a positive lock is fitted.

The tiller can be attached either with a stainless steel cap or by gluing and screwing into place with wood screws. I like the glued job because the tiller can never have play in it. With the tiller glued in position, it is necessary to drill a hole through the tiller, directly in line with the fittings, to take the gudgeon pin.

CLEATS

The Clam cleat is one of the latest and most efficient methods of securing lines, although I think it has a limited life when working under heavy loads or with hard laid rope. This type of rope, once it slips in the cleat, will burn flats on the inside, making the ridges of the Clams ineffective. Main advantage is that the line can just be put down in one and it is held where it falls, whereas with the cam cleat the line must be pulled through to gain entry between the cams. It is sometimes difficult, when you have something pulled on as hard as possible, to get the extra inch to enter it into a cam cleat.

The Clams are available in several sizes to fit different diameter ropes and are available with fairlead incorporated. One of their few drawbacks is their bulk—especially in the larger sizes. Finding fixing points in lightly constructed hulls where the fitting runs athwartships is another difficulty and must be planned for. This is where the old cam cleat still has its place; it can be conveniently screwed into a very narrow stringer or outer gunwale.

The old-fashioned double-ended cleat still has its uses, especially on larger yachts, and must be big enough to hold the size rope intended for it. Where a line has to be bounced up, such as a halyard, and then cleated, a cleat must be selected that has a running side and a jambing side. The jam wedge must be within the cleat and not between the cleat and the deck.